NON SANZ DROICT.

DISCARD

SHAKE-SPEARES

SONNETS.

Neuer before Imprinted.

AT LONDON
By *G. Eld* for *T. T.* and are
to be folde by *Iohn Wright,* dwelling
at Chriſt Church gate.
1 6 0 9.

Title page of the 1609 Quarto of the *Sonnets*.

William Shakespeare

The Complete Nondramatic Poetry

The Sonnets

Edited by William Burto
Introduction by W. H. Auden

Narrative Poems

Edited by William Burto
Introduction by William Empson

With New and Updated Critical Essays and a Revised Bibliography

THE SIGNET CLASSICS SHAKESPEARE
General Editor: Sylvan Barnet

SIGNET CLASSICS

SIGNET CLASSICS
Published by New American Library, a division of
Penguin Group (USA) Inc., 375 Hudson Street,
New York, New York 10014, USA
Penguin Group (Canada), 90 Eglinton Avenue East, Suite 700, Toronto,
Ontario M4P 2Y3, Canada (a division of Pearson Penguin Canada Inc.)
Penguin Books Ltd., 80 Strand, London WC2R 0RL, England
Penguin Ireland, 25 St. Stephen's Green, Dublin 2,
Ireland (a division of Penguin Books Ltd.)
Penguin Group (Australia), 250 Camberwell Road, Camberwell, Victoria 3124,
Australia (a division of Pearson Australia Group Pty. Ltd.)
Penguin Books India Pvt. Ltd., 11 Community Centre, Panchsheel Park,
New Delhi - 110 017, India
Penguin Group (NZ), 67 Apollo Drive, Rosedale, North Shore 0632,
New Zealand (a division of Pearson New Zealand Ltd.)
Penguin Books (South Africa) (Pty.) Ltd., 24 Sturdee Avenue,
Rosebank, Johannesburg 2196, South Africa

Penguin Books Ltd., Registered Offices:
80 Strand, London WC2R 0RL, England

Published by Signet Classics, an imprint of New American Library,
a division of Penguin Group (USA) Inc.

First Signet Classics Printing (Second Revised Edition), April 2008
10 9 8 7 6 5 4 3 2 1

The Sonnets:
    Copyright © William Burto, 1964, 1989
    Introduction copyright © W. H. Auden, 1964
    Copyright © Sylvan Barnet, 1963, 1989, 2008
Narrative Poems:
    Copyright © William Burto, 1968
    Introduction copyright © William Empson, 1968
    Copyright © Sylvan Barnet, 1963, 1989, 2008
All rights reserved

Contents

Shakespeare: An Overview

Biographical Sketch

Between the record of his baptism in Stratford on 26 April 1564 and the record of his burial in Stratford on 25 April 1616, some forty official documents name Shakespeare, and many others name his parents, his children, and his grandchildren. Further, there are at least fifty literary references to him in the works of his contemporaries. More facts are known about William Shakespeare than about any other playwright of the period except Ben Jonson. The facts should, however, be distinguished from the legends. The latter, inevitably more engaging and better known, tell us that the Stratford boy killed a calf in high style, poached deer and rabbits, and was forced to flee to London, where he held horses outside a playhouse. These traditions are only traditions; they may be true, but no evidence supports them, and it is well to stick to the facts.

Mary Arden, the dramatist's mother, was the daughter of a substantial landowner; about 1557 she married John Shakespeare, a tanner, glove-maker, and trader in wool, grain, and other farm commodities. In 1557 John Shakespeare was a member of the council (the governing body of Stratford), in 1558 a constable of the borough, in 1561 one of the two town chamberlains, in 1565 an alderman (entitling him to the appellation of "Mr."), in 1568 high bailiff— the town's highest political office, equivalent to mayor. After 1577, for an unknown reason he drops out of local politics. What *is* known is that he had to mortgage his wife's property, and that he was involved in serious litigation.

The birthday of William Shakespeare, the third child and the eldest son of this locally prominent man, is unrecorded, but the Stratford parish register records that the infant was baptized on 26 April 1564. (It is quite possible that he was born on 23 April, but this date has probably been assigned by tradition because it is the date on which, fifty-two years later, he died, and perhaps because it is the feast day of St. George, patron saint of England.) The attendance records of the Stratford grammar school of the period are not extant, but it is reasonable to assume that the son of a prominent local official attended the free school—it had been established for the purpose of educating males precisely of his class—and received substantial training in Latin. The masters of the school from Shakespeares seventh to fifteenth years held Oxford degrees; the Elizabethan curriculum excluded mathematics and the natural sciences but taught a good deal of Latin rhetoric, logic, and literature, including plays by Plautus, Terence, and Seneca.

On 27 November 1582 a marriage license was issued for the marriage of Shakespeare and Anne Hathaway, eight years his senior. The couple had a daughter, Susanna, in May 1583. Perhaps the marriage was necessary, but perhaps the couple had earlier engaged, in the presence of witnesses, in a formal "troth plight," which would render their children legitimate even if no further ceremony were performed. In February 1585, Anne Hathaway bore Shakespeare twins, Hamnet and Judith.

That Shakespeare was born is excellent; that he married and had children is pleasant; but that we know nothing about his departure from Stratford to London or about the beginning of his theatrical career is lamentable and must be admitted. We would gladly sacrifice details about his children's baptism for details about his earliest days in the theater. Perhaps the poaching episode is true (but it is first reported almost a century after Shakespeare's death), or perhaps he left Stratford to be a schoolmaster, as another tradition holds; perhaps he was moved (like Petruchio in *The Taming of the Shrew*) by

> Such wind as scatters young men through the world,
> To seek their fortunes farther than at home
> Where small experience grows.

(1.2.49–51)

In 1592, thanks to the cantankerousness of Robert Greene, we have our first reference, a snarling one, to Shakespeare as an actor and playwright. Greene, a graduate of St. John's College, Cambridge, had become a playwright and a pamphleteer in London, and in one of his pamphlets he warns three university-educated playwrights against an actor who has presumed to turn playwright:

> There is an upstart crow, beautified with our feathers, that with his *tiger's heart wrapped in a player's hide* supposes he is as well able to bombast out a blank verse as the best of you, and being an absolute Johannes-factotum [i.e., jack-of-all-trades] is in his own conceit the only Shake-scene in a country.

The reference to the player, as well as the allusion to Aesop's crow (who strutted in borrowed plumage, as an actor struts in fine words not his own), makes it clear that by this date Shakespeare had both acted and written. That Shakespeare is meant is indicated not only by *Shake-scene* but also by the parody of a line from one of Shakespeare's plays, *3 Henry VI*: "O, tiger's heart wrapped in a woman's hide" (1.4.137). If in 1592 Shakespeare was prominent enough to be attacked by an envious dramatist, he probably had served an apprenticeship in the theater for at least a few years.

In any case, although there are no extant references to Shakespeare between the record of the baptism of his twins in 1585 and Greene's hostile comment about "Shake-scene" in 1592, it is evident that during some of these "dark years" or "lost years" Shakespeare had acted and written. There are a number of subsequent references to him as an actor. Documents indicate that in 1598 he is a "principal comedian," in 1603 a "principal tragedian," in 1608 he is one of the "men players." (We do not have, however, any solid information about which roles he may have played; later traditions say he played Adam in *As You Like It* and the ghost in *Hamlet*, but nothing supports the assertions. Probably his role as dramatist came to supersede his role as actor.) The profession of actor was not for a gentleman, and it occasionally drew the scorn of university men like Greene, who resented writing speeches for persons less educated than themselves, but it was respectable enough; players, if prosperous, were in effect members of the bourgeoisie, and there is nothing to suggest that Stratford considered William Shakespeare less than a solid citizen. When, in 1596, the Shakespeares were granted a coat of arms—i.e., the right to be considered gentlemen—the grant was made to Shakespeare's father, but probably William Shakespeare had arranged the matter on his own behalf. In subsequent transactions he is occasionally styled a gentleman.

Although in 1593 and 1594 Shakespeare published two narrative poems dedicated to the Earl of Southampton, *Venus and Adonis* and *The Rape of Lucrece*, and may well have written most or all of his sonnets in the middle nineties, Shakespeare's literary activity seems to have been almost entirely devoted to the theater. (It may be significant that the two narrative poems were written in years when the plague closed the theaters for several months.) In 1594 he was a charter member of a theatrical company called the Chamberlain's Men, which in 1603 became the royal company, the King's Men, making Shakespeare the king's playwright. Until he retired to Stratford (about 1611, apparently), he was with this remarkably stable company. From 1599 the company acted primarily at the Globe theater, in which Shakespeare held a one-tenth interest. Other Elizabethan dramatists are known to have acted, but no other is known also to have been entitled to a share of the profits.

Shakespeare's first eight published plays did not have his name on them, but this is not remarkable; the most popular play of the period, Thomas Kyd's *The Spanish Tragedy*, went through many editions without naming Kyd, and Kyd's authorship is known only because a book on the profession of acting happens to quote (and attribute to Kyd) some lines on the interest of Roman emperors in the drama. What is remarkable is that after 1598 Shakespeare's name commonly appears on printed plays—some of which are not his. Presumably his name was a drawing card, and publishers used it to attract potential buyers. Another indication of his popularity comes from Francis Meres, author of *Palladis Tamia: Wit's Treasury* (1598). In this anthology of snippets accompanied by an essay on literature, many playwrights are mentioned, but Shakespeare's name occurs more often than any other, and Shakespeare is the only playwright whose plays are listed.

From his acting, his playwriting, and his share in a playhouse, Shakespeare seems to have made considerable money. He put it to work, making substantial investments in Stratford real estate. As early as 1597 he bought New Place, the second-largest house in Stratford. His family moved in soon afterward, and the house remained in the family until a granddaughter died in 1670. When Shakespeare made his will in 1616, less than a month before he died, he sought to leave his property intact to his descendants. Of small bequests to relatives and to friends (including three actors, Richard Burbage, John Heminges, and Henry Condell), that to his wife of the second-best bed has provoked the most comment. It has sometimes been taken as a sign of an unhappy marriage (other supposed signs are the apparently hasty marriage, his wife's seniority of eight years, and his residence in London without his family). Perhaps the second-best bed was the bed the couple had slept in, the best bed being reserved for visitors. In any case, had Shakespeare not excepted it, the bed would have gone (with the rest of his household possessions) to his daughter and her husband.

On 25 April 1616 Shakespeare was buried within the chancel of the church at Stratford. An unattractive monument to his memory, placed on a wall near the grave, says that he died on 23 April. Over the grave itself are the lines, perhaps by Shakespeare, that (more than his literary fame) have kept his bones undisturbed in the crowded burial ground, where old bones were often dislodged to make way for new:

Good friend, for Jesus' sake forbear
To dig the dust enclosed here.
Blessed be the man that spares these stones
And cursed be he that moves my bones.

A Note on the Anti-Stratfordians, Especially Baconians and Oxfordians

Not until 1769—more than a hundred and fifty years after Shakespeare's death—is there any record of anyone expressing doubt about Shakespeare's authorship of the plays and poems. In 1769, however, Herbert Lawrence nominated Francis Bacon (1561–1626) in *The Life and Adventures of Common Sense*. Since then, at least two dozen other nominees have been offered, including Christopher Marlowe, Sir Walter Raleigh, Queen Elizabeth I, and Edward de Vere, 17th earl of Oxford. The impulse behind all anti-Stratfordian movements is the scarcely concealed snobbish opinion that "the man from Stratford" simply could not have written the plays because he was a country fellow without a university education and without access to high society. Anyone, the argument goes, who used so many legal terms, medical terms, nautical terms, and so forth, and who showed some familiarity with classical writing, must have attended a university, and anyone who knew so much about courtly elegance and courtly deceit must himself have moved among courtiers. The plays do indeed reveal an author whose interests were exceptionally broad, but specialists in any given field—law, medicine, arms and armor, and so on—soon find that the plays do not reveal deep knowledge in specialized matters; indeed, the playwright often gets technical details wrong.

The claim on behalf of Bacon, forgotten almost as soon as it was put forth in 1769, was independently reasserted by Joseph C. Hart in 1848. In 1856 it was reaffirmed by W. H. Smith in a book, and also by Delia Bacon in an article; in 1857 Delia Bacon published a book, arguing that Francis Bacon had directed a group of intellectuals who wrote the plays.

Francis Bacon's claim has largely faded, perhaps because it was advanced with such evident craziness by Ignatius Donnelly, who in *The Great Cryptogram* (1888) claimed to break a code in the plays that proved Bacon had written not only the plays attributed to Shakespeare but also other Renaissance works, for instance the plays of Christopher Marlowe and the essays of Montaigne.

Consider the last two lines of the Epilogue in *The Tempest*:

> As you from crimes would pardoned be,
> Let your indulgence set me free.

What was Shakespeare—sorry, Francis Bacon, Baron Verulam—*really* saying in these two lines? According to Baconians, the lines are an anagram reading, "Tempest of Francis Bacon, Lord Verulam; do ye ne'er divulge me, ye words." Ingenious, and it is a pity that in the quotation the letter *a* appears only twice in the cryptogram, whereas in the deciphered message it appears three times. Oh, no problem; just alter "Verulam" to "Verul'm" and it works out very nicely.

Most people understand that with sufficient ingenuity one can torture any text and find in it what one wishes. For instance: Did Shakespeare have a hand in the King James Version of the Bible? It was nearing completion in 1610, when Shakespeare was forty-six years old. If you look at the 46th Psalm and count forward for forty-six words, you will find the word *shake*. Now if you go to the end of the psalm and count backward forty-six words, you will find the word *spear*. Clear evidence, according to some, that Shakespeare slyly left his mark in the book.

Bacon's candidacy has largely been replaced in the twentieth century by the candidacy of Edward de Vere (1550–1604), 17th earl of Oxford. The basic ideas behind the Oxford theory, advanced at greatest length by Dorothy and Charlton Ogburn in *This Star of England* (1952, rev. 1955), a book of 1297 pages, and by Charlton Ogburn in *The Mysterious William Shakespeare* (1984), a book of 892 pages, are these: (1) The man from Stratford could not possibly have had the mental equipment and the experience to have written the plays—only a courtier could have written them; (2) Oxford had the requisite background (social position, education, years at Queen Elizabeth's court); (3) Oxford did not wish his authorship to be known for two basic reasons: writing for the public theater was a vulgar pursuit, and the plays show so much courtly and royal disreputable behavior that they would have compromised Oxford's position at court. Oxfordians offer countless details to support the claim. For example, Hamlet's phrase "that ever I was born to set it right" (1.5.89) barely conceals "E. Ver, I was born to set it right," an unambiguous announcement of de Vere's authorship, according to *This Star of England* (p. 654). A second example: Consider Ben Jonson's poem entitled "To the Memory of My Beloved Master William Shakespeare," prefixed to the first collected edition of Shakespeare's plays in 1623. According to Oxfordians, when Jonson in this poem speaks of the author of the plays as the "swan of Avon," he is alluding not to William Shakespeare, who was born and died in Stratford-on-Avon and who throughout his adult life owned property there; rather, he is alluding to Oxford, who, the Ogburns say, used "William Shakespeare" as his pen name, and whose manor at Bilton was on the Avon River. Oxfordians do not offer any evidence that Oxford took a pen name, and they do not care that Oxford had sold the manor in 1581, forty-two years before Jonson wrote his poem. Surely a reference to the Shakespeare who was born in Stratford, who had returned to Stratford, and who had died there only seven years before Jonson wrote the poem is more plausible. And exactly why Jonson, who elsewhere also spoke of Shakespeare as a playwright, and why Heminges and Condell, who had acted with Shakespeare for about twenty years, should speak of Shakespeare as the author in their dedication in the 1623 volume of collected plays is never adequately explained by Oxfordians. Either Jonson, Heminges and Condell, and numerous others were in on the conspiracy, or they were all duped—equally unlikely alternatives. Another difficulty in the Oxford theory is that Oxford died in 1604, and some of the plays are clearly indebted to works and events later than 1604. Among the Oxfordian responses are: At his death Oxford left some plays, and in later years these were touched up by hacks, who added the material that points to later dates. *The Tempest*, almost universally regarded as one of Shakespeare's greatest plays and pretty clearly dated to 1611, does indeed date from a period after the death of Oxford, but it is a crude piece of work that should not be included in the canon of works by Oxford.

The anti-Stratfordians, in addition to assuming that the author must have been a man of rank and a university man, usually assume two conspiracies: (1) a conspiracy in Elizabethan and Jacobean times, in which a surprisingly large number of persons connected with the theater knew that the actor Shakespeare did not write the plays attributed to him but for some reason or other pretended that he did; (2) a conspiracy of today's Stratfordians, the professors who teach Shakespeare in the colleges and universities, who are said to have a vested interest in preserving Shakespeare as the author of the plays they teach. In fact, (1) it is inconceivable that the secret of Shakespeare's nonauthorship could have been preserved by all of the people who supposedly were in on the conspiracy, and (2) academic fame awaits any scholar today who can disprove Shakespeare's authorship.

The Stratfordian case is convincing not only because hundreds or even thousands of anti-Stratford arguments—of the sort that say "ever I was born" has the secret double meaning "E. Ver, I was born"—add up to nothing at all but also because irrefutable evidence connects the man from Stratford with the London theater and with the authorship of particular plays. The anti-Stratfordians do not seem to understand that it is not enough to dismiss the Stratford case by saying that a fellow from the provinces simply couldn't have written the plays. Nor do they understand that it is not enough to dismiss all of the evidence connecting Shakespeare with the plays by asserting that it is perjured.

The Shakespeare Canon

We return to William Shakespeare. Thirty-seven plays as well as some nondramatic poems are generally held to constitute the Shakespeare canon, the body of authentic works. The exact dates of composition of most of the works are highly uncertain, but evidence of a starting point and/or of a final limiting point often provides a framework for informed guessing. For example, *Richard II* cannot be earlier than 1595, the publication date of some material to which it is indebted; *The Merchant of Venice* cannot be later than 1598, the year Francis Meres mentioned it. Sometimes arguments for a date hang on an alleged topical allusion, such as the lines about the unseasonable weather in *A Midsummer*

Night's Dream, 2.1.81–117, but such an allusion, if indeed it is an allusion to an event in the real world, can be variously interpreted, and in any case there is always the possibility that a topical allusion was inserted years later, to bring the play up-to-date. Dates are often attributed on the basis of style, and although conjectures about style usually rest on other conjectures (such as Shakespeare's development as a playwright, or the appropriateness of lines to character), sooner or later one must rely on one's literary sense. There is no documentary proof, for example, that *Othello* is not as early as *Romeo and Juliet*, but one feels that *Othello* is a later, more mature work, and because the first record of its performance is 1604, one is glad enough to set its composition at that date and not push it back into Shakespeare's early years. (*Romeo and Juliet* was first published in 1597, but evidence suggests that it was written a little earlier.) The following chronology, then, is indebted not only to facts but also to informed guesswork and sensitivity. The dates, necessarily imprecise for some works, indicate something like a scholarly consensus concerning the time of original composition. Some plays show evidence of later revision.

Plays. The first collected edition of Shakespeare, published in 1623, included thirty-six plays. These are all accepted as Shakespeare's, though for one of them, *Henry VIII*, he is thought to have had a collaborator. A thirty-seventh play, *Pericles*, published in 1609 and attributed to Shakespeare on the title page, is also widely accepted as being partly by Shakespeare even though it is not included in the 1623 volume. Still another play not in the 1623 volume, *The Two Noble Kinsmen*, was first published in 1634, with a title page attributing it to John Fletcher and Shakespeare. Probably most students of the subject now believe that Shakespeare did indeed have a hand in it. Of the remaining plays attributed at one time or another to Shakespeare, only one, *Edward III*, anonymously published in 1596, is now regarded by some scholars as a serious candidate. The prevailing opinion, however, is that this rather simple-minded play is not Shakespeare's; at most he may have revised some passages, chiefly scenes with the Countess of

Salisbury. We include *The Two Noble Kinsmen* but do not include *Edward III* in the following list.

1588–94	*The Comedy of Errors*
1588–94	*Love's Labor's Lost*
1589–91	*2 Henry VI*
1590–91	*3 Henry VI*
1589–92	*1 Henry VI*
1592–93	*Richard III*
1589–94	*Titus Andronicus*
1593–94	*The Taming of the Shrew*
1592–94	*The Two Gentlemen of Verona*
1594–96	*Romeo and Juliet*
1594–96	*The Merchant of Venice*
1595	*Richard II*
1595–96	*A Midsummer Night's Dream*
1596–97	*King John*
1596–97	*1 Henry IV*
1597	*The Merry Wives of Windsor*
1597–98	*2 Henry IV*
1598–99	*Much Ado About Nothing*
1598–99	*Henry V*
1599	*Julius Caesar*
1599–1600	*As You Like It*
1599–1600	*Twelfth Night*
1600–1601	*Hamlet*
1601–1602	*Troilus and Cressida*
1602–1604	*All's Well That Ends Well*
1603–1604	*Othello*
1604	*Measure for Measure*
1605–1606	*King Lear*
1605–1606	*Macbeth*
1606–1607	*Antony and Cleopatra*
1605–1608	*Timon of Athens*
1607–1608	*Coriolanus*
1607–1608	*Pericles*
1609–10	*Cymbeline*
1610–11	*The Winter's Tale*
1611	*The Tempest*

| 1612–13 | *Henry VIII* |
| 1613 | *The Two Noble Kinsmen* |

Poems

1592–93	*Venus and Adonis*
1593–94	*The Rape of Lucrece*
1593–1600	*Sonnets*
1600–1601	*The Phoenix and the Turtle*

A Brief Survey of the Nondramatic Works

We sometimes forget that Shakespeare was known to his fellows not only as a dramatist but also as a poet, specifically as a writer of love poetry in the vein of the Roman poet Ovid. In 1598 Francis Meres, comparing English poets with ancient Greek and Roman poets and with contemporary Italian poets, wrote that "the sweete wittie soule of Ovid lives in mellifluous & hony-tongued Shakespeare, witnes his *Venus and Adonis,* his *Lucrece,* his sugred *Sonnets* among his private friends, &c."

Two Long Narratives:
Venus and Adonis and *Lucrece*

Shakespeare's first work to appear in print was not a play but a narrative poem, *Venus and Adonis* (1593). The status of poet was higher than that of playwright in Elizabethan times: Professional poets depended on courtly patronage, whereas most playwrights depended on the pennies of the general public. It is likely that Shakespeare thought, at least for a while, that his poetry rather than his plays would bring him lasting fame. This hypothesis receives some support from the fact that in the dedication to *Venus and Adonis* (to the Earl of Southampton) Shakespeare speaks of the poem as "the first heir of my invention" although he had written at least a half dozen plays by this date. Second, like *Venus and Adonis, The Rape of Lucrece* (his other long narrative poem) was published in a remarkably accurate text, again with a dedication by the author to Southampton. Shakespeare thus apparently had a hand in the publication of these poems, but he never concerned himself with the publication of the plays, and he wrote no further dedications.

Leisure time to write the two narratives was probably afforded by the plague, which closed the London theaters from the summer of 1592 to the spring of 1594. *Venus and Adonis,* an artful erotic poem of 1,194 lines rhyming *ababcc,* derives chiefly from Book 10 of Ovid's *Metamorphoses.* Shakespeare's poem was calculated to please his noble patron, the youthful Earl of Southampton (1573–1624), whose taste presumably had been developed by ornate and erotic mythological pieces such as Thomas Lodge's *Scylla's Metamorphosis* (1589), a poem that, treating the love of the sea god Glaucus for Silla, uses the same six-line stanza as *Venus and Adonis.* Marlowe's *Hero and Leander* (1593 or earlier, although not published until 1598) belongs to the same school of serious yet predominantly witty and decorative poetry.

Venus and Adonis has been much praised for its realistic passages about birds (86–87), horses (259–318), the doe (875–76), and especially the hare (679–708), but however we may value these passages, which seem derived from Warwickshire memories, the poem as a whole produces the effect not of realism but of most cunning artifice. It is less a photograph or an Impressionist painting than a tapestry, an elaborately wrought piece with the erotic mythological pictures that are mentioned in *The Taming of the Shrew,* where in fact a picture of Venus (Cytherea) and Adonis is specified, and the sedges (grasslike plants) are said to "wanton" (play amorously) with the wind:

> Doest thou love pictures? We will fetch thee straight
> Adonis painted by a running brook
> And Cytherea all in sedges hid,
> Which seem to move and wanton with her breath
> Even as the waving sedges play with wind. (Induction 2: 49–53)

Similarly, in *Venus and Adonis* a passage about nature usually is less a description of creatures moving in external nature than a presentation of abstract types set in a hothouse.

Or we can vary the figure and see the poem as William Hazlitt did, when, calling attention to the frigidity of this poem about passion, he characterized it as an icehouse. For Elizabethan readers, however, the poem was not cold but hot, and it is best understood when regarded as a Renaissance erotic mythological piece. Bruce Smith, in an essay written for this volume (page 391), astutely noting that the poem invites voyeurism, calls attention to line 343: "O, what a sight was wistly [i.e., attentively] to view." Perhaps the most famous passage in the poem is the following, with its infamous reference to "bottom-grass" (valley grass, but . . .). In the second line "ivory pale" means "ivory fence," i.e., Venus's arms that encircle Adonis.

> "Fondling," she saith, "since I have hemmed thee here
> Within the circuit of this ivory pale,
> I'll be a park, and thou shalt be my deer:
> Feed where thou wilt, on mountain or in dale;
>   Graze on my lips, and if those hills be dry,
>   Stray lower, where the pleasant fountains lie.
>
> "Within this limit is relief enough,
> Sweet bottom-grass, and high delightful plain,
> Round rising hillocks, brakes obscure and rough,
> To shelter thee from tempest and from rain.
>   Then be my deer since I am such a park;
>   No dog shall rouse thee though a thousand bark.   (229–40)

Attempts to enliven *Venus and Adonis* by finding in it anticipations of Shakespeare's later plays—*A Midsummer Night's Dream* and *As You Like It* (love in the woods), *All's Well That Ends Well* (a self-centered young man), *Antony and Cleopatra* (a destructive beauty)—do not quite work. But *Venus and Adonis* worked for its contemporary readers: There were at least ten editions of the poem in Shakespeare's lifetime; a contemporary writer, Gabriel Harvey, noted that "the younger sort takes much delight in Shakespeare's *Venus and Adonis*"; and in *The First Part of the Return from Parnassus,* a satiric play probably staged in 1599 by undergraduates at St. John's College, Cambridge, the foolish courtier Gullio says, "I'll worship sweet master

Shakespeare, and to honor him will lay his *Venus and Adonis* under my pillow." Bruce Smith, in the essay in this volume, helps today's readers to see what Shakespeare's contemporaries saw in the poem.

In 1594 Shakespeare followed this bid for noble patronage with the publication of a second poem dedicated to Southampton, *Lucrece,* the "graver labour" he had promised in the dedication to *Venus.* The title page calls the poem *Lucrece* but the running head calls it *The Rape of Lucrece*; not until the sixth quarto edition of 1616 was the poem entitled *The Rape of Lucrece.* Like *Venus and Adonis, Lucrece* draws its central narrative from Ovid, this time from a book called *Fasti* (festivals). The poem, 1,855 lines, written in a seven-line stanza known as rhyme royal *(ababbcc),* can be thought of as a tragic mini-epic. In its depiction of Tarquin, who, overcome by passion, sacrifices honor and gains only self-loathing and enmity, Shakespeare touches on the irony that is central to tragedy, and indeed, in *Macbeth,* Shakespeare was later to mention Tarquin. Here, first, is the passage from *Macbeth*:

> Now o'er the one half-world
> Nature seems dead, and wicked dreams abuse
> The curtained sleep; witchcraft celebrates
> Pale Hecate's offerings; and withered murder,
> Alarumed by his sentinel, the wolf,
> Whose howl's his watch, thus with his stealthy pace,
> With Tarquin's ravishing strides, towards his design
> Moves like a ghost.   (*Macbeth,* 2.1.49–56)

And here is the passage, some ten years earlier, from *Lucrece*:

> Now stole upon the time the dead of night,
> When heavy sleep had closed up mortal eyes.
> No comfortable star did lend his light,
> No noise but owls, and wolves' death-boding cries;
> Now serves the season that they may surprise
> The silly lambs: pure thoughts are dead and still,
> While lust and murder wakes to stain and kill.
>   (*Lucrece,* 162–68)

In Lucrece's lamentations, and especially in Tarquin's internal debates, the universal stuff of tragedy is set forth in a narrative form, yet the final effect is far from tragic, for like *Venus and Adonis* the poem is so richly heraldic, so formal in its contrasts that the manner overcomes the matter. It is a web of decorative (and sometimes very beautiful) passages; it is longer than *Venus and Adonis* (and fourteen times as long as its source), but the increased length is due not to additional action but to even greater elaboration of the little there is. It is not much to modern taste, but it greatly pleased its contemporaries; by 1616, the year of Shakespeare's death, it had gone through at least six editions. The dour Gabriel Harvey, who said, as we have already seen, "The younger sort takes much delight in Shakespeare's *Venus and Adonis,*" went on to add that Shakespeare's "*Lucrece,* and his *Hamlet, Prince of Denmark,* have it in them to please the wiser sort."

And in fact, in recent years, doubtless because of the development of feminist and gender criticism, interest in *Venus and Adonis* and *Lucrece* has markedly increased. Today's "wiser sort" are helping the rest of us to enjoy the poem.

Sonnets

Among the nondramatic poems, the sonnets have won widespread praise. They belong to a genre made famous in Italy by Petrarch (1304–74); Petrarch was imitated in England by Wyatt and by Surrey, some of whose poems were published in 1557 in a book that is usually called *Tottel's Miscellany.* But sonneteering did not become a national pastime in England until 1591, when the posthumous publication of Sir Philip Sidney's *Astrophel and Stella* started the vogue. The Italian or Petrarchan sonnet is basically a two-part poem, consisting of an octave rhyming *abbaabba* and (normally in a somewhat different tone of voice) a sestet rhyming *cdecde* or *cdcdcd,* or another variant. The English sonnet (sometimes called Shakespearean, though Shakespeare did not invent the form) is a four-part poem, consisting of three quatrains and a couplet:

abab cdcd efef gg. The couplet normally provides a syntac-
tically independent aphoristic summary. But the thought of
the sonnet does not always follow the rhyme scheme—that
is, it does not always break after each quatrain. In a good
number of Shakespeare's sonnets, the chief turn comes, as
in an Italian sonnet, after the eighth line.

Shakespeare's *Sonnets* was not published until 1609, but
surely most and possibly all of the 154 poems had been
written at least a decade earlier. The exact date of composi-
tion is unknown, but the early and middle nineties seem rea-
sonable for most of them. (There are also sonnets in *Love's
Labor's Lost* and *Romeo and Juliet,* plays of the middle
nineties.) In 1598 Francis Meres alluded to Shakespeare's
"sugred sonnets." "Sugared" is appropriate for at least some
of them: There are poems that show a delight in ingenious
conceits of the kind we associate with the earlier plays. But
other sonnets are masterful in an apparent simplicity of
utterance that, coupled with a depth of view, makes the
poems among the world's greatest. If the best sonnets were
written before 1598 (rather than shortly before publication
in 1609), Shakespeare achieved maturity in the sonnet more
quickly than in the drama.

The 154 poems do not narrate a continuous story, but
there are groups of related sonnets; for example, Sonnets
1–17 are all written to an aristocratic young man, urging
him to beget an heir. Although the sonnets may be indebted
to some contact that Shakespeare had with members of the
aristocracy, they cannot be read as sheer autobiography
(though of course they often ring true). The usual motifs of
Elizabethan sonnets can be found—for instance the poet
eternizes his patron, and the eye and the heart are at war—
but there is also a new range of feeling that has affinities
with *Lucrece* and therefore approaches a tragic view. For
instance, in *Lucrece* Shakespeare gives us this insight into
one kind of tragic experience:

> Those that much covet are with gain so fond
> That what they have not, that which they possess
> They scatter and unloose it from their bond,
> And so by hoping more they have but less;
> Or, gaining more, the profit of excess

Is but to surfeit, and such griefs sustain
That they prove bankrout in this poor rich gain.   (134–40)

After he rapes Lucrece, Tarquin is compared to a "full-fed hound or gorgèd hawk," now loathing what he had before pursued:

His taste delicious, in digestion souring,
Devours his will, that lived by foul devouring.   (699–700)

Every poem is complete in itself and ought not to be reduced or expanded to coincide with any other poem, but we can see in these passages from *Lucrece* something akin to Sonnet 129, a passionate analysis of lust before, during, and after consummation. (In the first line of this sonnet, "Th' expense of spirit" is the expenditure of vital power, and more specifically, perhaps, of semen. In line 9 the first word, "Made," is often emended to "mad," but it can be taken as equivalent to "Made mad.")

Th' expense of spirit in a waste of shame
Is lust in action; and, till action, lust
Is perjured, murd'rous, bloody, full of blame,
Savage, extreme, rude, cruel, not to trust;   4
Enjoyed no sooner but despisèd straight;
Past reason hunted, and no sooner had,
Past reason hated as a swallowed bait
On purpose laid to make the taker mad;   8
Made in pursuit, and in possession so;
Had, having, and in quest to have, extreme;
A bliss in proof, and proved, a very woe,
Before, a joy proposed; behind, a dream.   12
    All this the world well knows, yet none knows well
    To shun the heaven that leads men to this hell.

Not all Shakespeare's sonnets, of course, are like this, and our interest in the tragedies ought not to lead us to concentrate on poems about lust or the destructive will to the exclusion of, say, those celebrations of beauty that are equally impressive. In short, the sonnets are remarkably varied—

some readers who cherish a consistent story would say they are disordered. There is a young aristocrat and a dark lady (who was the poet's mistress and who also has had an affair with the young man), both of whom evoke varying degrees of admiration and distress from the speaker of the sonnets. If we look for a dominant subject, we perhaps find it in the opposition of Time to Nature. Time is a destroyer, as in the first four lines of Sonnet 65:

> Since brass, nor stone, nor earth, nor boundless sea,
> But sad mortality o'ersways their power,
> How with this rage shall beauty hold a plea,
> Whose action is no stronger than a flower?

But Nature engenders anew; although human beings, empires, and the seasons all decay, the poet affirms that there *is* such a thing as the "marriage of true minds," and his words re-create his subject, conferring on beauty a new existence that may arrest or at least seem to arrest the triumph of Time. If this inadequate description has any truth in it, the world of the sonnets is very near to that of the great plays. Indeed, even the seemingly curious emphasis in the sonnets that the young man beget an heir helps to align them with a common motif in the plays, the loss (in the tragedies) of an old aristocratic order and the restoration (in the comedies) of an old aristocratic order that had for a while been submerged.

A Lover's Complaint

A Lover's Complaint, a poem of 329 lines in the same seven-line stanza as *Lucrece* (the stanza is called rhyme royal, and the rhyme scheme is *ababbcc*), was first issued by the bookseller Thomas Thorpe, in 1609, in the volume that also contained Shakespeare's *Sonnets.* The sole evidence that it is by Shakespeare is the fact that the other poems in the book—the sonnets—unquestionably are by Shakespeare. Further, the *Sonnets* by themselves are of sufficient bulk to have made a book—that is, there was no need to add an inauthentic poem simply to pad the volume. And it has been argued that *A Lover's Complaint* is connected to the sonnets by virtue of similar characters (an older man, a young woman, and a seductive young man) and by similar motifs (for instance, deception). These arguments favoring attribution to Shakespeare do not seem compelling, and many scholars have doubted the attribution, chiefly because the work strikes them as undistinguished and because it doesn't sound like Shakespeare—it doesn't seem good enough to be Shakespeare's. Only recently, however, did Brian Vickers, in *Shakespeare, "A Lover's Complaint," and Sir John Davies of Hereford* (2007) make a highly convincing case that (a) the poem is not by Shakespeare and (b) it is almost surely by Sir John Davies (1569–1616).

Briefly, in his immensely learned book, Vickers offers evidence that the vocabulary (often archaic), the imagery, the rhetoric, the sentence structure, and the rhymes differ from Shakespeare's practice as we know it in the accepted works. Take the matter of vocabulary: True, in any given play by Shakespeare a reader encounters some words not used elsewhere by him, but in *A Lover's Complaint*—a short work—one finds twenty-three words not used elsewhere by Shakespeare, and in fact the number is closer to fifty if one counts words that he did use elsewhere but with a different meaning. Or take the matter of rhyme: First, in *A Lover's Complaint* there is about twice the amount of syntactical inversion in order to create a rhyme or fit the meter as there is in *Venus and Adonis* and *Lucrece*. Second, in *A Lover's Complaint,* the author repeats eleven pairs of rhyming words in what is a pretty short work, a practice unparalleled in Shakespeare's other poems. Vickers plausibly takes this repetition to show a lack of imagination, and it seems impossible to disagree with him. It's not a matter of a critic saying that he finds the work inferior. If that were the issue, one might reply that other critics do not find it inferior, and we cannot reject from the canon whatever seems not to suit our taste. Vickers convincingly shows, I think, that the poem is weak *by the standards of the time.*

In short, the editor of the Signet Classics Shakespeare believes that Vickers has proved his case—Shakespeare did not write *A Lover's Complaint,* and the probable author is Sir John Davies—but out of a deference to tradition, the editor retains the poem. Several good scholars have in the past argued on behalf of its authenticity—the most notable are McDonald P. Jackson, John Kerrigan, and Kenneth Muir—and the present editor is mindful of the words of Samuel Johnson, who, explaining his conservative reluctance to emend a text unless it made no sense whatever, said, "I have adopted the Roman sentiment, that it is more honorable to save a citizen than to kill an enemy."

A Lover's Complaint belongs to a genre (from the Middle Ages through the seventeenth century) called the *complaint,* a lament, in this case a pastoral complaint because most of it is uttered by a shepherdess. Usually such a poem is a monologue in which the speaker laments his or her unhappy experience with love, but other causes of unhappiness such as poverty may also be the subject. ("The Complaint of Chaucer to His Purse" is a famous comic example.) Often, as in *A Lover's Complaint,* a woman is the speaker, telling a tale of lost virginity and betrayal. More precisely, the speaker in this poem is not the woman but a poet-narrator who tells the reader (stanzas 1–8) that he overheard a woman lamenting and saw her speak to an old shepherd (stanzas 9–10). Then the poet-narrator reports verbatim her words (from line 71 onward). Within her speech she reports the words (177–280) of her faithless seducer, so we get, in short, the narrator's voice at the start, his report of the maiden's voice, and her report of the faithless lover's voice.

The Phoenix and the Turtle

One other short poem, indeed much shorter than *A Lover's Complaint,* is widely attributed to Shakespeare, and in the opinion of the editor, the attribution is undoubtedly correct. This is *The Phoenix and the Turtle,* published with Shakespeare's name but without a title in Robert Chester's collection entitled *Love's Martyr* (1601), dedicated to Sir John Salusbury (also Salisbury). Chester's poem, a very long narrative in the style Shakespeare used in *Venus and Adonis,* is followed by a title page that says, "Hereafter follow diverse poetical essays on the former subject, viz the turtle and the phoenix done by the best and chiefest of our

modern writers." Fourteen poems, including one attributed
to Shakespeare, follow this title page. In *Love's Martyr*
Shakespeare's poem is untitled; it was not called *The
Phoenix and the Turtle* until 1807, and today it is sometimes
called *The Phoenix and Turtle,* or (more conservatively)
some editors use the first line ("Let the bird of loudest lay")
as the title. Whatever its title, it has gained universal praise
only since the early twentieth century, probably because in
the 1920s admirers of John Donne and the other meta-
physical poets helped to educate subsequent taste to appre-
ciate this incantational, funereal, philosophical poem that,
drawing on logic, theology, and mythology, speaks about
the transcendence of human love. The motif is conveyed
through the symbols of the phoenix, a legendary bird that
resurrects itself from its own ashes, and the turtle—that is,
the turtledove—an emblem of constancy in love.

All poems are (as Aristotle instructed us some 2,500
years ago) made out of words that are arranged harmo-
niously. They are also *about* something, and here is where
disagreement can arise, but perhaps we can agree on one
thing further: The world that the poet gives us, however
much it may look like our own, however much it may echo
our own thoughts (as, for instance, in Robert Frost's "But I
have promises to keep, / And miles to go before I sleep, /
And miles to go before I sleep"), is a world of the poet's
own creation. In the example just given, Frost invites us to
overhear his invented speaker as he meditates "Between the
woods and frozen lake, / The darkest evening of the year."
This is not any old place at any old time: Frost has invented
a very special place and a very special time, "The darkest
evening of the year." But Frost is not our topic, and I intro-
duce him merely to make the point that every poem takes us
into an invented world, a world that may seem familiar but
also is nevertheless new and something very strange. Take
the first stanza of *The Phoenix and the Turtle*:

> Let the bird of loudest lay,
> On the sole Arabian tree,
> Herald sad and trumpet be
> To whose sound chaste wings obey.

Exactly which species of bird is "the bird of loudest lay," i.e., of loudest song? Is it the mythical phoenix, which was reputed to live in Arabia—but which later in the poem is said to be dead—or is it some other bird, perhaps the nightingale, or perhaps the crane, which traditionally was said to be notably loud? Or maybe it doesn't matter? What matters most, perhaps, is that Shakespeare abruptly brings the reader into a strange world, a world where a poet can order a bird— the "bird of loudest lay"—to summon (as a herald and as a trumpeter) other birds to assemble. But notice that this herald, this trumpeter, is not to summon *all* birds; no, the summons is addressed only to those birds who are of "chaste wings." It is a world of birds, but of birds who are very like human beings, some good, some bad. In fact, the second stanza banishes at least one bird:

> But thou, shrieking harbinger,
> Foul precurrer of the fiend,
> Augur of the fever's end
> To this troop come thou not near.

Possibly the "shrieking harbinger" who is the precursor of the devil and who can predict whether the victim of the fever will live or die is the screech owl, but again we can't be sure. What we *can* be sure of is this: Because we are reading a poem, we are being drawn into a very special world, like Frost's special world that is specifically yet mysteriously set "Between the woods and frozen lake, / The darkest evening of the year."

Readers are invited to enjoy this visit to the poet's world, but of course, even though we are enchanted by the music (notably the alliteration in "*L*et," "*l*oudest *l*ay" in the first line), we inevitably also want to know, "What does it mean? What is the poem about?" Yes, it is about some sort of mysterious unity, some sort of love that was so perfect that the two lovers were one:

> So they loved, as love in twain
> Had the essence but in one:
> Two distincts, division none,
> Number there in love was slain.

The lovers of course were two ("twain") but in essence they were one; they were "distinct" beings, but paradoxically, miraculously, there was no "division" between them. Who in the world were these two perfect lovers represented by the phoenix and the turtledove? Because the title page to Robert Chester's book describes Chester's poem as "allegorically shadowing the truth of Love," literary historians have provided several allegorical interpretations, and have assumed that the interpretations are relevant also to Shakespeare's poem. For example: The phoenix represents Queen Elizabeth, the turtle Essex; or the birds represent Elizabeth and her subjects, or Elizabeth and Salusbury (the dedicatee), or Salusbury and his wife. If there is an historical allegory, yes, we ought to try to unearth it, but such an allegorical reading probably will not enhance the poem for today's readers. Perhaps we will do better to think about the poem as a celebration of the mystery of a perfect human love that although now lost continues (because of Shakespeare's creation) to serve us as an inspiration.

   Venus and Adonis can be coupled with *Lucrece,* and each sonnet can be coupled with the remaining 153, but *The Phoenix and the Turtle* stands alone. Still, in its faith in the power of a love that transcends reason, a love in which individuals are mysteriously joined and yet, equally mysteriously, retain their identity, it earns its place in a story that includes the sonnets, *Romeo and Juliet,* and *Antony and Cleopatra.*

Short Poems in *The Passionate Pilgrim,* and Rejected Recent Candidates

   In 1599 William Jaggard, a publisher who in 1623 was to issue the earliest collected edition of Shakespeare's plays, published a collection of twenty poems—four of them are sonnets on the subject of Venus and Adonis—that he attributed to Shakespeare. Jaggard was doubtless cashing in on the popularity of *Venus and Adonis* and *Lucrece.* This 1599 volume in fact was a second edition, but of the first edition only two sheets remain, so the date (1598 or 1599) of the first edition is uncertain. Of the twenty poems, five are certainly by Shakespeare: Two of these five—the first two in the book—are sonnets that reappear with minor differences as Sonnets 138 and 144 in the 1609 volume of Shakespeare's *Sonnets*; the other three are lyrical passages from an early play by Shakespeare, *Love's Labor's Lost*, first published in 1598. Nine of the remaining fifteen poems are unquestionably by authors other than Shakespeare, including Richard Barnfield, Christopher Marlowe, and Sir Walter Raleigh. The remaining poems—conventionally numbered 7, 10, 13, 14, 15, and 18—may or may not be Shakespeare's. Of these six, only one, "Crabbèd age and youth," has aroused any enthusiasm. The truth is, no one seems to care greatly whether Shakespeare did or did not write them.

By way of contrast, in recent years strong passions have been aroused by two poems that certain proponents have claimed are by Shakespeare. In 1985 Gary Taylor announced (*Times Literary Supplement,* December 20, 1985, page 1447) that he had found in a seventeenth-century manuscript collection of poems, housed in the Bodleian Library, Oxford, a previously unknown poem by Shakespeare, "Shall I die?" Here is the opening stanza:

> Shall I die? Shall I fly
> Lovers' baits and deceits,
>   sorrow breeding?
> Shall I fend? Shall I send?
> Shall I shew, and not rue
>   my proceeding?
> In all duty her beauty
> Binds me her servant for ever,
>   If she scorn, I mourn,
> I retire to despair, joying never.

And so on, for eight additional stanzas. Aware that the poem is unimpressive, Taylor conjectured that the "conventionality of much of its imagery" and its "obsessive rhyming" indicate that it was an early work. Taylor based his case for Shakespeare's authorship chiefly on two things: First, in the manuscript the poem is assigned to "William Shakespeare" and, second, the poem shares many verbal

parallels with Shakespeares known works . To respond to
the first point first: Because it is not known who compiled
the manuscript, or when in the early seventeenth century it
was compiled, the attribution to Shakespeare carries very
little weight. Further, the poem appears also in a manuscript
at Yale, in the Beinecke Library, where it is *not* attributed
to Shakespeare. As for the parallel words and phrases,
many are commonplace: Expressions such as "my dove,"
"so rare," "win love's prize," and "but alas" appear in the
works of other writers; it really doesn't matter that Taylor
finds fifty-two parallels. No matter how many such expres-
sions can be found in Shakespeare, they add up to nothing.
Further, the rhyme "love" and "dove," which Taylor uses as
evidence, really is counterevidence: True, it appears both in
"Shall I die?" and in *Romeo and Juliet,* but in the play
Shakespeare's Mercutio mocks it as trite.

"Shall I die" was included in the Oxford edition of
Shakespeare's works—Taylor was an editor of the Oxford
volume—and this trivial poem was also included in editions
of the complete works published by Houghton Mifflin,
Norton, and Longman, presumably because each publisher
feared that if it did not use the poem it would be open to the
charge that its volume was not truly "complete." Several
scholars have decisively demonstrated the inadequacy of
Taylor's argument (notably Donald W. Foster in *Shake-
speare Quarterly* 38 [1987]: 58–77, and Thomas A.
Pendleton in *Review of English Studies* 15 [1989]: 323–51),
and Houghton Mifflin, Norton, and Longman now have
dropped (or will in the next reprint drop) this poem. Only
the Oxford edition, edited by Stanley Wells and Gary
Taylor, 2nd edition (2005), retains it, in the face of almost
universal rejection by scholars.

In the last decades of the twentieth century, a second non-
Shakespearean poem was much discussed as an addition to
the canon. In 1989 Donald W. Foster published *Elegy by
W. S. A Study in Attribution,* in which on stylometric evi-
dence he tentatively argued that Shakespeare was the author
of "A Funerall Elegye in Memory of the late Vertuous
Maister William Peeter of Whipton Neere Excester," pub-
lished in 1612 with a title page that attributes it to "W.S."
Foster later published additional arguments on the topic,

notably in *PMLA* 111 (1996): 1080–1105 and *PMLA* 112 (1997): 432–34. Early in 1996 Foster had achieved some fame by correctly identifying, on the basis of a computer analysis of stylistic similarities, *Newsweek* columnist Joe Klein as the author of the anonymous *Primary Colors,* a novel based on Bill Clinton's first campaign. Klein had good reasons for wishing to remain anonymous, but why would Shakespeare—the chief dramatist of the time—keep his authorship anonymous? And why would Peter's family, if they had been able to persuade so famous a figure to write an elegy, not reveal the author's name?

Most readers of "A Funeral Elegy" probably find the poem uninteresting—the diction vague and Latinate, the image of the deceased fuzzy, the poem overlong—but Foster argued that the issue is to be resolved not by matters of taste but by stylometrics, by statistical procedures. Claiming that he was not relying on taste, nor on aesthetic preference, which is subjective, but on statistical evidence, for instance a preference for old forms such as *whiles, hath, doth,* and the relatively unusual practice of using *who* for inanimate objects, Foster concluded that "A Funeral Elegy" belonged to Shakespeare. He was at least sufficiently persuasive so that the one-volume editions of Shakespeare published by Houghton Mifflin, Longman, and Norton included the poem, although the editors of the Houghton Mifflin and Longman volumes expressed thoughtful reservations. Shortly thereafter several scholars (notably Brian Vickers, in a book called *"Counterfeiting" Shakespeare* [2002] and Gilles D. Monsarrat in the May 2002 issue of *Review of English Studies*) convincingly argued that by Foster's own stylistic tests (e.g., a preference for *whiles* over *while,* for *doth* over *does*) the poem more closely resembles the writing of John Ford than of Shakespeare. In June 2002 Foster withdrew his argument. Presumably the poem will be withdrawn from all the one-volume editions that now include it.

The Signet Classics Shakespeare has never included either "Shall I die?" or "A Funeral Elegy."

Sylvan Barnet

The
Sonnets

Introduction

Probably, more nonsense has been talked and written, more intellectual and emotional energy expended in vain, on the sonnets of Shakespeare than on any other literary work in the world. Indeed, they have become the best touchstone I know of for distinguishing the sheep from the goats, those, that is, who love poetry for its own sake and understand its nature, from those who only value poems either as historical documents or because they express feelings or beliefs of which the reader happens to approve.

It so happens that we know almost nothing about the historical circumstances under which Shakespeare wrote these sonnets: we don't know to whom they are addressed or exactly when they were written, and, unless entirely new evidence should turn up, which is unlikely, we never shall.

This has not prevented many very learned gentlemen from displaying their scholarship and ingenuity in conjecture. Though it seems to me rather silly to spend much time upon conjectures which cannot be proved true or false, that is not my real objection to their efforts. What I really object to is their illusion that, if they were successful, if the identity of the Friend, the Dark Lady, the Rival Poet, etc., could be established beyond doubt, this would in any way illuminate our understanding of the sonnets themselves.

Their illusion seems to me to betray either a complete misunderstanding of the nature of the relation between art and life or an attempt to rationalize and justify plain vulgar idle curiosity.

Idle curiosity is an ineradicable vice of the human mind. All of us like to discover the secrets of our neighbors, particularly the ugly ones. This has always been so, and, probably, always will be. What is relatively new, however—it is scarcely to be found before the latter half of the eighteenth century—is a blurring of the borderline between the desire for truth and idle curiosity, until, today, it has been so thoroughly erased that we can indulge in the latter without the slightest pangs of conscience. A great deal of what today passes for scholarly research is an activity no different from that of reading somebody's private correspondence when he is out of the room, and it doesn't really make it morally any better if he is out of the room because he is in his grave.

In the case of a man of action—a ruler, a statesman, a general—the man is identical with his biography. In the case of any kind of artist, however, who is a maker not a doer, his biography, the story of his life, and the history of his works are distinct. In the case of a man of action, we can distinguish in a rough and ready way between his private personal life and his public life, but both are lives of action and, therefore, capable of affecting each other. The political interests of a king's mistress, for example, may influence his decisions on national policy. Consequently, the historian, in his search for truth, is justified in investigating the private life of a man of action to the degree that such discoveries throw light upon the history of his times which he had a share in shaping, even if the victim would prefer such secrets not to be known.

The case of any artist is quite different. Art history, the comparison of one work with another, one artistic epoch with another, the study of influences and changes of style is a legitimate study. The late J. B. Leishman's book, *Themes and Variations in Shakespeare's Sonnets*, is an admirable example of such an enquiry. Even the biography of an artist, if his life as a man was sufficiently interesting, is permissible, provided that the biographer and his readers realize that such an account throws no light whatsoever upon the artist's work. The relation between his life and his works is at one and the same time too self-evident to require comment—every work of art is, in one sense, a self-disclosure—and too complicated ever to unravel. Thus, it is self-evident that Catullus's love for Lesbia was the experience which inspired his love poems, and that, if either of them had had a different character, the poems would have been different, but no amount of research into their lives can tell us why Catullus wrote the actual poems he did, instead of an infinite number of similar poems he might have written instead, why, indeed, he wrote any, or why those he did are good. Even if one could question a poet himself about the relation between some poem of his and the events which provoked him to write it, he could not give a satisfactory answer, because even the most "occasional" poem, in the Goethean sense, involves not only the occasion but the whole life experience of the poet, and he himself cannot identify all the contributing elements.

Further, it should be borne in mind that most genuine artists would prefer that no biography be written. A genuine artist believes he has been put on earth to fulfill a certain function determined by the talent with which he has been entrusted. His personal life is, naturally, of concern to himself and, he hopes, to his personal friends, but he does not think it is or ought to be of any concern to the public. The one thing a writer, for example, hopes for, is attentive readers of his writings. He hopes they will study the text closely enough to spot misprints. Shakespeare would be grateful to many scholars, beginning with Malone, who have suggested sensible emendations to the Q text. And he hopes that they will read with patience and intelligence so as to extract as much meaning from the text as possible. If the shade of Shakespeare has read Professor William Empson's explication of "They that have power to hurt and will do none" (Sonnet 94), he may have wondered to himself, "Now, did I *really* say all that?", but he will certainly be grateful to Mr. Empson for his loving care.

Not only would most genuine writers prefer to have no biography written; they would also prefer, were it practically feasible, that their writings were published anonymously.

Shakespeare is in the singularly fortunate position of being, to all intents and purposes, anonymous. Hence the existence of persons who spend their lives trying to prove that his plays were written by someone else. (How odd it is that Freud should have been a firm believer in the Earl of Oxford theory.)

So far as the sonnets are concerned, the certain facts are just two in number. Two of the sonnets, "When my love swears that she is made of truth" (138), and "Two loves I have, of comfort and despair" (144), appeared in *The Passionate Pilgrim*, a poetic miscellany printed in 1599, and the whole collection was published by G. Eld for T. T. in 1609 with a dedication "To.The.Onlie.Begetter.Of.These.Insuing.Sonnets. Mr. W.H." Meres's reference in 1598 to "sugred Sonnets" by Shakespeare is inconclusive: the word *sonnet* was often used as a general term for a lyric, and even if Meres was using it in the stricter sense, we do not know if the sonnets he was referring to are the ones we have.

Aside from the text itself, this is all we know for certain and all we are ever likely to know. On philological grounds, I am inclined to agree with those scholars who take the word *begetter* to mean procurer, so that Mr. W.H. is not the friend who inspired most of the sonnets, but the person who secured the manuscript for the publisher.

So far as the date of their composition is concerned, all we know for certain is that the relation between Shakespeare and the Friend lasted at least three years:

> Three April perfumes in three hot Junes burned,
> Since first I saw you fresh, which yet are green. (104)

The fact that the style of the sonnets is nearer to that of the earlier plays than the later is not conclusive proof that their composition was contemporary with the former, because a poet's style is always greatly influenced by the particular verse form he is employing. As Professor C. S. Lewis has said: "If Shakespeare had taken an hour off from the composition of *Lear* to write a sonnet, the sonnet might not have been in the style of *Lear*." On the whole, I think an early date is a more plausible conjecture than a late one, because the experiences the sonnets describe seem to me to be more likely to befall a younger man than an older.

Let us, however, forget all about Shakespeare the man, leave the speculations about the persons involved, the names, already or in the future to be put forward, Southampton, Pembroke, Hughes, etc., to the foolish and the idle, and consider the sonnets themselves.

The first thing which is obvious after reading through the one hundred and fifty-four sonnets as we have them, is that they are not in any kind of planned sequence. The only semblance of order is a division into two unequal heaps—Sonnets 1 to 126 are addressed to a young man, assuming, which is probable but not certain, that there is only one young man addressed, and Sonnets 127–154 are addressed to a dark-haired woman. In both heaps, a triangle situation is referred to in which Shakespeare's friend and his mistress betray him by

having an affair together, which proves that the order is not
chronological. Sonnets 40 and 42, "Take all my loves, my love,
yea take them all," "That thou hast her, it is not all my grief,"
must be more or less contemporary with 144 and 152, "Two
loves I have, of comfort and despair," "In loving thee thou
know'st I am forsworn."

Nor in the two sets considered separately is it possible to be-
lieve that the order is chronological. Sometimes batches of
sonnets occur which clearly belong together—for example, the
opening series 1–17, in which the friend is urged to marry,
though, even here, 15 seems not to belong, for marriage is not
mentioned in it. At other times, sonnets which are similar in
theme are widely separated. To take a very trivial example, in
77 Shakespeare speaks of giving his friend a commonplace
book.

> Look what thy memory cannot contain,
> Commit to these waste blanks.

And in 122, he speaks of a similar gift from his friend to him.

> Thy gift, thy tables, are within my brain.

Surely, it is probable that they exchanged gifts and that these
sonnets belong together.

The serious objection, however, to the order of Sonnets
1–126 as the Q text prints them is psychological. Sonnets ex-
pressing feelings of unalloyed happiness and devotion are
mixed with others expressing grief and estrangement. Some
speak of injuries done to Shakespeare by his friend, others of
some scandal in which the friend was involved, others again of
some infidelity on Shakespeare's part in a succession which
makes no kind of emotional sense.

Any passionate relationship can go through and survive
painful crises, and become all the stronger for it. As Shake-
speare writes in Sonnet 119:

> O, benefit of ill: now I find true
> That better is by evil still made better;
> And ruined love, when it is built anew,
> Grows fairer than at first, more strong, far greater.

But forgiveness and reconciliation do not obliterate memory of the past. It is not possible to return to the innocent happiness expressed before any cloud appeared on the sky. It is not, it seems to me, possible to believe that, *after* going through the experiences described in Sonnets 40–42, Shakespeare would write either Sonnet 53,

> In all external grace, you have some part,
> But you like none, none you, for constant heart

or 105,

> Let not my love be called idolatry,
> Nor my beloved as an idol show,
> Since all alike my songs and praises be
> To one, of one, still such, and ever so.
> Kind is my love today, tomorrow kind,
> Still constant in a wondrous excellence.

If the order is not chronological, it cannot, either, be a sequence planned by Shakespeare for publication. Any writer with an audience in mind knows that a sequence of poems must climax with one of the best. Yet the sequence as we have it concludes with two of the worst of the sonnets, trivial conceits about, apparently, going to Bath to take the waters. Nor, when preparing for publication, will an author leave unrevised what is obviously a first draft, like Sonnet 99 with its fifteen lines.

A number of scholars have tried to rearrange the sonnets into some more logical order, but such efforts can never be more than conjecture, and it is best to accept the jumble we have been given.

If the first impression made by the sonnets is of their haphazard order, the second is of their extremely uneven poetic value.

After the 1609 edition, the sonnets were pretty well forgotten for over a century and a half. In 1640 Benson produced an extraordinary hodgepodge in which one hundred and forty-six of them were arranged into seventy-two poems with invented titles, and some of the *he*'s and *him*'s changed to *she*'s and *her*'s. It was not until 1780 that a significant critical text was made by Malone. This happened to be a period when critics condemned the sonnet as a form. Thus Steevens could write in 1766:

> Quaintness, obscurity, and tautology are to be regarded as the constituent parts of this exotic species of composition. . . . I am one of those who should have wished it to have expired in the country where it was born. . . . [A sonnet] is composed in the highest strain of affectation, pedantry, circumlocution, and nonsense.

And of Shakespeare's essays in this form:

> The strongest act of Parliament that could be framed would fail to compel readers unto their service.

Even when this prejudice against the sonnet as such had begun to weaken, and even after Bardolatry had begun, adverse criticism of the sonnets continued.

Thus Wordsworth, who was as responsible as anyone for rehabilitating the sonnet as a form (though he employed the Petrarchan, not the Shakespearean, kind), remarked:

> These sonnets beginning at CXXVII to his mistress are worse than a puzzle-peg. They are abominably harsh, obscure, and worthless. The others are for the most part much better, have many fine lines and passages. They are also in many places warm with passion. Their chief faults—and heavy ones they are—are sameness, tediousness, quaintness, and elaborate obscurity.

Hazlitt:
> If Shakespeare had written nothing but his sonnets . . . he would . . . have been assigned to the class of cold, artificial writers, who had no genuine sense of nature or passion.

Keats:
> They seem to be full of fine things said unintentionally—in the intensity of working out conceits.

Landor:
> Not a single one is very admirable. . . . They are hot and pothery: there is much condensation, little delicacy; like

raspberry jam without cream, without crust, without bread;
to break its viscidity.

In this century we have reacquired a taste for the conceit, as we
have for baroque architecture, and no longer think that artifice
is incompatible with passion. Even so, no serious critic of po-
etry can possibly think that all the sonnets are equally good.

On going through the hundred and fifty-four of them, I find
forty-nine which seem to me excellent throughout, a good
number of the rest have one or two memorable lines, but there
are also several which I can only read out of a sense of
duty. For the inferior ones we have no right to condemn Shake-
speare unless we are prepared to believe, a belief for which
there is no evidence, that he prepared or intended them all to be
published.

Considered in the abstract, as if they were Platonic Ideas,
the Petrarchan sonnet seems to be a more esthetically satisfy-
ing form than the Shakespearean. Having only two different
rhymes in the octave and two in the sestet, each is bound by
rhyme into a closed unity, and the asymmetrical relation of 8
to 6 is pleasing. The Shakespearean form, on the other hand,
with its seven different rhymes, almost inevitably becomes
a lyric of three symmetrical quatrains, finished off with an
epigrammatic couplet. As a rule Shakespeare shapes his
rhetorical argument in conformity with this, that is to say,
there is usually a major pause after the fourth, the eighth, and
the twelfth line. Only in one case, Sonnet 86, "Was it the proud
full sail of his great verse," does the main pause occur in
the middle of the second quatrain, so that the sonnet divides
into 6.6.2.

It is the concluding couplet in particular which, in the
Shakespearean form, can be a snare. The poet is tempted to
use it, either to make a summary of the preceding twelve
lines which is unnecessary, or to draw a moral which is too
glib and trite. In the case of Shakespeare himself, though there
are some wonderful couplets, for example the conclusion
of 61,

> For thee watch I, whilst thou dost wake elsewhere,
> From me far off, with others all too near,

or 87,

> Thus have I had thee as a dream doth flatter,
> In sleep a king, but waking no such matter,

all too often, even in some of the best, the couplet lines are the weakest and dullest in the sonnet, and, coming where they do at the end, the reader has the sense of a disappointing anticlimax.

Despite all this, it seems to me wise of Shakespeare to have chosen the form he did rather than the Petrarchan. Compared with Italian, English is so poor in rhymes that it is almost impossible to write a Petrarchan sonnet in it that sounds effortless throughout. In even the best examples from Milton, Wordsworth, Rossetti, for example, one is almost sure to find at least one line the concluding word of which does not seem inevitable, the only word which could accurately express the poet's meaning; one feels it is only there because the rhyme demanded it.

In addition, there are certain things which can be done in the Shakespearean form which the Petrarchan, with its sharp division between octave and sestet, cannot do. In Sonnet 66, "Tired with all these, for restful death I cry," and 129, "Th' expense of spirit in a waste of shame," Shakespeare is able to give twelve single-line *exempla* of the wretchedness of this world and the horrors of lust, with an accumulative effect of great power.

In their style, two characteristics of the sonnets stand out. Firstly, their *cantabile*. They are the work of someone whose ear is unerring. In his later blank verse, Shakespeare became a master of highly complicated effects of sound and rhythm, and the counterpointing of these with the sense, but in the sonnets he is intent upon making his verse as melodious, in the simplest and most obvious sense of the word, as possible, and there is scarcely a line, even in the dull ones, which sounds harsh or awkward. Occasionally, there are lines which foreshadow the freedom of his later verse. For example:

> Not mine own fears nor the prophetic soul
> Of the wide world dreaming on things to come.   (107)

But, as a rule, he keeps the rhythm pretty close to the metrical base. Inversion, except in the first foot, is rare, and so is trisyllabic substitution. The commonest musical devices are alliteration—

> Then were not summer's distillation left,
> A liquid prisoner pent in walls of glass   (5)

> Let me not to the marriage of true minds
> Admit impediments . . .   (116)

and the careful patterning of long and short vowels—

> How many a holy and obsequious tear   (31)

> Nor think the bitterness of absence sour   (57)

> So far from home into my deeds to pry.   (61)

The second characteristic they display is a mastery of every possible rhetorical device. The reiteration, for example, of words with either an identical or a different meaning—

> love is not love
> Which alters when it alteration finds,
> Or bends with the remover to remove.   (116)

Or the avoidance of monotony by an artful arithmetical variation of theme or illustration.

Here, I cannot do better than to quote (interpolating lines where appropriate) Professor C. S. Lewis on Sonnet 18. "As often," he says, "the theme begins at line 9,

> But thy eternal summer shall not fade,

occupying four lines, and the application is in the couplet:

> So long as men can breathe or eyes can see,
> So long lives this, and this gives life to thee.

Line 1

> Shall I compare thee to a summer's day

proposes a simile. Line 2

> Thou art more lovely and more temperate

corrects it. Then we have two one-line *exempla* justifying the correction

> Rough winds do shake the darling buds of May,
> And summer's lease hath all too short a date:

then a two-line *exemplum* about the sun

> Sometime too hot the eye of heaven shines,
> And often is his gold complexion dimmed:

then two more lines

> And every fair from fair sometime declines,
> By chance, or nature's changing course, untrimmed

which do not, as we had expected, add a fourth *exemplum* but generalize. Equality of length in the two last variations is thus played off against difference of function."*

The visual imagery is usually drawn from the most obviously beautiful natural objects, but, in a number, a single metaphorical conceit is methodically worked out, as in 87,

> Farewell, thou art too dear for my possessing,

where the character of an emotional relationship is worked out in terms of a legal contract.

In the inferior sonnets, such artifices may strike the reader as artificial, but he must reflect that, without the artifice, they might be much worse than they are. The worst one can say, I think, is that rhetorical skill enables a poet to write a poem for which genuine inspiration is lacking which, had he lacked such skill, he would not have written at all.

On the other hand those sonnets which express passionate emotions, whether of adoration or anger or grief or disgust, owe a very great deal of their effect precisely to Shakespeare's artifice, for without the restraint and distancing which the rhetorical devices provide, the intensity and immediacy of the emotion might have produced, not a poem, but an embarrassing "human

*English Literature in the Sixteenth Century. Oxford: Clarendon Press, 1954, p. 507.

document." Wordsworth defined poetry as emotion recollected in tranquillity. It seems highly unlikely that Shakespeare wrote many of these sonnets out of recollected emotion. In his case, it is the artifice that makes up for the lack of tranquillity.

If the vagueness of the historical circumstances under which the sonnets were written has encouraged the goats of idle curiosity, their matter has given the goats of ideology a wonderful opportunity to display their love of simplification at the expense of truth. Confronted with the extremely odd story they tell, with the fact that, in so many of them, Shakespeare addresses a young man in terms of passionate devotion, the sound and sensible citizen, alarmed at the thought that our Top-Bard could have had any experience with which he is unfamiliar, has either been shocked and wished that Shakespeare had never written them, or, in defiance of common sense, tried to persuade himself that Shakespeare was merely expressing in somewhat hyperbolic terms, such as an Elizabethan poet might be expected to use, what any normal man feels for a friend of his own sex. The homosexual reader, on the other hand, determined to secure our Top-Bard as a patron saint of the Homintern, has been uncritically enthusiastic about the first one hundred and twenty-six of the sonnets, and preferred to ignore those to the Dark Lady in which the relationship is unequivocally sexual, and the fact that Shakespeare was a married man and a father.

Dag Hammerskjöld, in a diary found after his death and just recently published in Sweden, makes an observation to which both the above types would do well to listen.

> How easy Psychology has made it for us to dismiss the perplexing mystery with a label which assigns it a place in the list of common aberrations.

That we are confronted in the sonnets by a mystery rather than by an aberration is evidenced for me by the fact that men and women whose sexual tastes are perfectly normal, but who enjoy and understand poetry, have always been able to read them as expressions of what they understand by the word *love*, without finding the masculine pronoun an obstacle.

I think that the *primary* experience—complicated as it

became later—out of which the sonnets to the friend spring was a mystical one.

All experiences which may be called mystical have certain characteristics in common.

(1) The experience is "given." That is to say, it cannot be induced or prolonged by an effort of will, though the openness of any individual to receive it is partly determined by his age, his psychophysical make-up, and his cultural milieu.

(2) Whatever the contents of the experience, the subject is absolutely convinced that it is a revelation of reality. When it is over, he does not say, as one says when one awakes from a dream: "Now I am awake and conscious again of the real world." He says, rather: "For a while the veil was lifted and a reality revealed which in my 'normal' state is hidden from me."

(3) With whatever the vision is concerned, things, human beings, or God, they are experienced as numinous, clothed in glory, charged with an intense being-thereness.

(4) Confronted by the vision, the attention of the subject, in awe, joy, dread, is absolutely absorbed in contemplation and, while the vision lasts, his self, its desires and needs, are completely forgotten.

Natural mystical experiences, visions that is to say, concerned with created beings, not with a creator God, and without overt religious content, are of two kinds, which one might call the Vision of Dame Kind and the Vision of Eros.

The classic descriptions of the first are to be found, of course, in certain of Wordsworth's poems, like *The Prelude*, the Immortality Ode, "Tintern Abbey," and "The Ruined Cottage." It is concerned with a multiplicity of creatures, inanimate and animate, but not with persons, though it may include human artifacts. If human beings do appear in it, they are always, I believe, total strangers to the subject, so that, so far as he is concerned, they are not persons. It would seem that, in our culture, this vision is not uncommon in childhood, but rare in adults.

The Vision of Eros, on the other hand, is concerned with a single person, who is revealed to the subject as being of infinite sacred importance. The classic descriptions of it are to be found in Plato's *Symposium*, Dante's *La Vita Nuova*, and some of these sonnets by Shakespeare.

It can, it seems, be experienced before puberty. If it occurs later, though the subject is aware of its erotic nature, his own desire is always completely subordinate to the sacredness of the beloved person who is felt to be infinitely superior to the lover. Before anything else, the lover desires the happiness of the beloved.

The Vision of Eros is probably a much rarer experience than most people in our culture suppose, but, when it is genuine, I do not think it makes any sense to apply to it terms like heterosexual or homosexual. Such terms can only be legitimately applied to the profane erotic experiences with which we are all familiar, to lust, for example, an interest in another solely as a sexual object, and that combination of sexual desire and *philia*, affection based upon mutual interests, values, and shared experiences which is the securest basis for a happy marriage.

That, in the Vision of Eros, the erotic is the medium, not the cause, is proved, I think, by the fact, on which all who have written about it with authority agree, that it cannot long survive an actual sexual relationship. Indeed, it is very doubtful if the Vision can ever be mutual: the story of Tristan and Isolde is a myth, not an instance of what can historically occur. To be receptive to it, it would seem that the subject must be exceptionally imaginative. Class feelings also seem to play a role; no one, apparently, can have such a vision about an individual who belongs to a social group which he has been brought up to regard as inferior to his own, so that its members are not, for him, fully persons.

The medium of the Vision is, however, undoubtedly erotic. Nobody who was unconscious of an erotic interest on his part would use the frank, if not brutal, sexual image which Shakespeare employs in speaking of his friend's exclusive interest in women.

> But since she pricked thee out for women's pleasure,
> Mine be thy love, and thy love's use their treasure. (20)

The beloved is always beautiful in the impersonal sense of the word as well as the personal. It is unfortunate that we have to use the same words, beauty and beautiful, to mean two quite different things. If I say: "Elizabeth has a beautiful figure" or "a beautiful profile," I am referring to an objective, publicly recognizable property, and, so long as the objects are members of the same class, I can compare one with another and arrange them along a scale of beauty. That is why it is possible to hold dog shows, beauty competitions, etc., or for a sculptor to state in mathematical terms the proportions of the ideal male or female figure. This kind of beauty is a gift of Nature's, depending upon a lucky combination of genes and the luck of good health, and a gift which Nature can, and, in due time, always does, take away. The reaction of the spectator to it is either impersonal admiration or impersonal sexual desire. Moral approval is not involved. It is perfectly possible for me to say: "Elizabeth has a beautiful figure, but she is a monster."

If, on the other hand, I say: "Elizabeth has a beautiful face or a beautiful expression," though I am still referring to something physical—I could not make the statement if I were blind—I am speaking of something which is personal, a unique face which cannot be compared with that of anyone else, and for which I hold Elizabeth personally responsible. Nature has had nothing to do with it. This kind of beauty is always associated with the notion of moral goodness. It is impossible to imagine circumstances in which I could say: "Elizabeth has a beautiful expression but she is a monster." And it is this kind of beauty which arouses in the beholder feelings, not of impersonal admiration or lust, but of personal love.

The Petrarchan distinction, employed by Shakespeare in a number of his sonnets, between the love of the eye and the love of the heart, is an attempt, I think, to express the difference between these two kinds of beauty and our response to them.

In the Vision of Eros, both are always present. The beloved is always beautiful in both the public and the personal sense. But, to the lover, the second is the more important. Dante certainly thought that Beatrice was a girl whose beauty everybody would admire, but it wouldn't have entered his head to compare her for beauty with other Florentine girls of the same age.

Both Plato and Dante attempt to give a religious explanation of the Vision. Both, that is to say, regard the love inspired by a created human being as intended to lead the lover towards the love of the uncreated source of all beauty. The difference between them is that Plato is without any notion of what we mean by a person, whether human or Divine; he can only think in terms of the individual and the universal, and beauty, for him, is always beauty in the impersonal sense. Consequently, on the Platonic ladder, the love of an individual must be forgotten in the love of the universal; what we should call infidelity becomes a moral duty. How different is Dante's interpretation. Neither he nor Beatrice tells us exactly what he had done which had led him to the brink of perdition, but both speak of it as a lack of fidelity on Dante's part to his love for Beatrice. In Paradise, she is with him up until the final moment when he turns from her towards "The Eternal Fountain" and, even then, he knows that her eyes are turned in the same direction. Instead of the many rungs of the Platonic ladder, there is only one step for the lover to take, from the person of the beloved creature to the Person of their common Creator.

It is consistent with Shakespeare's cast of mind as we meet it in the plays, where it is impossible to be certain what his personal beliefs were on any subject, that the sonnets should contain no theory of love: Shakespeare contents himself with simply describing the experience.

Though the primary experience from which they started was, I believe, the Vision of Eros, that is, of course, not all they are about. For the vision to remain undimmed, it is probably necessary that the lover have very little contact with the beloved, however nice a person she (or he) may be. Dante, after all, only saw Beatrice once or twice, and she probably knew little about him. The story of the sonnets seems to me to be the story of an agonized struggle by Shakespeare to preserve the glory of the vision he had been granted in a relationship, lasting at least three years, with a person who seemed intent by his actions upon covering the vision with dirt.

As outsiders, the impression we get of his friend is one of a young man who was not really very nice, very conscious of his good looks, able to switch on the charm at any moment, but essentially frivolous, cold-hearted, and self-centered, aware, probably, that he had some power over Shakespeare—if he thought about it at all, no doubt he gave it a cynical explanation—but with no conception of the intensity of the feelings he had, unwittingly, aroused. Somebody, in fact, rather like Bassanio in *The Merchant of Venice*.

The sonnets addressed to the Dark Lady are concerned with that most humiliating of all erotic experiences, sexual infatuation—*Vénus toute entière à sa proie attachée*.

Simple lust is impersonal, that is to say the pursuer regards himself as a person but the object of his pursuit as a thing, to whose personal qualities, if she has any, he is indifferent, and, if he succeeds, he expects to be able to make a safe getaway as soon as he becomes bored. Sometimes, however, he gets trapped. Instead of becoming bored, he becomes sexually obsessed, and the girl, instead of conveniently remaining an object, becomes a real person to him, but a person whom he not only does not love, but actively dislikes.

No other poet, not even Catullus, has described the anguish, self-contempt, and rage produced by this unfortunate condition so well as Shakespeare in some of these sonnets, 141, for example, "In faith I do not love thee with my eyes," or 151, "Love is too young to know what conscience is."

Aside from the opening seventeen sonnets urging his friend to marry—which may well, as some scholars have suggested, have been written at the suggestion of some member of the young man's family—aside from these, and half a dozen elegant trifles, what is astonishing about the sonnets, especially when one remembers the age in which they were written, is the impression they make of naked autobiographical confession. The Elizabethans were not given to writing their autobiographies or to "unlocking their hearts." Donne's love poems were no doubt inspired by a personal passion, but this is hidden behind the public performance. It is not until Rousseau and the age of *Sturm und Drang* that confession becomes a literary genre. After the sonnets, I cannot think of anything in English poetry so seemingly autobiographical until Meredith's *Modern Love*, and even then, the personal events seem to be very carefully "posed."

It is impossible to believe either that Shakespeare wished them to be published or that he can have shown most of them to the young man and woman, whoever they were, to whom they are addressed. Suppose you had written Sonnet 57,

> Being your slave, what should I do but tend
> Upon the hours and times of your desire?

Can you imagine showing it to the person you were thinking of? Vice versa, what on earth would you feel, supposing someone you knew handed you the sonnet and said: "This is about you"?

Though Shakespeare may have shown the sonnets to one or two intimate literary friends—it would appear that he must have—he wrote them, I am quite certain, as one writes a diary, for himself alone, with no thought of a public.

When the sonnets are really obscure, they are obscure in the way that a diary can be, in which the writer does not bother to explain references which are obvious to him, but an outsider cannot know. For example, in the opening lines of Sonnet 125

> Were't aught to me I bore the canopy,
> With my extern the outward honoring.

It is impossible for the reader to know whether Shakespeare is simply being figurative or whether he is referring to some ceremony in which he actually took part, or, if he is, what that ceremony can have been. Again, the concluding couplet of 124 remains impenetrable.

> To this I witness call the fools of Time,
> Which die for goodness, who have lived for crime.

Some critics have suggested that this is a cryptic reference to the Jesuits who were executed on charges of high treason. This may be so, but there is nothing in the text to prove it, and even if it is so, I fail to understand their relevance as witnesses to Shakespeare's love which no disaster or self-interest can affect.

How the sonnets came to be published—whether Shakespeare gave copies to some friend who then betrayed him, or whether some enemy stole them—we shall probably never know. Of one thing I am certain: Shakespeare must have been horrified when they were published.

The Elizabethan age was certainly as worldly-wise and no more tolerant, perhaps less, than our own. After all, sodomy was still a capital offense. The poets of the period, like Marlowe and Barnfield, whom we know to have been homosexual, were very careful not to express their feelings in the first person, but in terms of classical mythology. Renaissance Italy had the reputation for being tolerant on this subject, yet, when Michelangelo's nephew published his sonnets to Tomasso de Cavalieri, which are much more restrained than Shakespeare's, for the sake of his uncle's reputation he altered the sex, just as Benson was to do with Shakespeare in 1640.

Shakespeare must have known that his sonnets would be read by many readers in 1609 as they are read by many today— with raised eyebrows. Though I believe such a reaction to be due to a misunderstanding, one cannot say that it is not understandable.

In our culture, we have good reason to be skeptical when anyone claims to have experienced the Vision of Eros, and even to doubt if it ever occurs, because half our literature, popular and highbrow, ever since the Provençal poets made the disastrous mistake of trying to turn a mystical experience into a social cult, is based on the assumption that what is, probably, a rare experience, is one which almost everybody has or ought to have; if they don't, then there must be something wrong with them. We know only too well how often, when a person speaks of having "fallen in love" with X, what he or she really feels could be described in much cruder terms. As La Rochefoucauld observed:

> True love is like seeing ghosts: we all talk about it, but few of us have ever seen one.

It does not follow, however, that true love or ghosts cannot exist. Perhaps poets are more likely to experience it than others, or become poets because they have. Perhaps Hannah Arendt is right: "Poets are the only people to whom love is not only a crucial but an indispensable experience, which entitles them to mistake it for a universal one." In Shakespeare's case, what happened to his relations with his friend and his mistress, whether they were abruptly broken off in a quarrel, or slowly faded into indifference, is anybody's guess. Did Shakespeare later feel that the anguish at the end was not too great a price to pay for the glory of the initial vision? I hope so and believe so. Anyway, poets are tough and can profit from the most dreadful experiences.

There is a scene in *The Two Noble Kinsmen* which most scholars believe to have been written by Shakespeare and which, if he did, may very well be the last thing he wrote. In it there is a speech by Palamon in which he prays to Venus for her aid. The speech is remarkable, firstly, in its choice of examples of the power of the Goddess—nearly all are humiliating or horrid—and, secondly, for the intensity of the disgust expressed at masculine sexual vanity.

> Hail, Sovereign Queen of secrets, who has power
> To call the fiercest tyrant from his rage,
> And weep unto a girl; that hast the might
> Even with an eye-glance, to choke Mars's drum
> And turn th' alarm to whispers; that canst make
> A cripple flourish with his crutch, and cure him
> Before Apollo; that mayst force the King
> To be his subjects' vassal, and induce
> Stale gravity to dance; the polled bachelor—
> Whose youth, like wanton boys through bonfires,
> Have skipped thy flame—at seventy thou canst catch
> And make him, to the scorn of his hoarse throat,
> Abuse young lays of love: what godlike power
> Hast thou not power upon? . . .
> . . . Take to thy grace
> Me, thy vowed soldier, who do bear thy yoke
> As 'twere a wreath of roses, yet is heavier
> Than lead itself, stings more than nettles.
> I have never been foul-mouthed against thy law,
> Nev'r revealed secret, for I knew none; would not
> Had I kenned all that were; I never practised
> Upon man's wife, nor would the libels read
> Of liberal wits; I never at great feasts
> Sought to betray a beauty, but have blushed
> At simp'ring Sirs that did; I have been harsh
> To large confessors, and have hotly asked them
> If they had mothers: I had one, a woman,
> And women 'twere they wronged. I knew a man
> Of eighty winters, this I told them, who
> A lass of fourteen brided. 'Twas thy power
> To put life into dust; the aged cramp
> Had screwed his square foot round,
> The gout had knitted his fingers into knots,
> Torturing convulsions from his globy eyes,
> Had almost drawn their spheres, that what was life
> In him seemed torture: this anatomy
> Had by his young fair pheare a boy, and I
> Believed it was his, for she swore it was,
> And who would not believe her? Brief, I am

To those that prate, and have done, no companion;
To those that boast, and have not, a defier;
To those that would, and cannot, a rejoicer.
Yea, him I do not love, that tells close offices
The foulest way, nor names concealments in
The boldest language. Such a one I am,
And vow that lover never yet made sigh
Truer than I. O, then, most soft, sweet Goddess,
Give me the victory of this question, which
Is true love's merit, and bless me with a sign
Of thy great pleasure.

*Here music is heard, doves are seen to flutter; they fall again
upon their faces, then on their knees.*

Oh thou, that from eleven to ninety reign'st
In mortal bosoms, whose chase is this world,
And we in herds thy game; I give thee thanks
For this fair token, which, being laid unto
Mine innocent true heart, arms in assurance
My body to this business. Let us rise
And bow before the Goddess: Time comes on.

Exeunt. Still music of records.

W. H. Auden

TO THE ONLY BEGETTER OF

THESE ENSUING SONNETS

MR. W. H. ALL HAPPINESS

AND THAT ETERNITY

PROMISED

BY

OUR EVER-LIVING POET

WISHETH

THE WELL-WISHING

ADVENTURER IN

SETTING

FORTH

T.T.

The initials concluding the dedication are those of Thomas Thorpe, the publisher of the volume. The identity of Mr. W. H. is uncertain. Most persons who write on the subject have felt it too prosaic to hold that Mr. W. H. was simply a person who brought the poems into the publisher's hands; rather, they have sought to identify him with the friend to whom many of the poems are addressed. The favorite candidates are William Herbert, Earl of Pembroke (and one of the dedicatees of the First Folio), and Henry Wriothesley, Earl of Southampton (to whom Shakespeare dedicated *Venus and Adonis* and *Lucrece*). But it is unlikely that an earl would be addressed as "Mr." Yet another candidate is Sir William Hervey, third husband of Southampton's mother; his advocates say that Hervey was the "begetter" in the sense that he may have encouraged Shakespeare to write the sonnets urging the young man (allegedly Southampton) to wed.

1

From fairest creatures we desire increase,
That thereby beauty's rose might never die,
But as the riper should by time decease,
His tender heir might bear his memory;   *4*
But thou contracted to thine own bright eyes,
Feed'st thy light's flame with self-substantial fuel,
Making a famine where abundance lies,
Thyself thy foe, to thy sweet self too cruel.   *8*
Thou that art now the world's fresh ornament,
And only herald to the gaudy spring,
Within thine own bud buriest thy content,
And, tender churl, mak'st waste in niggarding.   *12*
    Pity the world, or else this glutton be,
      To eat the world's due, by the grave and thee.

5 **contracted** betrothed 6 **self-substantial fuel** fuel of your own substance 10 **only** chief 11 **thy content** what you contain, i.e., potential fatherhood 12 **niggarding** hoarding 14 **world's due** i.e., propagation of the species 14 **by the grave and thee** i.e., by dying without children

2

When forty winters shall besiege thy brow,
And dig deep trenches in thy beauty's field,
Thy youth's proud livery, so gazed on now,
4 Will be a tottered weed of small worth held:
Then being asked where all thy beauty lies,
Where all the treasure of thy lusty days,
To say within thine own deep-sunken eyes,
8 Were an all-eating shame and thriftless praise.
How much more praise deserved thy beauty's use,
If thou couldst answer, "This fair child of mine
Shall sum my count, and make my old excuse,"
12 Proving his beauty by succession thine.
    This were to be new made when thou art old,
    And see thy blood warm when thou feel'st it cold.

2 **trenches** i.e., wrinkles 3 **livery** outward appearance 4 **tottered weed** tattered garment 6 **lusty** vigorous 8 **thriftless** unprofitable 9 **use** investment 11 **sum my count** even out my account 11 **my old excuse** excuse when I am old

3

Look in thy glass and tell the face thou viewest
Now is the time that face should form another,
Whose fresh repair if now thou not renewest,
Thou dost beguile the world, unbless some mother.   *4*
For where is she so fair whose uneared womb
Disdains the tillage of thy husbandry?
Or who is he so fond will be the tomb
Of his self-love to stop posterity?   *8*
Thou art thy mother's glass, and she in thee
Calls back the lovely April of her prime;
So thou through windows of thine age shalt see,
Despite of wrinkles, this thy golden time.   *12*
   But if thou live rememb'red not to be,
    Die single and thine image dies with thee.

3 **fresh repair** youthful state   4 **unbless some mother** leave some
woman unblessed with motherhood   5 **uneared** untilled   7 **fond**
foolish   8 **Of** because of   13 **rememb'red not to be** only to be
forgotten

4

Unthrifty loveliness, why dost thou spend
Upon thyself thy beauty's legacy?
Nature's bequest gives nothing but doth lend,
4   And being frank she lends to those are free.
Then, beauteous niggard, why dost thou abuse
The bounteous largess given thee to give?
Profitless usurer, why dost thou use
8   So great a sum of sums yet canst not live?
For having traffic with thyself alone,
Thou of thyself thy sweet self dost deceive.
Then how when Nature calls thee to be gone,
12   What acceptable audit canst thou leave?
     Thy unused beauty must be tombed with thee,
     Which, usèd, lives th' executor to be.

2 **beauty's legacy** inheritance of beauty   4 **frank . . . free** (both words mean "generous")   5 **niggard** miser   7 **use** (1) invest (2) use up   8 **live** (1) making a living (2) endure   9 **traffic** commerce   14 **lives** i.e., in a son

5

Those hours that with gentle work did frame
The lovely gaze where every eye doth dwell
Will play the tyrants to the very same
And that unfair which fairly doth excel;   *4*
For never-resting Time leads summer on
To hideous winter and confounds him there,
Sap checked with frost and lusty leaves quite gone,
Beauty o'ersnowed and bareness everywhere.   *8*
Then, were not summer's distillation left
A liquid prisoner pent in walls of glass,
Beauty's effect with beauty were bereft,
Nor it nor no remembrance what it was.   *12*
    But flowers distilled though they with winter meet,
    Leese but their show, their substance still lives sweet.

---

1 **hours** (disyllabic) 2 **gaze** object gazed on 4 **unfair** make
ugly 4 **fairly** in beauty 6 **confounds** destroys 9 **summer's
distillation** perfumes made from flowers 11 **Beauty's effect** i.e.,
the perfume 12 **Nor . . . nor** (there would be) neither . . . nor
14 **Leese but their show** lose only their outward form

6

Then let not winter's ragged hand deface
In thee thy summer ere thou be distilled.
Make sweet some vial; treasure thou some place
4   With beauty's treasure ere it be self-killed.
That use is not forbidden usury
Which happies those that pay the willing loan;
That's for thyself to breed another thee,
8   Or ten times happier be it ten for one.
Ten times thyself were happier than thou art,
If ten of thine ten times refigured thee:
Then what could death do if thou shouldst depart,
12   Leaving thee living in posterity?
 Be not self-willed, for thou art much too fair,
 To be death's conquest and make worms thine heir.

---

1 **ragged** rough   3 **treasure** enrich   5 **use** lending money at interest   6 **happies . . . loan** makes happy those who willingly pay the loan   9 **happier** luckier   10 **refigured** represented

7

Lo, in the orient when the gracious light
Lifts up his burning head, each under eye
Doth homage to his new-appearing sight,
Serving with looks his sacred majesty;   4
And having climbed the steep-up heavenly hill,
Resembling strong youth in his middle age,
Yet mortal looks adore his beauty still,
Attending on his golden pilgrimage;   8
But when from highmost pitch, with weary car,
Like feeble age he reeleth from the day,
The eyes, 'fore duteous, now converted are
From his low tract and look another way: 12
    So thou, thyself outgoing in thy noon,
    Unlooked on diest unless thou get a son.

1 **orient** east   1 **light** sun   2 **under** i.e., earthly   7 **looks** on-
lookers   9 **highmost pitch** zenith   9 **car** chariot (of Phoebus)
11 **converted** turned away   12 **tract** track   14 **get** beget

8

Music to hear, why hear'st thou music sadly?
Sweets with sweets war not, joy delights in joy.
Why lov'st thou that which thou receiv'st not gladly,
4   Or else receiv'st with pleasure thine annoy?
If the true concord of well tunèd sounds,
By unions married, do offend thine ear,
They do but sweetly chide thee, who confounds
8   In singleness the parts that thou shouldst bear.
Mark how one string, sweet husband to another,
Strikes each in each by mutual ordering;
Resembling sire, and child, and happy mother,
12   Who all in one, one pleasing note do sing;
    Whose speechless song, being many, seeming one,
    Sings this to thee, "Thou single wilt prove none."

1 **Music to hear** you who are music to hear   1 **sadly** gravely
7–8 **confounds . . . bear** i.e., destroys by playing singly the multiple
role (of husband and father) that you should play   9 **sweet husband
to another** i.e., tuned in unison (so that when struck, its partner vi-
brates)   14 **none** nothing

9

Is it for fear to wet a widow's eye
That thou consum'st thyself in single life?
Ah, if thou issueless shalt hap to die,
The world will wail thee like a makeless wife; 4
The world will be thy widow and still weep,
That thou no form of thee hast left behind,
When every private widow well may keep,
By children's eyes, her husband's shape in mind. 8
Look what an unthrift in the world doth spend,
Shifts but his place, for still the world enjoys it;
But beauty's waste hath in the world an end,
And kept unused, the user so destroys it: 12
    No love toward others in that bosom sits
    That on himself such murd'rous shame commits.

3 **issueless** childless　3 **hap** happen, chance　4 **makeless** mateless　5 **still** always　7 **private** individual　9 **Look what** whatever　9 **unthrift** prodigal　10 **his** its　14 **murd'rous shame** shameful murder

10

For shame, deny that thou bear'st love to any
Who for thyself art so unprovident.
Grant if thou wilt, thou art beloved of many,
4   But that thou none lov'st is most evident;
For thou art so possessed with murd'rous hate,
That 'gainst thyself thou stick'st not to conspire,
Seeking that beauteous roof to ruinate,
8   Which to repair should be thy chief desire.
O, change thy thought, that I may change my mind.
Shall hate be fairer lodged than gentle love?
Be as thy presence is, gracious and kind,
12   Or to thyself at least kind-hearted prove.
      Make thee another self for love of me,
      That beauty still may live in thine or thee.

6 **thou stick'st** you scruple   7 **roof** i.e., body (which houses the spirit)   11 **presence** appearance   14 **still** always

11

As fast as thou shalt wane, so fast thou grow'st
In one of thine, from that which thou departest;
And that fresh blood which youngly thou bestow'st
Thou mayst call thine, when thou from youth convertest.   *4*
Herein lives wisdom, beauty, and increase;
Without this, folly, age, and cold decay.
If all were minded so, the times should cease,
And threescore year would make the world away.   *8*
Let those whom Nature hath not made for store,
Harsh, featureless, and rude, barrenly perish.
Look whom she best endowed, she gave the more;
Which bounteous gift thou shouldst in bounty cherish.   *12*
    She carved thee for her seal, and meant thereby
    Thou shouldst print more, not let that copy die.

3 **youngly** in youth   4 **Thou . . . convertest** you . . . change   6 **Without this** beyond this course of action   7 **times** generations of men
9 **for store** as stock to draw upon   10 **featureless, and rude** ugly
and unrefined   11 **Look whom** whomever   13 **seal** stamp

12

When I do count the clock that tells the time,
And see the brave day sunk in hideous night;
When I behold the violet past prime,
4 And sable curls are silvered o'er with white;
When lofty trees I see barren of leaves,
Which erst from heat did canopy the herd,
And summer's green, all girded up in sheaves,
8 Borne on the bier with white and bristly beard;
Then of thy beauty do I question make,
That thou among the wastes of time must go,
Since sweets and beauties do themselves forsake,
12 And die as fast as they see others grow,
    And nothing 'gainst Time's scythe can make defense,
    Save breed, to brave him when he takes thee hence.

2 **brave** splendid   4 **sable** black   6 **erst** formerly   9 **question
make** entertain doubt   14 **Save breed, to brave** except offspring,
to defy

13

O, that you were yourself, but, love, you are
No longer yours than you yourself here live;
Against this coming end you should prepare,
And your sweet semblance to some other give.   *4*
So should that beauty which you hold in lease
Find no determination, then you were
Yourself again after your self's decease,
When your sweet issue your sweet form should bear.   *8*
Who lets so fair a house fall to decay,
Which husbandry in honor might uphold
Against the stormy gusts of winter's day
And barren rage of death's eternal cold?   *12*
    O, none but unthrifts! Dear my love, you know,
      You had a father; let your son say so.

3 **Against** in expectation of   5 **in lease** i.e., for a term   6 **determination** end   8 **issue** offspring   10 **husbandry** (1) thrift (2) marriage   13 **unthrifts** prodigals

14

Not from the stars do I my judgment pluck,
And yet methinks I have astronomy;
But not to tell of good or evil luck,
4   Of plagues, of dearths, or seasons' quality;
Nor can I fortune to brief minutes tell,
Pointing to each his thunder, rain, and wind,
Or say with princes if it shall go well
8   By oft predict that I in heaven find.
But from thine eyes my knowledge I derive,
And, constant stars, in them I read such art
As truth and beauty shall together thrive
12   If from thyself to store thou wouldst convert:
     Or else of thee this I prognosticate,
     Thy end is truth's and beauty's doom and date.

1 **pluck** derive   2 **astronomy** astrology   5 **fortune to brief minutes tell** i.e., predict the exact time of each happening   6 **Pointing** appointing   6 **his** its   8 **oft predict that** frequent prediction of what   10 **art** knowledge   11 **As** as that   12 **store** fertility   12 **convert** turn   14 **doom and date** end, Judgment Day

15

When I consider everything that grows
Holds in perfection but a little moment,
That this huge stage presenteth naught but shows
Whereon the stars in secret influence comment;   *4*
When I perceive that men as plants increase,
Cheerèd and checked even by the selfsame sky,
Vaunt in their youthful sap, at height decrease,
And wear their brave state out of memory;   *8*
Then the conceit of this inconstant stay
Sets you most rich in youth before my sight,
Where wasteful Time debateth with Decay,
To change your day of youth to sullied night;   *12*
    And, all in war with Time for love of you,
    As he takes from you, I engraft you new.

4 **in secret influence comment** i.e., exert a silent influence
6 **Cheerèd and checked** encouraged and rebuked 7 **Vaunt**
boast 8 **wear their brave state out of memory** wear out their
handsome condition until it is forgotten 9 **conceit** idea 9 **stay**
duration 11 **debateth** contends 14 **engraft** i.e., with eternizing
poetry

16

But wherefore do not you a mightier way
Make war upon this bloody tyrant Time?
And fortify yourself in your decay
4   With means more blessèd than my barren rhyme?
Now stand you on the top of happy hours,
And many maiden gardens, yet unset,
With virtuous wish would bear your living flowers,
8   Much liker than your painted counterfeit.
So should the lines of life that life repair,
Which this time's pencil, or my pupil pen,
Neither in inward worth nor outward fair
12 Can make you live yourself in eyes of men.
     To give away yourself keeps yourself still,
       And you must live, drawn by your own sweet skill.

---

6 **unset** unplanted   8 **counterfeit** portrait   9 **lines of life** lineal
descendants   10 **time's pencil** artist of the present day   11 **fair**
beauty   13 **give away yourself** i.e., to beget children   13 **keeps**
preserves

17

Who will believe my verse in time to come
If it were filled with your most high deserts?
Though yet heaven knows it is but as a tomb
Which hides your life and shows not half your parts.   *4*
If I could write the beauty of your eyes,
And in fresh numbers number all your graces,
The age to come would say "This poet lies,
Such heavenly touches ne'er touched earthly faces."   *8*
So should my papers, yellowed with their age,
Be scorned, like old men of less truth than tongue,
And your true rights be termed a poet's rage
And stretchèd meter of an antique song: *12*
  But were some child of yours alive that time,
  You should live twice, in it and in my rhyme.

2 **deserts** (rhymes with "parts") 4 **parts** good qualities 6 **numbers** verses 8 **touches** (1) strokes of pencil or brush (2) traits
11 **true rights** due praise 11 **rage** inspiration 12 **stretchèd meter** poetic exaggeration

18

Shall I compare thee to a summer's day?
Thou art more lovely and more temperate.
Rough winds do shake the darling buds of May,
4 And summer's lease hath all too short a date.
Sometime too hot the eye of heaven shines,
And often is his gold complexion dimmed;
And every fair from fair sometime declines,
8 By chance, or nature's changing course, untrimmed;
But thy eternal summer shall not fade,
Nor lose possession of that fair thou ow'st,
Nor shall Death brag thou wand'rest in his shade,
12 When in eternal lines to time thou grow'st.
  So long as men can breathe or eyes can see,
  So long lives this, and this gives life to thee.

4 **lease** allotted time 4 **date** duration 7 **fair from fair** beautiful thing from beauty 8 **untrimmed** divested of ornament 10 **thou ow'st** you possess

19

Devouring Time, blunt thou the lion's paws,
And make the earth devour her own sweet brood;
Pluck the keen teeth from the fierce tiger's jaws,
And burn the long-lived phoenix in her blood;   *4*
Make glad and sorry seasons as thou fleets,
And do whate'er thou wilt, swift-footed Time,
To the wide world and all her fading sweets;
But I forbid thee one most heinous crime,   *8*
O, carve not with thy hours my love's fair brow,
Nor draw no lines there with thine antique pen.
Him in thy course untainted do allow,
For beauty's pattern to succeeding men.   *12*
   Yet do thy worst, old Time; despite thy wrong,
   My love shall in my verse ever live young.

---

4 **phoenix** mythical bird that periodically is consumed in flames and
arises renewed (symbol of immortality) 4 **in her blood** alive
10 **antique** (1) old (2) grotesque, antic 11 **untainted** untouched

20

A woman's face, with Nature's own hand painted,
Hast thou, the master mistress of my passion;
A woman's gentle heart, but not acquainted
4   With shifting change, as is false women's fashion;
An eye more bright than theirs, less false in rolling,
Gilding the object whereupon it gazeth;
A man in hue all hues in his controlling,
Which steals men's eyes and women's souls
8   amazeth.
And for a woman wert thou first created,
Till Nature as she wrought thee fell a-doting,
And by addition me of thee defeated,
12 By adding one thing to my purpose nothing.
    But since she pricked thee out for women's
        pleasure,
    Mine be thy love, and thy love's use their
        treasure.

1 **Nature's** i.e., not Art's   2 **master mistress** supreme mistress
(some editors hyphenate, indicating that in this case the "mistress" is
a "master")   2 **passion** love (or possibly love poems)   5 **rolling**
i.e., roving from one to another   7 **hue** appearance (both complex-
ion and form)   11 **defeated** defrauded   13 **pricked thee out**
(1) marked you out (2) added a phallus (cf. line 12)

21

So is it not with me as with that Muse,
Stirred by a painted beauty to his verse,
Who heaven itself for ornament doth use,
And every fair with his fair doth rehearse;   *4*
Making a couplement of proud compare
With sun and moon, with earth and sea's rich gems,
With April's first-born flowers, and all things rare
That heaven's air in this huge rondure hems.   *8*
O, let me true in love but truly write,
And then believe me, my love is as fair
As any mother's child, though not so bright
As those gold candles fixed in heaven's air: *12*
    Let them say more that like of hearsay well;
    I will not praise that purpose not to sell.

1 **Muse** poet 2 **Stirred** inspired 4 **fair** beautiful thing 4 **rehearse** mention, i.e., compare 5 **couplement** combination 5 **compare** comparison 8 **rondure** sphere, world 8 **hems** encircles
13 **that like of hearsay well** who delight in empty talk 14 **that** who

22

My glass shall not persuade me I am old,
So long as youth and thou are of one date,
But when in thee Time's furrows I behold,
⁴ Then look I death my days should expiate.
For all that beauty that doth cover thee
Is but the seemly raiment of my heart,
Which in thy breast doth live, as thine in me.
⁸ How can I then be elder than thou art?
O, therefore, love, be of thyself so wary
As I, not for myself, but for thee will,
Bearing thy heart, which I will keep so chary
¹² As tender nurse her babe from faring ill.
    Presume not on thy heart when mine is slain;
    Thou gav'st me thine, not to give back again.

2 **of one date** of the same age   4 **expiate** end   11 **chary** carefully   13 **Presume not on** do not lay claim to

23

As an unperfect actor on the stage,
Who with his fear is put besides his part,
Or some fierce thing replete with too much rage,
Whose strength's abundance weakens his own heart;   *4*
So I, for fear of trust, forget to say
The perfect ceremony of love's right,
And in mine own love's strength seem to decay,
O'ercharged with burden of mine own love's fight.   *8*
O, let my books be then the eloquence
And dumb presagers of my speaking breast,
Who plead for love, and look for recompense,
More than that tongue that more hath more expressed.   *12*
    O, learn to read what silent love hath writ.
    To hear with eyes belongs to love's fine wit.

5 **for fear of trust** fearing to trust myself   6 **right** (pun on
"rite")   9 **books** (possibly it should be emended to "looks," i.e.,
though silent, he hopes his looks will speak for him)   10 **dumb
presagers** silent foretellers   12 **more expressed** more often ex-
pressed   14 **wit** intelligence

24

Mine eye hath played the painter and hath steeled
Thy beauty's form in table of my heart;
My body is the frame wherein 'tis held,
4   And perspective it is best painter's art,
For through the painter must you see his skill,
To find where your true image pictured lies,
Which in my bosom's shop is hanging still,
8   That hath his windows glazèd with thine eyes.
Now see what good turns eyes for eyes have done:
Mine eyes have drawn thy shape, and thine for me
Are windows to my breast, wherethrough the sun
12 Delights to peep, to gaze therein on thee.
    Yet eyes this cunning want to grace their art,
    They draw but what they see, know not the heart.

1 **steeled** engraved   2 **table** tablet, picture   4 **perspective** (perhaps the idea is that the *frame*, in line 3, contributes to the perspective of the picture it encloses; some editors put a colon after *perspective*)   8 **his** its   8 **glazèd** covered as with glass   13 **cunning** ability   13 **want** lack

25

Let those who are in favor with their stars
Of public honor and proud titles boast,
Whilst I whom fortune of such triumph bars,
Unlooked for joy in that I honor most.   4
Great princes' favorites their fair leaves spread
But as the marigold at the sun's eye,
And in themselves their pride lies burièd,
For at a frown they in their glory die.   8
The painful warrior famousèd for might,
After a thousand victories once foiled,
Is from the book of honor rasèd quite,
And all the rest forgot for which he toiled.   12
    Then happy I that love and am beloved
    Where I may not remove, nor be removed.

4 **Unlooked for joy in that** unexpectedly enjoy that which   6 **But only**   9 **painful** painstaking   11 **rasèd quite** erased entirely

26

Lord of my love, to whom in vassalage
Thy merit hath my duty strongly knit,
To thee I send this written ambassage,
To witness duty, not to show my wit.
Duty so great, which wit so poor as mine
May make seem bare, in wanting words to show it,
But that I hope some good conceit of thine
In thy soul's thought, all naked, will bestow it;
Till whatsoever star that guides my moving
Points on me graciously with fair aspect,
And puts apparel on my tottered loving
To show me worthy of thy sweet respect.
    Then may I dare to boast how I do love thee;
    Till then, not show my head where thou mayst prove
    me.

4

8

12

3 **written ambassage** message   4 **wit** mental powers   6 **wanting** lacking   7 **conceit** thought   8 **all naked, will bestow** it will accept (give lodging to) my bare statement   9 **moving** life   10 **aspect** astrological influence   11 **tottered** tattered   14 **prove** test

27

Weary with toil, I haste me to my bed,
The dear repose for limbs with travel tired,
But then begins a journey in my head
To work my mind when body's work's expired;   *4*
For then my thoughts, from far where I abide,
Intend a zealous pilgrimage to thee,
And keep my drooping eyelids open wide,
Looking on darkness which the blind do see;   *8*
Save that my soul's imaginary sight
Presents thy shadow to my sightless view,
Which like a jewel hung in ghastly night,
Makes black night beauteous and her old face new.   *12*
   Lo, thus, by day my limbs, by night my mind,
    For thee, and for myself, no quiet find.

2 **travel** (1) labor (2) journeying   4 **To work** to set at work   6 **Intend** set out upon   9 **imaginary** imaginative   10 **shadow** image

28

How can I then return in happy plight
That am debarred the benefit of rest,
When day's oppression is not eased by night,
4 But day by night and night by day oppressed,
And each, though enemies to either's reign,
Do in consent shake hands to torture me,
The one by toil, the other to complain
8 How far I toil, still farther off from thee?
I tell the day, to please him, thou art bright
And dost him grace when clouds do blot the heaven;
So flatter I the swart-complexioned night,
12 When sparkling stars twire not, thou gild'st the even.
    But day doth daily draw my sorrows longer,
    And night doth nightly make grief's length seem stronger.

6 **shake hands** unite   7 **the other to complain** i.e., the night causes
me to complain   10 **dost him grace** i.e., shine for him   11 **swart-
complexioned** dark complexioned   12 **twire** twinkle (?)   12 **thou
gild'st the even** you brighten the evening

29

When, in disgrace with Fortune and men's eyes,
I all alone beweep my outcast state,
And trouble deaf heaven with my bootless cries,
And look upon myself and curse my fate,   *4*
Wishing me like to one more rich in hope,
Featured like him, like him with friends possessed,
Desiring this man's art, and that man's scope,
With what I most enjoy contented least;   *8*
Yet in these thoughts myself almost despising,
Haply I think on thee, and then my state,
Like to the lark at break of day arising
From sullen earth, sings hymns at heaven's gate;   *12*
   For thy sweet love rememb'red such wealth brings,
   That then I scorn to change my state with kings.

1 **disgrace** disfavor   3 **bootless** useless   6 **like him, like him** like
a second man, like a third man   7 **art** skill   7 **scope** mental power
10 **Haply** perchance   10 **state** i.e., condition   12 **sullen** gloomy

30

When to the sessions of sweet silent thought
I summon up remembrance of things past,
I sigh the lack of many a thing I sought,
4   And with old woes new wail my dear Time's waste.
Then can I drown an eye, unused to flow,
For precious friends hid in death's dateless night,
And weep afresh love's long since canceled woe,
8   And moan th' expense of many a vanished sight;
Then can I grieve at grievances foregone,
And heavily from woe to woe tell o'er
The sad account of fore-bemoanèd moan,
12   Which I new pay as if not paid before.
    But if the while I think on thee, dear friend,
    All losses are restored and sorrows end.

1 **sessions** sittings of a court or council   4 **new wail** newly bewail   4 **my dear Time's waste** Time's destruction of things dear to me   6 **dateless** endless   7 **canceled** i.e., because paid in full   8 **expense** loss   9 **foregone** former   10 **tell** count

31

Thy bosom is endearèd with all hearts
Which I by lacking have supposèd dead;
And there reigns love and all love's loving parts,
And all those friends which I thought buried. *4*
How many a holy and obsequious tear
Hath dear religious love stol'n from mine eye,
As interest of the dead, which now appear
But things removed that hidden in there lie. *8*
Thou art the grave where buried love doth live,
Hung with the trophies of my lovers gone,
Who all their parts of me to thee did give;
That due of many now is thine alone. *12*
　　Their images I loved I view in thee,
　　And thou, all they, hast all the all of me.

---

1 **endearèd** made more precious   5 **obsequious** funereal   6 **religious** worshipful   7 **interest** right   7 **which** who   10 **trophies** memorials   11 **parts** shares   12 **That due of many** that which was due to many

32

If thou survive my well-contented day,
When that churl Death my bones with dust shall cover,
And shalt by fortune once more resurvey

4 These poor rude lines of thy deceasèd lover,
Compare them with the bett'ring of the time,
And though they be outstripped by every pen,
Reserve them for my love, not for their rhyme,

8 Exceeded by the height of happier men.
O, then vouchsafe me but this loving thought:
"Had my friend's Muse grown with this growing age,
A dearer birth than this his love had brought,

12 To march in ranks of better equipage;
    But since he died, and poets better prove,
    Theirs for their style I'll read, his for his love."

1 **my well-contented day** i.e., my day of death whose arrival will content me   5 **bett'ring** improved poetry   7 **Reserve** preserve   8 **happier** more gifted   12 **of better equipage** better equipped

33

Full many a glorious morning have I seen
Flatter the mountain tops with sovereign eye,
Kissing with golden face the meadows green,
Gilding pale streams with heavenly alchemy;   4
Anon permit the basest clouds to ride
With ugly rack on his celestial face,
And from the forlorn world his visage hide,
Stealing unseen to west with this disgrace.   8
Even so my sun one early morn did shine,
With all triumphant splendor on my brow;
But out alack, he was but one hour mine,
The region cloud hath masked him from me now.   12
   Yet him for this my love no whit disdaineth;
   Suns of the world may stain when heaven's sun
     staineth.

2 **Flatter . . . eye** i.e., the sun, like a monarch's eye, flatters all that it
rests upon 5 **Anon** soon 5 **basest** darkest 6 **rack** vapory
clouds 7 **forlorn** forsaken 11 **out alack** alas 12 **region cloud**
clouds of the upper air 14 **stain** grow dim

34

Why didst thou promise such a beauteous day,
And make me travel forth without my cloak,
To let base clouds o'ertake me in my way,
4   Hiding thy brav'ry in their rotten smoke?
'Tis not enough that through the cloud thou break,
To dry the rain on my storm-beaten face,
For no man well of such a salve can speak,
8   That heals the wound, and cures not the disgrace.
Nor can thy shame give physic to my grief;
Though thou repent, yet I have still the loss.
Th' offender's sorrow lends but weak relief
12   To him that bears the strong offense's cross.
    Ah, but those tears are pearl which thy love sheeds,
    And they are rich and ransom all ill deeds.

3 **base** dark 4 **brav'ry** finery 4 **rotten smoke** unwholesome vapors 9 **physic** remedy 13 **sheeds** sheds 14 **ransom** atone for

35

No more be grieved at that which thou hast done:
Roses have thorns, and silver fountains mud,
Clouds and eclipses stain both moon and sun,
And loathsome canker lives in sweetest bud.   4
All men make faults, and even I in this,
Authorizing thy trespass with compare,
Myself corrupting, salving thy amiss,
Excusing thy sins more than thy sins are;   8
For to thy sensual fault I bring in sense—
Thy adverse party is thy advocate—
And 'gainst myself a lawful plea commence.
Such civil war is in my love and hate   12
    That I an accessory needs must be
    To that sweet thief which sourly robs from me.

---

3 **stain** darken 4 **canker** cankerworm (that destroys flowers)
6 **Authorizing** justifying 6 **with compare** by comparison 7 **salving thy amiss** palliating your misbehavior 8 **Excusing . . . are** i.e.,
offering excuses more abundant than your sins (?) 9 **to thy . . .
sense** perhaps: to your physical fault I add reason ("sense"); possibly,
however, "in sense" is a pun on "incense," i.e., my reason sweetens
your sins 13 **accessory** accomplice 14 **sourly** bitterly

36

Let me confess that we two must be twain,
Although our undivided loves are one.
So shall those blots that do with me remain,
4   Without thy help, by me be borne alone.
In our two loves there is but one respect,
Though in our lives a separable spite,
Which though it alter not love's sole effect,
8   Yet doth it steal sweet hours from love's delight.
I may not evermore acknowledge thee,
Lest my bewailèd guilt should do thee shame;
Nor thou with public kindness honor me,
12   Unless thou take that honor from thy name.
    But do not so; I love thee in such sort
    As, thou being mine, mine is thy good report.

---

5 **but one respect** only one regard   6 **separable spite** spiteful separation   7 **sole** unique   13–14 **But do . . . report** (this couplet is repeated in Sonnet 96)   14 **report** reputation

37

As a decrepit father takes delight
To see his active child do deeds of youth,
So I, made lame by Fortune's dearest spite,
Take all my comfort of thy worth and truth.   *4*
For whether beauty, birth, or wealth, or wit,
Or any of these all, or all, or more,
Entitled in their parts do crownèd sit,
I make my love engrafted to this store.   *8*
So then I am not lame, poor, nor despised
Whilst that this shadow doth such substance give
That I in thy abundance am sufficed
And by a part of all thy glory live.   *12*
    Look what is best, that best I wish in thee.
    This wish I have, then ten times happy me!

3 **dearest** most grievous 4 **of** from 5 **wit** intelligence 7 **Entitled in . . . sit** sit as king entitled to their places 8 **engrafted to this store** i.e., fused with and nourished by this abundance 13 **Look what** whatever

38

How can my Muse want subject to invent,
While thou dost breathe, that pour'st into my verse
Thine own sweet argument, too excellent
4 For every vulgar paper to rehearse?
O, give thyself the thanks, if aught in me
Worthy perusal stand against thy sight;
For who's so dumb that cannot write to thee
8 When thou thyself dost give invention light?
Be thou the tenth Muse, ten times more in worth
Than those old nine which rhymers invocate;
And he that calls on thee, let him bring forth
12 Eternal numbers to outlive long date.
    If my slight Muse do please these curious days,
    The pain be mine, but thine shall be the praise.

1 **want subject to invent** lack subject matter for creation   2 **that** who   3 **argument** subject   4 **vulgar paper** ordinary composition   4 **rehearse** repeat   5 **in me** of my writings   6 **stand against thy sight** meet your eyes, i.e., be written for you   7 **dumb** mute   8 **invention** imagination   10 **invocate** invoke   12 **numbers** verses   12 **long date** a distant era   13 **curious** critical   14 **pain** trouble

39

O, how thy worth with manners may I sing,
When thou art all the better part of me?
What can mine own praise to mine own self bring,
And what is't but mine own when I praise thee?   *4*
Even for this, let us divided live,
And our dear love lose name of single one,
That by this separation I may give
That due to thee which thou deserv'st alone.   *8*
O, absence, what a torment wouldst thou prove,
Were it not thy sour leisure gave sweet leave
To entertain the time with thoughts of love,
Which time and thoughts so sweetly dost deceive,   *12*
  And that thou teachest how to make one twain
  By praising him here who doth hence remain.

1 **with manners** i.e., without self-praise   5 **for** because of   11 **entertain** pass

40

Take all my loves, my love, yea take them all;
What hast thou then more than thou hadst before?
No love, my love, that thou mayst true love call;
4 All mine was thine, before thou hadst this more.
Then if for my love thou my love receivest,
I cannot blame thee for my love thou usest;
But yet be blamed, if thou this self deceivest
8 By willful taste of what thyself refusest.
I do forgive thy robb'ry, gentle thief,
Although thou steal thee all my poverty;
And yet love knows it is a greater grief
12 To bear love's wrong than hate's known injury.
    Lascivious grace, in whom all ill well shows,
    Kill me with spites; yet we must not be foes.

6 **for** because   6 **thou usest** you are intimate with   7 **this self**
i.e., your other self, the poet ("this self" is, however, often emended to
"thy self")   8 **willful taste** capricious enjoyment   10 **my poverty**
the little I have   12 **known** open   13 **Lascivious grace** i.e., you
who have such grace even when lascivious

41

Those pretty wrongs that liberty commits,
When I am sometime absent from thy heart,
Thy beauty and thy years full well befits,
For still temptation follows where thou art.   4
Gentle thou art, and therefore to be won;
Beauteous thou art, therefore to be assailed;
And when a woman woos, what woman's son
Will sourly leave her till she have prevailed?   8
Ay me, but yet thou might'st my seat forbear,
And chide thy beauty and thy straying youth,
Who lead thee in their riot even there
Where thou art forced to break a twofold truth: 12
    Hers, by thy beauty tempting her to thee,
    Thine, by thy beauty being false to me.

1 **pretty** petty (?)   1 **liberty** licentiousness   4 **still** always   9 **seat** place   11 **Who** which   11 **riot** revels   12 **truth** duty

42

That thou hast her, it is not all my grief,
And yet it may be said I loved her dearly;
That she hath thee is of my wailing chief,
4 A loss in love that touches me more nearly.
Loving offenders, thus I will excuse ye:
Thou dost love her, because thou know'st I love her,
And for my sake even so doth she abuse me,
8 Suff'ring my friend for my sake to approve her.
If I lose thee, my loss is my love's gain,
And losing her, my friend hath found that loss:
Both find each other, and I lose both twain,
12 And both for my sake lay on me this cross.
　　But here's the joy: my friend and I are one;
　　Sweet flattery! Then she loves but me alone.

---

3 **of my wailing chief** chief cause of my grief   4 **nearly** closely
7 **abuse** deceive   8 **approve** test, experience sensually   9 **love's**
mistress'

43

When most I wink, then do mine eyes best see,
For all the day they view things unrespected,
But when I sleep, in dreams they look on thee
And, darkly bright, are bright in dark directed.   *4*
Then thou, whose shadow shadows doth make bright,
How would thy shadow's form form happy show
To the clear day with thy much clearer light,
When to unseeing eyes thy shade shines so!   *8*
How would, I say, mine eyes be blessèd made,
By looking on thee in the living day,
When in dead night thy fair imperfect shade
Through heavy sleep on sightless eyes doth stay!   *12*
    All days are nights to see till I see thee,
    And nights bright days when dreams do show thee me.

---

1 **I wink** I close my eyes, i.e., I sleep   2 **unrespected** unregarded
5 **shadow shadows** image darkness   6 **thy shadow's form** the
body that casts your shadow   13 **are nights to see** look like nights

44

If the dull substance of my flesh were thought,
Injurious distance should not stop my way,
For then despite of space I would be brought,
4 From limits far remote, where thou dost stay.
No matter then although my foot did stand
Upon the farthest earth removed from thee;
For nimble thought can jump both sea and land,
8 As soon as think the place where he would be.
But, ah, thought kills me that I am not thought,
To leap large lengths of miles when thou art gone,
But that so much of earth and water wrought,
12 I must attend time's leisure with my moan,
    Receiving naught by elements so slow
    But heavy tears, badges of either's woe.

1 **dull substance** i.e., earth and water (in contrast to air and
fire) 2 **Injurious** malicious 4 **limits** districts 4 **where** to
where 6 **farthest earth removed** earth farthest removed 8 **he**
it 11 **wrought** compounded 12 **attend** await 14 **badges of ei-
ther's woe** i.e., earth's because heavy, water's because wet (and per-
haps because salty)

45

The other two, slight air and purging fire,
Are both with thee, wherever I abide;
The first my thought, the other my desire,
These present-absent with swift motion slide.   4
For when these quicker elements are gone
In tender embassy of love to thee,
My life, being made of four, with two alone
Sinks down to death, oppressed with melancholy;   8
Until life's composition be recured
By those swift messengers returned from thee,
Who even but now come back again, assured
Of thy fair health, recounting it to me.   12
   This told, I joy, but then no longer glad,
    I send them back again, and straight grow sad.

---

1 **two** i.e., of the four elements (see note on the first line of the pre-
vious sonnet)   1 **slight** insubstantial   4 **present-absent** now here,
now gone   7 **two alone** i.e., earth and water   9 **recured** restored
to health   10 **messengers** i.e., fire and air

46

Mine eye and heart are at a mortal war
How to divide the conquest of thy sight;
Mine eye my heart thy picture's sight would bar,
4   My heart mine eye the freedom of that right.
My heart doth plead that thou in him dost lie—
A closet never pierced with crystal eyes;
But the defendant doth that plea deny,
8   And says in him thy fair appearance lies.
To 'cide this title is impanelèd
A quest of thoughts, all tenants to the heart;
And by their verdict is determinèd
12   The clear eye's moiety, and the dear heart's part:
      As thus—mine eye's due is thy outward part,
      And my heart's right thy inward love of heart.

2 **conquest of thy sight** i.e., the right to gaze on you   10 **quest** inquest, jury   12 **moiety** portion

47

Betwixt mine eye and heart a league is took,
And each doth good turns now unto the other.
When that mine eye is famished for a look,
Or heart in love with sighs himself doth smother,   4
With my love's picture then my eye doth feast,
And to the painted banquet bids my heart.
Another time mine eye is my heart's guest
And in his thoughts of love doth share a part.   8
So, either by thy picture or my love,
Thyself away are present still with me;
For thou not farther than my thoughts canst move,
And I am still with them, and they with thee;   12
   Or, if they sleep, thy picture in my sight
   Awakes my heart to heart's and eye's delight.

1 **a league is took** an agreement is made   8 **his** i.e., the heart's
12 **still** always

48

How careful was I, when I took my way,
Each trifle under truest bars to thrust,
That to my use it might unusèd stay
4 From hands of falsehood, in sure wards of trust!
But thou, to whom my jewels trifles are,
Most worthy comfort, now my greatest grief,
Thou best of dearest, and mine only care,
8 Art left the prey of every vulgar thief.
Thee have I not locked up in any chest,
Save where thou art not, though I feel thou art,
Within the gentle closure of my breast,
12 From whence at pleasure thou mayst come and part;
    And even thence thou wilt be stol'n, I fear,
    For truth proves thievish for a prize so dear.

2 **trifle** i.e., in comparison with the person addressed 2 **truest** most trusty 4 **wards** cells 5 **to** in comparison with 8 **vulgar** common 9 **chest** (1) coffer (2) breast 14 **truth** honesty

49

Against that time, if ever that time come,
When I shall see thee frown on my defects,
Whenas thy love hath cast his utmost sum,
Called to that audit by advised respects;   *4*
Against that time when thou shalt strangely pass,
And scarcely greet me with that sun, thine eye,
When love, converted from the thing it was,
Shall reasons find of settled gravity.   *8*
Against that time do I ensconce me here
Within the knowledge of mine own desart,
And this my hand against myself uprear,
To guard the lawful reasons on thy part.   *12*
    To leave poor me thou hast the strength of laws,
    Since why to love I can allege no cause.

1 **Against** in preparation for   3 **cast his utmost sum** computed its
final reckoning   4 **advised respects** well-considered reasons
5 **strangely** with a reserved manner (like a stranger)   9 **ensconce
me** fortify myself   10 **desart** desert   11 **uprear** raise as a witness

50

How heavy do I journey on the way
When what I seek, my weary travel's end,
Doth teach that ease and that repose to say,
4   "Thus far the miles are measured from thy friend."
The beast that bears me, tired with my woe,
Plods dully on, to bear that weight in me,
As if by some instinct the wretch did know
8   His rider loved not speed, being made from thee.
The bloody spur cannot provoke him on,
That sometimes anger thrusts into his hide,
Which heavily he answers with a groan,
12   More sharp to me than spurring to his side;
    For that same groan doth put this in my mind:
    My grief lies onward and my joy behind.

1 **heavy** sadly

51

Thus can my love excuse the slow offense
Of my dull bearer, when from thee I speed:
From where thou art why should I haste me thence?
Till I return, of posting is no need.   *4*
O, what excuse will my poor beast then find
When swift extremity can seem but slow?
Then should I spur, though mounted on the wind,
In wingèd speed no motion shall I know.   *8*
Then can no horse with my desire keep pace;
Therefore desire, of perfect'st love being made,
Shall neigh (no dull flesh) in his fiery race;
But love, for love, thus shall excuse my jade: *12*
    Since from thee going he went willful slow,
    Towards thee I'll run and give him leave to go.

1 **slow offense** offense of slowness   4 **posting** riding hastily
6 **swift extremity** extreme swiftness   11 **neigh** i.e., in exultation in
its ethereal speed (?) (some editors emend to "weigh" with the mean-
ing that desire refuses to keep to the slow pace of the horse and will
not weigh down the horse's "dull flesh")   12 **jade** nag   14 **go** walk

52

So am I as the rich, whose blessèd key
Can bring him to his sweet up-lockèd treasure,
The which he will not ev'ry hour survey,
4   For blunting the fine point of seldom pleasure.
Therefore are feasts so solemn and so rare,
Since, seldom coming, in the long year set,
Like stones of worth they thinly placèd are,
8   Or captain jewels in the carcanet.
So is the time that keeps you as my chest,
Or as the wardrobe which the robe doth hide,
To make some special instant special blest,
12   By new unfolding his imprisoned pride.
        Blessèd are you whose worthiness gives scope,
        Being had, to triumph, being lacked, to hope.

1 **key** (rhymes with "survey")   4 **For** for fear of   4 **seldom plea-
sure** pleasure infrequently enjoyed   8 **captain** chief   8 **carcanet**
collar of jewels   12 **his** its

53

What is your substance, whereof are you made,
That millions of strange shadows on you tend?
Since everyone hath, every one, one shade,
And you, but one, can every shadow lend. 4
Describe Adonis, and the counterfeit
Is poorly imitated after you;
On Helen's cheek all art of beauty set,
And you in Grecian tires are painted new. 8
Speak of the spring and foison of the year;
The one doth shadow of your beauty show,
The other as your bounty doth appear,
And you in every blessèd shape we know. 12
    In all external grace you have some part,
    But you like none, none you, for constant heart.

---

2 **strange shadows** images not your own (the images of Adonis, Helen, spring, and autumn in the following lines) 2 **tend** wait on 3 **shade** shadow 4 **And you ... lend** i.e., and you, though one, can provide a variety of good traits (?) 5 **counterfeit** picture 8 **tires** attire 9 **foison** rich harvest

54

O, how much more doth beauty beauteous seem,
By that sweet ornament which truth doth give!
The rose looks fair, but fairer we it deem
4   For that sweet odor which doth in it live.
The canker blooms have full as deep a dye,
As the perfumèd tincture of the roses,
Hang on such thorns, and play as wantonly,
8   When summer's breath their maskèd buds discloses;
But, for their virtue only is their show,
They live unwooed and unrespected fade,
Die to themselves. Sweet roses do not so;
12 Of their sweet deaths are sweetest odors made.
    And so of you, beauteous and lovely youth,
        When that shall vade, by verse distills your truth.

2 **truth** fidelity   5 **canker blooms** dog roses (which lack the perfume of the damask rose)   6 **tincture** color   7 **wantonly** unrestrainedly   8 **maskèd** hidden   8 **discloses** opens   9 **for** because   9 **virtue only** only merit   10 **unrespected** unregarded   12 **are sweetest odors made** perfumes are made   14 **vade** depart, perish   14 **by verse distills your truth** by means of verse your essence is distilled ("by" is often emended to "my")

55

Not marble, nor the gilded monuments
Of princes, shall outlive this pow'rful rhyme,
But you shall shine more bright in these contents
Than unswept stone, besmeared with sluttish time.   *4*
When wasteful war shall statues overturn,
And broils root out the work of masonry,
Nor Mars his sword nor war's quick fire shall burn
The living record of your memory.   *8*
'Gainst death and all oblivious enmity
Shall you pace forth; your praise shall still find room
Even in the eyes of all posterity
That wear this world out to the ending doom.   *12*
    So, till the judgment that yourself arise,
    You live in this, and dwell in lovers' eyes.

3 **these contents** i.e., the contents of this poem   4 **Than** than
in   4 **stone** memorial tablet in the floor of a church   6 **broils** skir-
mishes   7 **Nor . . . nor** neither . . . nor   7 **Mars his sword** Mars'
sword   7 **burn** (either metaphorically governs "Mars his sword" as
well as "war's quick fire," or the verb governing "Mars his sword" is
omitted)   9 **all oblivious enmity** all enmity that brings oblivion (?)
enmity that brings oblivion to all (?)   12 **wear this world out**
outlasts this world   13 **judgment that** Judgment Day when
14 **lovers'** admirers'

56

Sweet love, renew thy force; be it not said
Thy edge should blunter be than appetite,
Which but today by feeding is allayed,
4 Tomorrow sharp'ned in his former might.
So, love, be thou; although today thou fill
Thy hungry eyes even till they wink with fullness,
Tomorrow see again, and do not kill
8 The spirit of love with a perpetual dullness.
Let this sad int'rim like the ocean be
Which parts the shore where two contracted new
Come daily to the banks, that, when they see
12 Return of love, more blest may be the view;
  Or call it winter, which being full of care,
  Makes summer's welcome thrice more wished,
    more rare.

---

1 **love** spirit of love, i.e., not the beloved   2 **edge** keenness   2 **appetite** lust   6 **wink** shut in sleep   9 **sad int'rim** period of estrangement (?)   10 **contracted new** newly betrothed

57

Being your slave, what should I do but tend
Upon the hours and times of your desire?
I have no precious time at all to spend,
Nor services to do till you require.   4
Nor dare I chide the world-without-end hour
Whilst I, my sovereign, watch the clock for you,
Nor think the bitterness of absence sour
When you have bid your servant once adieu.   8
Nor dare I question with my jealous thought
Where you may be, or your affairs suppose,
But, like a sad slave, stay and think of naught
Save where you are how happy you make those.   12
   So true a fool is love that in your will,
   Though you do anything, he thinks no ill.

1 **tend** wait 5 **world-without-end** seemingly endless 7 **Nor
think** nor dare I think 9 **question** dispute 10 **suppose** guess
at 13 **will** desire (with a pun on Shakespeare's first name)

58

That god forbid that made me first your slave
I should in thought control your times of pleasure,
Or at your hand th' account of hours to crave,
4   Being your vassal bound to stay your leisure.
O, let me suffer, being at your beck,
Th' imprisoned absence of your liberty;
And patience, tame to sufferance, bide each check,
8   Without accusing you of injury.
Be where you list, your charter is so strong
That you yourself may privilege your time
To what you will; to you it doth belong
12   Yourself to pardon of self-doing crime.
    I am to wait, though waiting so be hell,
    Not blame your pleasure, be it ill or well.

---

4 **stay your leisure** wait until you are unoccupied   6 **Th' imprisoned . . . liberty** the imprisonment brought to me by your freedom to absent yourself   7 **And patience . . . check** i.e., and patience, disciplined to accept suffering, endures every rebuke   8 **injury** injustice   9 **list** wish   9 **charter** privilege   10 **privilege** authorize   12 **self-doing** (1) done by one's self (2) done to one's self   13 **am to** must

59

If there be nothing new, but that which is
Hath been before, how are our brains beguiled,
Which, laboring for invention, bear amiss
The second burden of a former child!   *4*
O, that record could with a backward look,
Even of five hundred courses of the sun,
Show me your image in some antique book,
Since mind at first in character was done;   *8*
That I might see what the old world could say
To this composèd wonder of your frame;
Whether we are mended, or whe'r better they,
Or whether revolution be the same.   *12*
   O, sure I am the wits of former days
   To subjects worse have given admiring praise.

3 **for invention** i.e., to create something new   3–4 **bear . . . former child** futilely bring forth only a reproduction of what had already been created   5 **record** memory   6 **courses of the sun** years   8 **Since mind . . . done** since thought was first expressed in writing   10 **composèd wonder** wonderful composition   11 **mended** bettered   11 **whe'r** whether   12 **revolution be the same** i.e., cycles are repeated   13 **wits** men of intellect

60

Like as the waves make towards the pebbled shore,
So do our minutes hasten to their end;
Each changing place with that which goes before,
4 In sequent toil all forwards do contend.
Nativity, once in the main of light,
Crawls to maturity, wherewith being crowned,
Crooked eclipses 'gainst his glory fight,
8 And Time that gave doth now his gift confound.
Time doth transfix the flourish set on youth,
And delves the parallels in beauty's brow,
Feeds on the rarities of nature's truth,
12 And nothing stands but for his scythe to mow:
    And yet to times in hope my verse shall stand,
    Praising thy worth, despite his cruel hand.

4 **sequent** successive   5 **Nativity . . . light** i.e., the newborn, at first
in the ocean (metaphorical for "great expanse" or "flood") of light
7 **Crooked** malignant   8 **confound** destroy   9 **transfix** destroy
10 **delves the parallels** i.e., digs wrinkles   13 **times in hope** fu-
ture times

61

Is it thy will thy image should keep open
My heavy eyelids to the weary night?
Dost thou desire my slumbers should be broken
While shadows like to thee do mock my sight?   *4*
Is it thy spirit that thou send'st from thee
So far from home into my deeds to pry,
To find out shames and idle hours in me,
The scope and tenure of thy jealousy?   *8*
O no, thy love, though much, is not so great.
It is my love that keeps mine eye awake,
Mine own true love that doth my rest defeat,
To play the watchman ever for thy sake.   *12*
   For thee watch I, whilst thou dost wake elsewhere,
   From me far off, with others all too near.

4 **shadows** images 8 **The scope . . . jealousy** the aim and meaning
of your suspicion 11 **defeat** destroy 13 **watch** keep awake
13 **wake** revel at night (with a pun on "wake up in bed")

62

Sin of self-love possesseth all mine eye
And all my soul and all my every part;
And for this sin there is no remedy,
4   It is so grounded inward in my heart.
Methinks no face so gracious is as mine,
No shape so true, no truth of such account,
And for myself mine own worth do define,
8   As I all other in all worths surmount.
But when my glass shows me myself indeed,
Beated and chopped with tanned antiquity,
Mine own self-love quite contrary I read;
12   Self so self-loving were iniquity.
    'Tis thee, myself, that for myself I praise,
    Painting my age with beauty of thy days.

5 **gracious** attractive   8 **As** as though   8 **other** others   10 **chopped** creased   10 **antiquity** old age   13 **myself** my alter ego   13 **that for** whom as   14 **days** i.e., youth

63

Against my love shall be as I am now,
With Time's injurious hand crushed and o'erworn;
When hours have drained his blood and filled his brow
With lines and wrinkles, when his youthful morn ———   4
Hath traveled on to Age's steepy night,
And all those beauties whereof now he's king
Are vanishing, or vanished out of sight,
Stealing away the treasure of his spring;   8
For such a time do I now fortify
Against confounding Age's cruel knife,
That he shall never cut from memory
My sweet love's beauty, though my lover's life.   12
   His beauty shall in these black lines be seen,
    And they shall live, and he in them still green.

1 **Against** in expectation of the time when   5 **Age's steepy night**
i.e., old age, which precipitously leads to the darkness of death
9 **fortify** build defenses   10 **confounding** destructive   10 **knife**
i.e., Time's scythe   12 **my lover's life** (1) the life of my lover (2) the
life of me, the lover

64

When I have seen by Time's fell hand defaced
The rich proud cost of outworn buried age,
When sometime lofty towers I see down-razed,
4   And brass eternal slave to mortal rage;
When I have seen the hungry ocean gain
Advantage on the kingdom of the shore,
And the firm soil win of the wat'ry main,
8   Increasing store with loss and loss with store;
When I have seen such interchange of state,
Or state itself confounded to decay,
Ruin hath taught me thus to ruminate,
12 That Time will come and take my love away.
    This thought is as a death, which cannot choose
    But weep to have that which it fears to lose.

1 **fell** cruel   2 **cost** splendor   2 **age** past times   3 **sometime** once
4 **brass eternal** everlasting brass   4 **mortal rage** the rage of mortality   6 **Advantage** i.e., inroads   8 **Increasing store . . . store**
i.e., now one increases in abundance ("store") with the other's loss,
now one repairs its loss with abundance taken from the other
9 **state** condition (but in line 10 "state" = greatness)   10 **confounded** destroyed   14 **to have** because it has

65

Since brass, nor stone, nor earth, nor boundless sea,
But sad mortality o'ersways their power,
How with this rage shall beauty hold a plea,
Whose action is no stronger than a flower?   *4*
O, how shall summer's honey breath hold out
Against the wrackful siege of batt'ring days,
When rocks impregnable are not so stout,
Nor gates of steel so strong but Time decays?   *8*
O, fearful meditation, where, alack,
Shall Time's best jewel from Time's chest lie hid?
Or what strong hand can hold his swift foot back,
Or who his spoil of beauty can forbid?   *12*
    O, none, unless this miracle have might,
    That in black ink my love may still shine bright.

1 **Since** since there is neither   3 **rage** fury   3 **hold** maintain
4 **action** case, suit   6 **wrackful** destructive   8 **decays** causes
them to decay   10 **from Time's chest lie hid** i.e., conceal itself to
avoid being enclosed in Time's coffer   12 **spoil** plundering
14 **my love** my beloved

66

Tired with all these, for restful death I cry,
As, to behold desert a beggar born,
And needy nothing trimmed in jollity,
4   And purest faith unhappily forsworn,
And gilded honor shamefully misplaced,
And maiden virtue rudely strumpeted,
And right perfection wrongfully disgraced,
8   And strength by limping sway disabled,
And art made tongue-tied by authority,
And folly (doctorlike) controlling skill,
And simple truth miscalled simplicity,
12   And captive good attending captain ill.
    Tired with all these, from these would I be gone,
    Save that to die, I leave my love alone.

2 **As** for instance   2 **desert** a deserving person   3 **needy . . .
jollity** i.e., a nonentity, who is poor in virtues, festively attired
4 **unhappily forsworn** miserably perjured   5 **gilded** golden
7 **disgraced** disfigured   8 **limping sway** i.e., incompetent authority   10 **doctorlike** with the air of a learned man   11 **simple**
pure   11 **simplicity** stupidity   12 **attending** subordinated to

67

Ah, wherefore with infection should he live,
And with his presence grace impiety,
That sin by him advantage should achieve
And lace itself with his society?   *4*
Why should false painting imitate his cheek
And steal dead seeing of his living hue?
Why should poor beauty indirectly seek
Roses of shadow, since his rose is true?   *8*
Why should he live, now Nature bankrout is,
Beggared of blood to blush through lively veins,
For she hath no exchequer now but his,
And, proud of many, lives upon his gains?   *12*
   O, him she stores, to show what wealth she had,
   In days long since, before these last so bad.

---

1 **infection** an age of corruption   4 **lace** adorn   5 **false painting**
(possibly the reference is to the use of cosmetics or possibly to por-
traiture)   6 **dead seeing** the lifeless appearance (though perhaps
seeing should be emended to "seeming")   7 **poor** second-
rate   7 **indirectly** by imitation   8 **of shadow** painted (?)
9 **bankrout** bankrupt   10 **Beggared . . . veins** i.e., so impoverished
that it can blush only with the aid of cosmetics   11 **exchequer** trea-
sury (of natural beauty)   12 **proud** (perhaps "falsely proud," but
possibly should be emended to *prived*, i.e., deprived)

68

Thus is his cheek the map of days outworn,
When beauty lived and died as flowers do now,
Before these bastard signs of fair were born,
4   Or durst inhabit on a living brow;
Before the golden tresses of the dead,
The right of sepulchers, were shorn away
To live a second life on second head,
8   Ere beauty's dead fleece made another gay.
In him those holy antique hours are seen,
Without all ornament, itself and true,
Making no summer of another's green,
12   Robbing no old to dress his beauty new;
    And him as for a map doth Nature store,
    To show false Art what beauty was of yore.

1 **map** representation, picture   1 **days outworn** past times
3 **bastard signs of fair** false appearances (cosmetics, wigs) of
beauty   3 **born** (with pun on "borne")   9 **antique hours** ancient
times   10 **all** any   13 **store** preserve

69

Those parts of thee that the world's eye doth view
Want nothing that the thought of hearts can mend;
All tongues, the voice of souls, give thee that due,
Utt'ring bare truth, even so as foes commend.   *4*
Thy outward thus with outward praise is crowned,
But those same tongues that give thee so thine own
In other accents do this praise confound
By seeing farther than the eye hath shown.   *8*
They look into the beauty of thy mind,
And that in guess they measure by thy deeds;
Then, churls, their thoughts, although their eyes were
      kind,
To thy fair flower add the rank smell of weeds;   *12*
    But why thy odor matcheth not thy show,
    The soil is this, that thou dost common grow.

1 **parts** outward qualities   2 **Want** lack   4 **even so as foes com-**
. **mend** i.e., without exaggeration   6 **so thine own** i.e., your due
7 **confound** destroy   14 **soil** (1) ground (2) blemish

70

That thou art blamed shall not be thy defect,
For slander's mark was ever yet the fair;
The ornament of beauty is suspect,
4 A crow that flies in heaven's sweetest air.
So thou be good, slander doth but approve
Thy worth the greater, being wooed of time;
For canker vice the sweetest buds doth love,
8 And thou present'st a pure unstainèd prime.
Thou hast passed by the ambush of young days,
Either not assailed, or victor being charged;
Yet this thy praise cannot be so thy praise
12 To tie up envy, evermore enlarged.
    If some suspect of ill masked not thy show,
    Then thou alone kingdoms of hearts shouldst owe.

3 **The ornament of beauty is suspect** suspicion (because it always
seeks out the beautiful) is an ornament of beauty   5 **So** provided
that   5 **approve** prove   6 **wooed of time** i.e., tempted to evil by
the present times   7 **canker vice** vice like a cankerworm (which
preys on buds)   9 **ambush of young days** snares of youth
10 **charged** attacked   12 **To tie up envy** to overcome malice
12 **enlarged** at liberty   13 **If some . . . show** i.e., if some suspicion
of evil did not surround you   14 **owe** own

71

No longer mourn for me when I am dead
Than you shall hear the surly sullen bell
Give warning to the world that I am fled
From this vile world with vilest worms to dwell.   4
Nay, if you read this line, remember not
The hand that writ it, for I love you so
That I in your sweet thoughts would be forgot,
If thinking on me then should make you woe.   8
O, if, I say, you look upon this verse,
When I, perhaps, compounded am with clay,
Do not so much as my poor name rehearse,
But let your love even with my life decay,   12
   Lest the wise world should look into your moan,
   And mock you with me after I am gone.

72

O, lest the world should task you to recite
What merit lived in me that you should love
After my death, dear love, forget me quite,
4　For you in me can nothing worthy prove;
Unless you would devise some virtuous lie,
To do more for me than mine own desert,
And hang more praise upon deceasèd I
8　Than niggard truth would willingly impart.
O, lest your true love may seem false in this,
That you for love speak well of me untrue,
My name be buried where my body is,
12　And live no more to shame nor me nor you;
　　For I am shamed by that which I bring forth,
　　And so should you, to love things nothing worth.

1 **recite** tell　4 **prove** find　6 **desert** (rhymes with "impart")
8 **niggard** miserly　10 **untrue** untruly　11 **My name be** let my
name be　12 **nor . . . nor** neither . . . nor

73

That time of year thou mayst in me behold
When yellow leaves, or none, or few, do hang
Upon those boughs which shake against the cold,
Bare ruined choirs where late the sweet birds sang.   *4*
In me thou seest the twilight of such day
As after sunset fadeth in the west,
Which by and by black night doth take away,
Death's second self, that seals up all in rest   *8*
In me thou seest the glowing of such fire
That on the ashes of his youth doth lie,
As the deathbed whereon it must expire,
Consumed with that which it was nourished by.   *12*
   This thou perceiv'st, which makes thy love more
      strong,
   To love that well which thou must leave ere long.

4 **choirs** the part of the chancel in which the service is performed   7 **by and by** shortly   8 **Death's second self** i.e., sleep
8 **seals up** encloses (with a suggestion of sealing a coffin)   10 **That** as   14 **that** i.e., that substance, the poet

74

But be contented. When that fell arrest
Without all bail shall carry me away,
My life hath in this line some interest
4   Which for memorial still with thee shall stay.
When thou reviewest this, thou dost review
The very part was consecrate to thee.
The earth can have but earth, which is his due;
8   My spirit is thine, the better part of me.
So then thou hast but lost the dregs of life,
The prey of worms, my body being dead;
The coward conquest of a wretch's knife,
12   Too base of thee to be rememberèd.
   The worth of that is that which it contains,
   And that is this, and this with thee remains.

---

1 **fell** cruel   2 **Without all bail** i.e., without any possibility of re-
lease   3 **line** verse   3 **interest** part   4 **still** always   7 **his** its
11 **The coward conquest** i.e., conquest that even a coward can
make   11 **wretch's** Death's (or possibly Time's)   13–14 **The
worth . . . remains** i.e., the value of the body is in the spirit it con-
tains, and this spirit is in the poem and remains with you

75

So are you to my thoughts as food to life,
Or as sweet-seasoned showers are to the ground;
And for the peace of you I hold such strife
As 'twixt a miser and his wealth is found;   *4*
Now proud as an enjoyer, and anon
Doubting the filching age will steal his treasure;
Now counting best to be with you alone,
Then bettered that the world may see my pleasure;   *8*
Sometime all full with feasting on your sight,
And by and by clean starvèd for a look;
Possessing or pursuing no delight
Save what is had or must from you be took.   *12*
    Thus do I pine and surfeit day by day,
      Or gluttoning on all, or all away.

2 **sweet-seasoned** of the sweet season, spring   3 **peace of you** i.e.,
the peace I find because of you   5 **enjoyer** possessor   5 **anon** soon
6 **Doubting** fearing   8 **bettered** made happier   10 **by and by**
soon   10 **clean** wholly   14 **Or...or** either...or

76

Why is my verse so barren of new pride,
So far from variation or quick change?
Why with the time do I not glance aside
4   To new-found methods and to compounds strange?
Why write I still all one, ever the same,
And keep invention in a noted weed,
That every word doth almost tell my name,
8   Showing their birth, and where they did proceed?
O, know, sweet love, I always write of you,
And you and love are still my argument.
So all my best is dressing old words new,
12 Spending again what is already spent:
    For as the sun is daily new and old,
    So is my love still telling what is told.

1 **pride** adornment   3 **with the time** (1) following the present fashion (2) with the passage of time   4 **compounds** (1) compositions (2) compound words   5 **still all one** always one way   6 **invention** imaginative creation   6 **noted weed** well-known dress   8 **where** whence   10 **argument** theme

77

Thy glass will show thee how thy beauties wear,
Thy dial how thy precious minutes waste;
The vacant leaves thy mind's imprint will bear,
And of this book this learning mayst thou taste.   *4*
The wrinkles which thy glass will truly show,
Of mouthèd graves, will give thee memory;
Thou by thy dial's shady stealth mayst know
Time's thievish progress to eternity.   *8*
Look what thy memory cannot contain,
Commit to these waste blanks, and thou shalt find
Those children nursed, delivered from thy brain,
To take a new acquaintance of thy mind.   *12*
   These offices, so oft as thou wilt look,
    Small profit thee, and much enrich thy book.

---

2 **dial** sundial 3 **vacant leaves** i.e., the blank leaves (of a memo-
randum book, or "table" as in Sonnet 122) 6 **mouthèd** i.e., gap-
ing, openmouthed 6 **give thee memory** remind you 7 **shady
stealth** slowly moving shadow 9 **Look what** whatever 10 **waste
blanks** blank pages 11 **children** i.e., your thoughts 13 **offices**
duties (of looking at the mirror, the sundial, and the thoughts in the
book)

78

So oft have I invoked thee for my Muse
And found such fair assistance in my verse
As every alien pen hath got my use
4   And under thee their poesy disperse.
Thine eyes, that taught the dumb on high to sing
And heavy ignorance aloft to fly,
Have added feathers to the learnèd's wing,
8   And given grace a double majesty.
Yet be most proud of that which I compile,
Whose influence is thine, and born of thee.
In others' works thou dost but mend the style,
12 And arts with thy sweet graces gracèd be;
     But thou art all my art and dost advance
     As high as learning my rude ignorance.

3 **As** that   3 **alien pen** pen belonging to others   3 **got my use**
adopted my practice (either style or subject matter)   4 **under
thee** i.e., with you as patron   5 **on high** (1) aloud (2) loftily
8 **grace** excellence   9 **compile** write   10 **influence** inspiration
14 **rude** unrefined

79

Whilst I alone did call upon thy aid,
My verse alone had all thy gentle grace;
But now my gracious numbers are decayed,
And my sick Muse doth give another place.   *4*
I grant, sweet love, thy lovely argument
Deserves the travail of a worthier pen,
Yet what of thee thy poet doth invent
He robs thee of, and pays it thee again.   *8*
He lends thee virtue, and he stole that word
From thy behavior; beauty doth he give,
And found it in thy cheek; he can afford
No praise to thee but what in thee doth live.   *12*
    Then thank him not for that which he doth say,
    Since what he owes thee thou thyself dost pay.

3 **gracious numbers** pleasing verses   4 **give another place** yield
to another   5 **thy lovely argument** the theme of your loveli-
ness   11 **afford** offer   14 **owes** (poems are regarded as the poet's
repayment of obligation; see Sonnet 83, line 4)

80

O, how I faint when I of you do write,
Knowing a better spirit doth use your name,
And in the praise thereof spends all his might,
4   To make me tongue-tied speaking of your fame.
But since your worth, wide as the ocean is,
The humble as the proudest sail doth bear,
My saucy bark, inferior far to his,
8   On your broad main doth willfully appear.
Your shallowest help will hold me up afloat
Whilst he upon your soundless deep doth ride;
Or, being wracked, I am a worthless boat,
12   He of tall building, and of goodly pride.
     Then if he thrive, and I be cast away,
     The worst was this: my love was my decay.

1 **faint** waver   2 **better spirit** greater genius   6 **humble** humblest   6 **as** as well as   8 **willfully** boldly   10 **soundless** bottomless   11 **wracked** wrecked   11 **boat** small vessel (in contrast to a ship)   12 **tall building** sturdy construction   12 **pride** magnificence   14 **decay** cause of ruin

81

Or I shall live your epitaph to make,
Or you survive when I in earth am rotten.
From hence your memory death cannot take,
Although in me each part will be forgotten.   *4*
Your name from hence immortal life shall have,
Though I, once gone, to all the world must die.
The earth can yield me but a common grave,
When you entombèd in men's eyes shall lie.   *8*
Your monument shall be my gentle verse,
Which eyes not yet created shall o'erread,
And tongues to be your being shall rehearse
When all the breathers of this world are dead.   *12*
   You still shall live—such virtue hath my pen—
   Where breath most breathes, even in the mouths of
      men.

1 **Or** either   3 **From hence** from these poems (?) from the earth (?)
4 **in me each part** all of my qualities   5 **from hence** from these
poems   11 **rehearse** repeat   13 **virtue** power   14 **breath** life

82

I grant thou wert not married to my Muse,
And therefore mayst without attaint o'erlook
The dedicated words which writers use
4 Of their fair subject, blessing every book.
Thou art as fair in knowledge as in hue,
Finding thy worth a limit past my praise;
And therefore art enforced to seek anew
8 Some fresher stamp of the time-bettering days.
And do so, love; yet when they have devised
What strainèd touches rhetoric can lend,
Thou, truly fair, wert truly sympathized
12 In true plain words by thy true-telling friend:
    And their gross painting might be better used
    Where cheeks need blood; in thee it is abused.

1 **married to** closely joined to   2 **attaint** dishonor   2 **o'erlook**
read over   3 **dedicated** devoted (with a pun on dedications prefixed
to books)   5 **hue** (1) complexion (2) figure   6 **limit** reach
8 **stamp** impression   8 **time-bettering** improving   11 **fair** beau-
tiful   11 **truly sympathized** represented to the life

83

I never saw that you did painting need,
And therefore to your fair no painting set;
I found, or thought I found, you did exceed
The barren tender of a poet's debt;   4
And therefore have I slept in your report,
That you yourself, being extant, well might show
How far a modern quill doth come too short,
Speaking of worth, what worth in you doth grow.   8
This silence for my sin you did impute,
Which shall be most my glory, being dumb;
For I impair not beauty, being mute,
When others would give life and bring a tomb.   12
　　There lives more life in one of your fair eyes
　　Than both your poets can in praise devise.

2 **fair** beauty 4 **The barren . . . debt** i.e., the worthless offer that
the poet is obliged to make 5 **slept in your report** refrained from
praising you 7 **modern** trivial

84

Who is it that says most, which can say more
Than this rich praise, that you alone are you,
In whose confine immurèd is the store
4   Which should example where your equal grew?
Lean penury within that pen doth dwell,
That to his subject lends not some small glory,
But he that writes of you, if he can tell
8   That you are you, so dignifies his story.
Let him but copy what in you is writ,
Not making worse what nature made so clear,
And such a counterpart shall fame his wit,
12 Making his style admirèd everywhere.
     You to your beauteous blessings add a curse,
     Being fond on praise, which makes your praises worse.

1 **Who . . . more** i.e., who, having said the utmost, can say more
3–4 **In whose . . . grew** in whom is stored all the abundance which
would have to serve as a model for any equal   6 **his** its   10 **clear**
radiant   11 **fame his wit** make famous his mind   14 **fond on** fool-
ishly enamored of (but the sense seemed called for here is that the pa-
tron's excellence is such that it wreaks havoc with the poets who seek
to praise him)

85

My tongue-tied Muse in manners holds her still
While comments of your praise, richly compiled,
Reserve their character with golden quill
And precious phrase by all the Muses filed.   *4*
I think good thoughts whilst other write good words,
And, like unlettered clerk, still cry "Amen"
To every hymn that able spirit affords
In polished form of well-refinèd pen.   *8*
Hearing you praised, I say, " 'Tis so, 'tis true,"
And to the most of praise add something more;
But that is in my thought, whose love to you,
Though words come hindmost, holds his rank before.   *12*
   Then others for the breath of words respect,
   Me for my dumb thoughts, speaking in effect.

1 **in manners holds her still** is politely silent 2–3 **While . . . quill**
while comments in your praise, richly composed with golden pen, pre-
serve their features ("character" means both "writing" and "traits,"
"features") 4 **filed** polished 5 **other** others 6 **still** always
7 **able spirit affords** i.e., competent poets write 10 **most** utmost
13–14 **Then others . . . effect** i.e., then take notice of other poets for
their spoken words (but in "breath" there is a suggestion of their
insubstantiality), and of me for my silent thoughts, which, by their si-
lence, speak

86

Was it the proud full sail of his great verse,
Bound for the prize of all-too-precious you,
That did my ripe thoughts in my brain inhearse,
4   Making their tomb the womb wherein they grew?
Was it his spirit, by spirits taught to write
Above a mortal pitch, that struck me dead?
No, neither he, nor his compeers by night
8   Giving him aid, my verse astonishèd.
He, nor that affable familiar ghost
Which nightly gulls him with intelligence,
As victors, of my silence cannot boast;
12   I was not sick of any fear from thence.
        But when your countenance filled up his line,
        Then lacked I matter, that enfeebled mine.

1 **his** i.e., a rival poet's   3 **inhearse** enclose as in a coffin   6 **dead**
silent   8 **astonishèd** struck dumb   9 **familiar ghost** assisting
spirit   10 **gulls him with intelligence** deceives him with rumors (?)
13 **countenance filled up his line** (1) beauty was the subject of his
verse (2) approval polished his verse (if the quarto's "fild" is printed
"filed" instead of "filled")

87

Farewell, thou art too dear for my possessing,
And like enough thou know'st thy estimate.
The charter of thy worth gives thee releasing;
My bonds in thee are all determinate.   *4*
For how do I hold thee but by thy granting,
And for that riches where is my deserving?
The cause of this fair gift in me is wanting,
And so my patent back again is swerving.   *8*
Thyself thou gav'st, thy own worth then not knowing,
Or me, to whom thou gav'st it, else mistaking;
So thy great gift, upon misprision growing,
Comes home again, on better judgment making.   *12*
    Thus have I had thee as a dream doth flatter,
    In sleep a king, but waking no such matter.

2 **estimate** value 3 **charter** privilege 4 **bonds in** claims on
4 **determinate** expired 7 **wanting** lacking 8 **patent** privilege
8 **back again is swerving** returns (to you) 11 **upon misprision
growing** arising from a mistake

88

When thou shalt be disposed to set me light
And place my merit in the eye of scorn,
Upon thy side against myself I'll fight
4   And prove thee virtuous, though thou art forsworn.
With mine own weakness being best acquainted,
Upon thy part I can set down a story
Of faults concealed wherein I am attainted,
8   That thou in losing me shall win much glory.
And I by this will be a gainer too,
For, bending all my loving thoughts on thee,
The injuries that to myself I do,
12   Doing thee vantage, double-vantage me.
    Such is my love, to thee I so belong,
    That for thy right myself will bear all wrong.

1 **set me light** value me little   8 **That** so that   12 **vantage** advantage   14 **right** (1) good (2) privilege

89

Say that thou didst forsake me for some fault,
And I will comment upon that offense.
Speak of my lameness, and I straight will halt,
Against thy reasons making no defense.   4
Thou canst not, love, disgrace me half so ill,
To set a form upon desirèd change,
As I'll myself disgrace, knowing thy will.
I will acquaintance strangle and look strange;   8
Be absent from thy walks, and in my tongue
Thy sweet belovèd name no more shall dwell,
Lest I, too much profane, should do it wrong
And haply of our old acquaintance tell.   12
    For thee, against myself I'll vow debate,
    For I must ne'er love him whom thou dost hate.

1 **Say** i.e., assume 3 **halt** limp 4 **reasons** arguments 5 **disgrace** discredit 6 **To set . . . change** to give a good appearance to the change you desire (?) 7 **disgrace** disfigure 8 **acquaintance** i.e., familiarity 12 **haply** by chance 13 **debate** contention

90

Then hate me when thou wilt; if ever, now;
Now, while the world is bent my deeds to cross,
Join with the spite of fortune, make me bow,
4 And do not drop in for an after-loss.
Ah, do not, when my heart hath 'scaped this sorrow,
Come in the rearward of a conquered woe;
Give not a windy night a rainy morrow,
8 To linger out a purposed overthrow.
If thou wilt leave me, do not leave me last,
When other petty griefs have done their spite,
But in the onset come; so shall I taste
12 At first the very worst of fortune's might,
  And other strains of woe, which now seem woe,
  Compared with loss of thee will not seem so.

4 **after-loss** later loss   6 **Come in ... woe** i.e., come belatedly
when I have conquered my sorrow   8 **linger out** prolong   8 **pur-
posed** intended   13 **strains** kinds

91

Some glory in their birth, some in their skill,
Some in their wealth, some in their body's force,
Some in their garments, though newfangled ill,
Some in their hawks and hounds, some in their horse;   *4*
And every humor hath his adjunct pleasure,
Wherein it finds a joy above the rest,
But these particulars are not my measure;
All these I better in one general best.   *8*
Thy love is better than high birth to me,
Richer than wealth, prouder than garments' cost,
Of more delight than hawks or horses be;
And having thee, of all men's pride I boast: *12*
    Wretched in this alone, that thou mayst take
    All this away, and me most wretched make.

3 **newfangled ill** fashionably ugly   4 **horse** horses   5 **humor** temperament   5 **his** its   7 **measure** standard (of happiness)   12 **all men's pride** i.e., all that men take pride in

92

But do thy worst to steal thyself away,
For term of life thou art assurèd mine,
And life no longer than thy love will stay,
4   For it depends upon that love of thine.
Then need I not to fear the worst of wrongs,
When in the least of them my life hath end.
I see a better state to me belongs
8   Than that which on thy humor doth depend.
Thou canst not vex me with inconstant mind,
Since that my life on thy revolt doth lie.
O, what a happy title do I find,
12   Happy to have thy love, happy to die!
        But what's so blessèd-fair that fears no blot?
        Thou mayst be false, and yet I know it not.

6 **the least of them** i.e., any sign that the friend's love is cooling   8 **humor** caprice   10 **Since . . . lie** since my life ends if you desert me   11 **happy title** title to happiness

93

So shall I live, supposing thou art true,
Like a deceivèd husband; so love's face
May still seem love to me, though altered new,
Thy looks with me, thy heart in other place.   *4*
For there can live no hatred in thine eye;
Therefore in that I cannot know thy change.
In many's looks, the false heart's history
Is writ in moods and frowns and wrinkles strange,   *8*
But heaven in thy creation did decree
That in thy face sweet love should ever dwell;
Whate'er thy thoughts or thy heart's workings be,
Thy looks should nothing thence but sweetness tell.   *12*
   How like Eve's apple doth thy beauty grow
   If thy sweet virtue answer not thy show.

94

They that have pow'r to hurt and will do none,
That do not do the thing they most do show,
Who, moving others, are themselves as stone,
4   Unmovèd, cold, and to temptation slow:
They rightly do inherit heaven's graces,
And husband nature's riches from expense,
They are the lords and owners of their faces,
8   Others but stewards of their excellence:
The summer's flow'r is to the summer sweet,
Though to itself it only live and die,
But if that flow'r with base infection meet,
12   The basest weed outbraves his dignity:
    For sweetest things turn sourest by their deeds,
    Lilies that fester smell far worse than weeds.

2 **do show** (1) seem to do (?) (2) show they could do (?) 6 **husband**
manage prudently 6 **expense** loss 8 **stewards** custodians
12 **outbraves his** surpasses its

95

How sweet and lovely dost thou make the shame
Which, like a canker in the fragrant rose,
Doth spot the beauty of thy budding name!
O, in what sweets dost thou thy sins enclose!   *4*
That tongue that tells the story of thy days,
Making lascivious comments on thy sport,
Cannot dispraise, but in a kind of praise;
Naming thy name blesses an ill report.   *8*
O, what a mansion have those vices got
Which for their habitation chose out thee,
Where beauty's veil doth cover every blot,
And all things turns to fair that eyes can see!   *12*
    Take heed, dear heart, of this large privilege;
    The hardest knife ill-used doth lose his edge.

2 **canker** cankerworm (that feeds on blossoms)   6 **sport** amorous
dalliance   14 **his** its

96

Some say thy fault is youth, some wantonness,
Some say thy grace is youth and gentle sport;
Both grace and faults are loved of more and less;
4   Thou mak'st faults graces that to thee resort.
As on the finger of a thronèd queen
The basest jewel will be well esteemed,
So are those errors that in thee are seen
8   To truths translated and for true things deemed.
How many lambs might the stern wolf betray,
If like a lamb he could his looks translate;
How many gazers might'st thou lead away,
12   If thou wouldst use the strength of all thy state!
     But do not so; I love thee in such sort
      As, thou being mine, mine is thy good report.

2 **gentle sport** amorous dalliance (a more favorable interpretation
of the "wantonness" of line 1)   3 **of more and less** by people high
and low   8 **translated** transformed   9 **stern** cruel   12 **state** emi-
nent position   13–14 (this couplet ends Sonnet 36)   14 **report**
reputation

97

How like a winter hath my absence been
From thee, the pleasure of the fleeting year!
What freezings have I felt, what dark days seen,
What old December's bareness everywhere!   *4*
And yet this time removed was summer's time,
The teeming autumn, big with rich increase,
Bearing the wanton burden of the prime,
Like widowed wombs after their lords' decease.   *8*
Yet this abundant issue seemed to me
But hope of orphans and unfathered fruit;
For summer and his pleasures wait on thee,
And, thou away, the very birds are mute;   *12*
    Or, if they sing, 'tis with so dull a cheer,
    That leaves look pale, dreading the winter's near.

2 **pleasure of the fleeting year** i.e., the summer (normally the pleas-
ant part of the year, but like a winter because of the friend's
absence)   6 **teeming** pregnant   7 **Bearing ... prime** i.e., bear-
ing the load conceived in the wantonness of the spring ("prime" =
spring)   9 **issue** offspring   11 **his** its

98

From you have I been absent in the spring,
When proud-pied April, dressed in all his trim,
Hath put a spirit of youth in everything,
4   That heavy Saturn laughed and leaped with him,
Yet nor the lays of birds, nor the sweet smell
Of different flowers in odor and in hue,
Could make me any summer's story tell,
8   Or from their proud lap pluck them where they grew.
Nor did I wonder at the lily's white,
Nor praise the deep vermilion in the rose;
They were but sweet, but figures of delight,
12   Drawn after you, you pattern of all those.
    Yet seemed it winter still, and, you away,
    As with your shadow I with these did play.

---

2 **proud-pied** gorgeously variegated 2 **trim** ornamental dress
4 **That** so that 4 **heavy Saturn** (the planet Saturn was thought to
cause gloominess) 5 **nor . . . nor** neither . . . nor 5 **lays** songs
7 **summer's story** i.e., pleasant stories suitable for summer ("a sad
tale's best for winter") 14 **shadow** portrait

99

The forward violet thus did I chide:
Sweet thief, whence didst thou steal thy sweet that smells
If not from my love's breath? The purple pride
Which on thy soft cheek for complexion dwells   4
In my love's veins thou hast too grossly dyed.
The lily I condemnèd for thy hand,
And buds of marjoram had stol'n thy hair;
The roses fearfully on thorns did stand,   8
One blushing shame, another white despair;
A third, nor red nor white, had stol'n of both,
And to his robb'ry had annexed thy breath;
But for his theft, in pride of all his growth   12
A vengeful canker eat him up to death.
    More flowers I noted, yet I none could see,
    But sweet or color it had stol'n from thee.

1 **forward** early 3 **purple** (Shakespeare often does not distinguish
between purple and crimson) 3 **pride** splendor 6 **condemnèd
for thy hand** condemned for stealing the whiteness of your hand
8 **fearfully** uneasily 13 **canker eat** cankerworm ate

100

Where art thou, Muse, that thou forget'st so long
To speak of that which gives thee all thy might?
Spend'st thou thy fury on some worthless song,
4 Dark'ning thy pow'r to lend base subjects light?
Return, forgetful Muse, and straight redeem
In gentle numbers time so idly spent,
Sing to the ear that doth thy lays esteem,
8 And gives thy pen both skill and argument.
Rise, resty Muse, my love's sweet face survey,
If Time have any wrinkle graven there;
If any, be a satire to decay
12 And make Time's spoils despisèd everywhere.
  Give my love fame faster than Time wastes life;
  So thou prevent'st his scythe and crooked knife.

3 **fury** poetic enthusiasm 6 **numbers** verses 7 **lays** songs
8 **argument** subject 9 **resty** torpid 10 **If** to see if 11 **be a satire to decay** satirize decay

101

O truant Muse, what shall be thy amends
For thy neglect of truth in beauty dyed?
Both truth and beauty on my love depends;
So dost thou too, and therein dignified.   4
Make answer, Muse, wilt thou not haply say,
"Truth needs no color, with his color fixed,
Beauty no pencil, beauty's truth to lay;
But best is best, if never intermixed"?   8
Because he needs no praise, wilt thou be dumb?
Excuse not silence so, for't lies in thee
To make him much outlive a gilded tomb,
And to be praised of ages yet to be.   12
    Then do thy office, Muse; I teach thee how
    To make him seem, long hence, as he shows now.

3 **love** beloved   4 **dignified** you are dignified   5 **haply** per-
chance   6 **color** artificial color, disguise   6 **his color fixed** its un-
changeable color   7 **to lay** i.e., to put on canvas   8 **intermixed**
i.e., with the inadequate words of the Muse   13 **do thy office** per-
form your duty

102

My love is strength'ned, though more weak in
      seeming;
I love not less, though less the show appear.
That love is merchandized whose rich esteeming
4   The owner's tongue doth publish everywhere.
Our love was new, and then but in the spring,
When I was wont to greet it with my lays,
As Philomel in summer's front doth sing
8   And stops her pipe in growth of riper days.
Not that the summer is less pleasant now
Than when her mournful hymns did hush the night,
But that wild music burdens every bough,
12   And sweets grown common lose their dear delight.
    Therefore, like her, I sometime hold my tongue,
    Because I would not dull you with my song.

2 **show** outward manifestation   3 **merchandized** offered for sale,
hawked   3 **esteeming** value   6 **lays** songs   7 **Philomel** the
nightingale   7 **front** forefront   8 **riper** later   11 **But that** i.e.,
but it seems so because

103

Alack, what poverty my Muse brings forth,
That, having such a scope to show her pride,
The argument all bare is of more worth
Than when it hath my added praise beside.   *4*
O, blame me not if I no more can write!
Look in your glass, and there appears a face
That overgoes my blunt invention quite,
Dulling my lines and doing me disgrace.   *8*
Were it not sinful then, striving to mend,
To mar the subject that before was well?
For to no other pass my verses tend
Than of your graces and your gifts to tell;   *12*
    And more, much more, than in my verse can sit
    Your own glass shows you when you look in it.

1 **poverty** inferior matter   2 **pride** splendor   3 **argument** theme
3 **all bare** i.e., of itself   7 **overgoes my blunt invention** exceeds
my awkward creation   8 **disgrace** discredit   9 **mend** improve
11 **pass** purpose

104

To me, fair friend, you never can be old,
For as you were when first your eye I eyed,
Such seems your beauty still. Three winters cold
4   Have from the forests shook three summers' pride,
Three beauteous springs to yellow autumn turned
In process of the seasons have I seen,
Three April perfumes in three hot Junes burned,
8   Since first I saw you fresh, which yet are green.
Ah, yet doth beauty, like a dial hand,
Steal from his figure, and no pace perceived;
So your sweet hue, which methinks still doth stand,
12 Hath motion, and mine eye may be deceived;
    For fear of which, hear this, thou age unbred:
    Ere you were born was beauty's summer dead.

4 **pride** splendor   10 **his figure** its numeral (with a pun on "figure,"
the friend's appearance)   11 **sweet hue** fair appearance   11 **still**
(1) motionless (2) always, forever   13 **unbred** unborn

105

Let not my love be called idolatry,
Nor my belovèd as an idol show,
Since all alike my songs and praises be
To one, of one, still such, and ever so.   *4*
Kind is my love today, tomorrow kind,
Still constant in a wondrous excellence;
Therefore my verse, to constancy confined,
One thing expressing, leaves out difference.   *8*
Fair, kind, and true is all my argument,
Fair, kind, and true, varying to other words;
And in this change is my invention spent,
Three themes in one, which wondrous scope affords.   *12*
    Fair, kind, and true have often lived alone,
     Which three till now never kept seat in one.

4 **still** always 5 **Kind** naturally benevolent 8 **difference** variety 9 **Fair** beautiful 9 **argument** theme 11 **And in . . . spent** i.e., and in variations on this theme I expend all my imagination

106

When in the chronicle of wasted time
I see descriptions of the fairest wights,
And beauty making beautiful old rhyme
In praise of ladies dead and lovely knights;
Then, in the blazon of sweet beauty's best,
Of hand, of foot, of lip, of eye, of brow,
I see their antique pen would have expressed
Even such a beauty as you master now.
So all their praises are but prophecies
Of this our time, all you prefiguring,
And, for they looked but with divining eyes,
They had not still enough your worth to sing:
   For we, which now behold these present days,
   Have eyes to wonder, but lack tongues to praise.

4

8

12

1 **wasted** past   2 **wights** people   4 **lovely** attractive   5 **blazon**
commemorative description   11 **for** because   11 **divining** guess-
ing   12 **still** yet (the common emendation to "skill" is unnecessary)
13 **For** for even

107

Not mine own fears nor the prophetic soul
Of the wide world dreaming on things to come
Can yet the lease of my true love control,
Supposed as forfeit to a confined doom.   *4*
The mortal moon hath her eclipse endured,
And the sad augurs mock their own presage,
Incertainties now crown themselves assured,
And peace proclaims olives of endless age.   *8*
Now with the drops of this most balmy time
My love looks fresh, and Death to me subscribes,
Since, spite of him, I'll live in this poor rhyme,
While he insults o'er dull and speechless tribes: *12*
    And thou in this shalt find thy monument,
      When tyrants' crests and tombs of brass are spent.

3 **lease** allotted time   4 **Supposed ... doom** i.e., though it is thought
doomed to expire after a limited time   5 **The mortal moon ... en-
dured** (numerous commentators claim that this line dates the sonnet;
among interpretations are: 1588, when the Spanish Armada, thought
to have assumed a crescent formation, was destroyed; 1595, when the
moon underwent a total eclipse; 1595, when Queen Elizabeth I sur-
vived a critical period in her horoscope; 1599, when Queen Elizabeth
survived an illness)   6–7 **And the sad ... assured** and the prophets
of gloom are mocked by their own predictions now that uncertainties
yield to assurance (?)   10 **to me subscribes** acknowledges me as his
superior   12 **insults** triumphs   14 **spent** consumed

108

What's in the brain that ink may character
Which hath not figured to thee my true spirit?
What's new to speak, what now to register,
4   That may express my love or thy dear merit?
Nothing, sweet boy, but yet, like prayers divine,
I must each day say o'er the very same;
Counting no old thing old, thou mine, I thine,
8   Even as when first I hallowed thy fair name.
So that eternal love in love's fresh case
Weighs not the dust and injury of age,
Nor gives to necessary wrinkles place,
12   But makes antiquity for aye his page,
  Finding the first conceit of love there bred
  Where time and outward form would show it dead.

1 **character** write 2 **figured** shown 9 **fresh case** youthful appearance 10 **Weighs not** cares not for 12 **for aye his page** forever his servant 13 **conceit** conception

109

O, never say that I was false of heart,
Though absence seemed my flame to qualify.
As easy might I from myself depart
As from my soul, which in thy breast doth lie.   *4*
That is my home of love; if I have ranged,
Like him that travels, I return again,
Just to the time, not with the time exchanged,
So that myself bring water for my stain.   *8*
Never believe, though in my nature reigned
All frailties that besiege all kinds of blood,
That it could so preposterously be stained
To leave for nothing all thy sum of good;   *12*
    For nothing this wide universe I call
    Save thou, my Rose; in it thou art my all.

2 **qualify** moderate   5 **ranged** wandered   7 **Just** punctual   7 **ex-
changed** changed   10 **blood** flesh, temperament

110

Alas, 'tis true I have gone here and there
And made myself a motley to the view,
Gored mine own thoughts, sold cheap what is most dear,
4 Made old offenses of affections new.
Most true it is that I have looked on truth
Askance and strangely; but, by all above,
These blenches gave my heart another youth,
8 And worse essays proved thee my best of love.
Now all is done, have what shall have no end.
Mine appetite I never more will grind
On newer proof, to try an older friend,
12 A god in love, to whom I am confined.
    Then give me welcome, next my heaven the best,
    Even to thy pure and most loving breast.

2 **motley** jester 3 **Gored** wounded 4 **affections** passions
5 **truth** fidelity 6 **strangely** in a reserved manner 7 **blenches**
side glances (?) 8 **worse essays** trials of worse friendships (?)
9 **have what shall have no end** take what shall be eternal 11 **proof**
experiment 11 **try** test 13 **next** next to

111

O, for my sake do you with Fortune chide,
The guilty goddess of my harmful deeds,
That did not better for my life provide
Than public means which public manners breeds.   *4*
Thence comes it that my name receives a brand,
And almost thence my nature is subdued
To what it works in, like the dyer's hand.
Pity me then, and wish I were renewed,   *8*
Whilst, like a willing patient, I will drink
Potions of eisel 'gainst my strong infection;
No bitterness that I will bitter think,
Nor double penance, to correct correction.   *12*
   Pity me then, dear friend, and I assure ye
   Even that your pity is enough to cure me.

3 **That** who   3 **life** livelihood   4 **Than . . . breeds** than earning a
livelihood by satisfying the public, which engenders vulgar manners
5 **brand** stigma   6–7 **subdued/To** subjected to   10 **eisel** vinegar
(used as a preventative against the plague)

112

Your love and pity doth th' impression fill,
Which vulgar scandal stamped upon my brow;
For what care I who calls me well or ill,
4   So you o'er-green my bad, my good allow?
You are my all the world, and I must strive
To know my shames and praises from your tongue;
None else to me, nor I to none alive,
8   That my steeled sense or changes right or wrong.
In so profound abysm I throw all care
Of others' voices, that my adder's sense
To critic and to flatterer stoppèd are.
12 Mark how with my neglect I do dispense:
     You are so strongly in my purpose bred,
     That all the world besides methinks are dead.

1 **doth th' impression fill** effaces the scar   2 **stamped** (allusion to branding felons)   4 **allow** approve   6 **shames** faults   7–8 **None else . . . wrong** only you can change my sense of what is right and wrong (?)   9 **profound** deep   10 **adder's sense** i.e., deaf ears (adders were thought to be deaf)   12 **Mark how . . . dispense** listen to how I excuse ("dispense with") my neglect (i.e., of others)   13 **in my purpose bred** grown in my mind   14 **That all . . . dead** that I think only you have life

113

Since I left you, mine eye is in my mind,
And that which governs me to go about
Doth part his function and is partly blind,
Seems seeing, but effectually is out;   *4*
For it no form delivers to the heart   .
Of bird, of flow'r, or shape, which it doth latch.
Of his quick objects hath the mind no part,
Nor his own vision holds what it doth catch;   *8*
For if it see the rud'st or gentlest sight,
The most sweet favor or deformèd'st creature,
The mountain, or the sea, the day, or night,
The crow, or dove, it shapes them to your feature.   *12*
   Incapable of more, replete with you,
   My most true mind thus maketh mine eye untrue.

3 **Doth part . . . blind** i.e., performs only part of its function, receiving images but not conveying them to the mind or "heart"   3, 7, 8 **his** its   4 **effectually** in reality   6 **latch** catch sight of   7 **quick** fleeting   10 **favor** face   13 **Incapable of** unable to take in   14 **true** faithful

114

Or whether doth my mind, being crowned with you,
Drink up the monarch's plague, this flattery?
Or whether shall I say mine eye saith true,
4   And that your love taught it this alchemy,
To make of monsters, and things indigest,
Such cherubins as your sweet self resemble,
Creating every bad a perfect best
8   As fast as objects to his beams assemble?
O, 'tis the first, 'tis flatt'ry in my seeing,
And my great mind most kingly drinks it up.
Mine eye well knows what with his gust is 'greeing,
12 And to his palate doth prepare the cup.
      If it be poisoned, 'tis the lesser sin
      That mine eye loves it and doth first begin.

1, 3 **Or whether** (indicates alternative questions)   1 **being crowned
with you** made a king by possessing you   2 **this flattery** i.e., false
appearances (such as surround a monarch) as specified in the previ-
ous sonnet   5 **indigest** formless   6 **cherubins** angelic creatures
8 **to his beams assemble** appear to his eye (the eye was thought to
cast beams; see Sonnet 20, line 6)   11 **with his gust is 'greeing**
agrees with the mind's taste   14 **That** since

115

Those lines that I before have writ do lie,
Even those that said I could not love you dearer.
Yet then my judgment knew no reason why
My most full flame should afterwards burn clearer.   *4*
But reckoning Time, whose millioned accidents
Creep in 'twixt vows and change decrees of kings,
Tan sacred beauty, blunt the sharp'st intents,
Divert strong minds to th' course of alt'ring things.   *8*
Alas, why, fearing of Time's tyranny,
Might I not then say, "Now I love you best,"
When I was certain o'er incertainty,
Crowning the present, doubting of the rest?   *12*
    Love is a babe; then might I not say so,
    To give full growth to that which still doth grow.

5 **millioned accidents** innumerable happenings   7 **Tan** i.e., darken,
coarsen   8 **Divert** alter   12 **Crowning** glorifying   13 **then**
therefore   13 **so** i.e., "Now I love you best" (line 10)

116

Let me not to the marriage of true minds
Admit impediments; love is not love
Which alters when it alteration finds,
4   Or bends with the remover to remove.
O, no, it is an ever-fixèd mark
That looks on tempests and is never shaken;
It is the star to every wand'ring bark,
8   Whose worth's unknown, although his height be
          taken.
Love's not Time's fool, though rosy lips and cheeks
Within his bending sickle's compass come;
Love alters not with his brief hours and weeks,
12   But bears it out even to the edge of doom.
     If this be error and upon me proved,
     I never writ, nor no man ever loved.

2 **impediments** (an echo of the marriage service in the Book of Common Prayer: "If any of you know cause or just impediment . . .")
5 **mark** seamark   7 **the star** the North Star   8 **Whose worth's . . . taken** whose value (e.g., to mariners) is inestimable although the star's altitude has been determined   9 **fool** plaything   10 **compass** range, circle   11 **his** Time's   12 **bears it out** survives   12 **edge of doom** Judgment Day   13 **upon** against

117

Accuse me thus: that I have scanted all
Wherein I should your great deserts repay,
Forgot upon your dearest love to call,
Whereto all bonds do tie me day by day;   *4*
That I have frequent been with unknown minds,
And given to time your own dear-purchased right;
That I have hoisted sail to all the winds
Which should transport me farthest from your sight.   *8*
Book both my willfulness and errors down,
And on just proof surmise accumulate;
Bring me within the level of your frown,
But shoot not at me in your wakened hate;   *12*
    Since my appeal says I did strive to prove
    The constancy and virtue of your love.

1 **scanted all** given only grudgingly   5 **frequent** intimate   5 **unknown minds** i.e., nonentities   6 **given to time** squandered on other people of the time   9 **Book** write down in a book   10 **surmise accumulate** add suspicions   11 **level** range, aim   13 **appeal** plea 13 **prove** test

118

Like as to make our appetites more keen
With eager compounds we our palate urge,
As to prevent our maladies unseen,
4   We sicken to shun sickness when we purge;
Even so, being full of your ne'er-cloying sweetness,
To bitter sauces did I frame my feeding;
And, sick of welfare, found a kind of meetness
8   To be diseased ere that there was true needing.
Thus policy in love, t' anticipate
The ills that were not, grew to faults assured,
And brought to medicine a healthful state,
12   Which, rank of goodness, would by ill be cured.
    But thence I learn, and find the lesson true,
    Drugs poison him that so fell sick of you.

2 **eager compounds** tart sauces   2 **urge** stimulate   3 **prevent**
forestall   6 **bitter sauces** i.e., undesirable people   6 **frame**
direct   7 **sick of welfare** gorged with well-being   7 **meetness** fit-
ness   9 **policy** prudence   11 **medicine** i.e., the need of medicine
12 **rank of** gorged with

119

What potions have I drunk of Siren tears
Distilled from limbecks foul as hell within,
Applying fears to hopes and hopes to fears,
Still losing when I saw myself to win!   4
What wretched errors hath my heart committed,
Whilst it hath thought itself so blessèd never!
How have mine eyes out of their spheres been fitted
In the distraction of this madding fever!   8
O, benefit of ill: now I find true
That better is by evil still made better;
And ruined love, when it is built anew,
Grows fairer than at first, more strong, far greater.   12
   So I return rebuked to my content,
    And gain by ills thrice more than I have spent.

2 **limbecks** alembics 3 **Applying** i.e., as an ointment 4 **Still** always 6 **so blessèd never** never so blessed 7 **spheres** sockets 7 **fitted** forced by fits

120

That you were once unkind befriends me now,
And for that sorrow which I then did feel
Needs must I under my transgression bow,
4 Unless my nerves were brass or hammered steel.
For if you were by my unkindness shaken,
As I by yours, y'have passed a hell of time,
And I, a tyrant, have no leisure taken
8 To weigh how once I suffered in your crime.
O, that our night of woe might have rememb'red
My deepest sense how hard true sorrow hits,
And soon to you, as you to me then, tend'red
12 The humble salve which wounded bosoms fits!
      But that your trespass now becomes a fee;
      Mine ransoms yours, and yours must ransom me.

2 **for** because of   4 **nerves** sinews   7–8 **no leisure . . . weigh** not
taken the time to consider   9 **night of woe** i.e., estrangement
9 **rememb'red** reminded   11 **soon** as soon   11 **tend'red** offered
12 **humble salve** balm of humility   12 **fits** suits   13 **that your
trespass** that trespass of yours   13 **fee** compensation   14 **ransoms**
atones for

121

'Tis better to be vile than vile esteemed
When not to be receives reproach of being,
And the just pleasure lost, which is so deemed
Not by our feeling, but by others' seeing.   *4*
For why should others' false adulterate eyes
Give salutation to my sportive blood?
Or on my frailties why are frailer spies,
Which in their wills count bad what I think good?   *8*
No, I am that I am, and they that level
At my abuses reckon up their own;
I may be straight though they themselves be bevel.
By their rank thoughts my deeds must not be shown,   *12*
    Unless this general evil they maintain:
    All men are bad and in their badness reign.

2 **being** i.e., being vile   3 **just** legitimate   3 **so** i.e., vile   6 **Give salutation to** act on   6 **sportive** wanton   8 **in their wills** i.e., willfully (?)   9 **that** who (an echo of Exodus 3:14)   9 **level** aim   10 **abuses** transgressions   11 **bevel** i.e., crooked   12 **rank** corrupt

122

Thy gift, thy tables, are within my brain
Full charactered with lasting memory,
Which shall above that idle rank remain
4 Beyond all date, even to eternity;
Or, at the least, so long as brain and heart
Have faculty by nature to subsist,
Till each to rased oblivion yield his part
8 Of thee, thy record never can be missed.
That poor retention could not so much hold,
Nor need I tallies thy dear love to score.
Therefore to give them from me was I bold,
12 To trust those tables that receive thee more.
    To keep an adjunct to remember thee
    Were to import forgetfulness in me.

1 **tables** memorandum books   2 **charactered** written   3 **that idle rank** that useless series of leaves   7 **rased oblivion** oblivion which erases   7 **his** its   9 **That poor retention** i.e., the memorandum books   10 **tallies** accounting devices   12 **those tables** i.e., the mind   14 **import** imply

123

No, Time, thou shalt not boast that I do change.
Thy pyramids built up with newer might
To me are nothing novel, nothing strange;
They are but dressings of a former sight.   *4*
Our dates are brief, and therefore we admire
What thou dost foist upon us that is old,
And rather make them born to our desire
Than think that we before have heard them told.   *8*
Thy registers and thee I both defy,
Not wond'ring at the present, nor the past;
For thy records and what we see doth lie,
Made more or less by thy continual haste.   *12*
   This I do vow, and this shall ever be:
   I will be true despite thy scythe and thee.

2 **pyramids** (possibly an allusion to Egyptian obelisks erected in Rome by Pope Sextus 1586–89; more likely an allusion to triumphal structures erected in London to welcome James I in 1603; most likely a reference to all monuments)   5 **dates** allotted times   5 **admire** regard with wonder   7 **born to our desire** turn them into the new things we wish to see   9 **registers** records

124

If my dear love were but the child of state,
It might for Fortune's bastard be unfathered,
As subject to Time's love, or to Time's hate,
4   Weeds among weeds, or flowers with flowers
            gathered.
No, it was builded far from accident;
It suffers not in smiling pomp, nor falls
Under the blow of thrallèd discontent,
8   Whereto th' inviting time our fashion calls.
It fears not Policy, that heretic,
Which works on leases of short-numb'red hours,
But all alone stands hugely politic,
12   That it nor grows with heat, nor drowns with showers.
        To this I witness call the fools of Time,
        Which die for goodness, who have lived for crime.

1 **love** i.e., the emotion, not the person   1 **but** only   1 **child of
state** i.e., product of externals such as wealth and power   2 **for For-
tune's bastard be unfathered** i.e., be marked as the bastard son of
Fortune   5 **accident** chance   7 **thrallèd discontent** discontent of
persons oppressed   9 **Policy, that heretic** i.e., unprincipled self-
interest which is faithless   11 **all alone stands hugely politic** i.e.,
only love is infinitely prudent   12 **That it nor . . . nor** since it nei-
ther . . . nor   13 **fools of Time** playthings of Time (?) time-servers (?)
14 **Which . . . crime** i.e., who at the last minute repent their crimi-
nal lives

125

Were't aught to me I bore the canopy,
With my extern the outward honoring,
Or laid great bases for eternity,
Which proves more short than waste or ruining?   *4*
Have I not seen dwellers on form and favor
Lose all and more by paying too much rent,
For compound sweet forgoing simple savor,
Pitiful thrivers, in their gazing spent?   *8*
No, let me be obsequious in thy heart,
And take thou my oblation, poor but free,
Which is not mixed with seconds, knows no art,
But mutual render, only me for thee.   *12*
　　Hence, thou suborned informer! A true soul
　　When most impeached stands least in thy control.

1 **Were't aught** would it be anything   1 **canopy** (borne over an eminent person)   2 **extern** outward action   5 **dwellers on form and favor** i.e., those who make much of appearance and external beauty   6 **paying too much rent** i.e., obsequiousness   7 **simple** pure   8 **Pitiful . . . spent** pitiable creatures who use themselves up in looking at outward honor   9 **obsequious** devoted   11 **seconds** i.e., baser matter   11 **art** artifice   12 **render** surrender   13 **suborned informer** perjured witness   14 **impeached** accused

126

O thou, my lovely boy, who in thy power
Dost hold Time's fickle glass, his sickle hour,
Who hast by waning grown, and therein show'st
4   Thy lovers withering, as thy sweet self grow'st;
If Nature, sovereign mistress over wrack,
As thou goest onwards, still will pluck thee back,
She keeps thee to this purpose, that her skill
8   May Time disgrace and wretched minutes kill.
Yet fear her, O thou minion of her pleasure;
She may detain, but not still keep her treasure.
       Her audit, though delayed, answered must be,
12   And her quietus is to render thee.

2 **glass** mirror   2 **hour** hourglass   3 **by waning grown** i.e., by
growing older growing more beautiful   5 **wrack** destruction
6, 10 **still** always   9 **minion** favorite   11 **audit** final account
11 **answered** paid   12 **quietus** final settlement   12 **render** sur-
render

127

In the old age black was not counted fair,
Or, if it were, it bore not beauty's name.
But now is black beauty's successive heir,
And beauty slandered with a bastard shame;   *4*
For since each hand hath put on nature's power,
Fairing the foul with art's false borrowed face,
Sweet beauty hath no name, no holy bower,
But is profaned, if not lives in disgrace.   *8*
Therefore my mistress' eyes are raven black,
Her eyes so suited, and they mourners seem,
At such who, not born fair, no beauty lack,
Sland'ring creation with a false esteem: *12*
    Yet so they mourn, becoming of their woe,
    That every tongue says beauty should look so.

1 **old age** i.e., age of chivalry   1 **black** i.e., brunette   1 **fair** beautiful (with a pun on the obvious meaning)   3 **successive heir** legitimate heir   4 **And beauty . . . shame** i.e., blond beauty is defamed as illegitimate   5 **put on** taken over   6 **art's false borrowed face** i.e., cosmetics   7 **Sweet** natural, i.e., blond   11 **At** for   13 **becoming of** gracing

128

How oft, when thou, my music, music play'st
Upon that blessèd wood whose motion sounds
With thy sweet fingers when thou gently sway'st
4　The wiry concord that mine ear confounds,
Do I envy those jacks that nimble leap
To kiss the tender inward of thy hand,
Whilst my poor lips, which should that harvest reap,
8　At the wood's boldness by thee blushing stand.
To be so tickled, they would change their state
And situation with those dancing chips
O'er whom thy fingers walk with gentle gait,
12　Making dead wood more blest than living lips.
　　Since saucy jacks so happy are in this,
　　Give them thy fingers, me thy lips to kiss.

2 **wood** keys (of the spinet or virginal)　2 **motion** movement
3 **thou gently sway'st** you gently direct　4 **wiry concord** harmony
of the strings　4 **confounds** delightfully overcomes　5 **jacks** (de-
vices which pluck the strings, but here probably misused for keys; in
line 13, there is a pun on the meaning "fellows")　9 **they** i.e., the
poet's lips

5–6 There are always some who cannot bear to think that the Swan of
Avon could ever make a mistake about anything. A certain E. W. Nay-
lor explains these lines as follows. "The lady, having removed the rail
which ordinarily stops the 'jacks' from jumping right out of the in-
strument when the keys are struck, was leaning over her work, testing
it by striking the defective note, and holding the 'tender inward' of her
hand over the 'jack' to prevent it from flying to the other end of the
room."
　　　　　　　　　　　　　　　　　　　　　　　　　　W.H.A.

129

Th' expense of spirit in a waste of shame
Is lust in action; and, till action, lust
Is perjured, murd'rous, bloody, full of blame,
Savage, extreme, rude, cruel, not to trust;   *4*
Enjoyed no sooner but despisèd straight;
Past reason hunted, and no sooner had,
Past reason hated as a swallowed bait
On purpose laid to make the taker mad;   *8*
Made in pursuit, and in possession so;
Had, having, and in quest to have, extreme;
A bliss in proof, and proved, a very woe,
Before, a joy proposed; behind, a dream.   *12*
    All this the world well knows, yet none knows well
    To shun the heaven that leads men to this hell.

1 **expense** expenditure   1 **spirit** vital power, semen   6,7 **Past** beyond   9 **Made** i.e., made mad (most editors emend to "Mad")   11 **in proof** while being experienced   11 **proved** i.e., when experienced   12 **dream** nightmare (?)   14 **heaven** the sensation (or place?) of bliss

130

My mistress' eyes are nothing like the sun;
Coral is far more red than her lips' red;
If snow be white, why then her breasts are dun;
4 If hairs be wires, black wires grow on her head.
I have seen roses damasked, red and white,
But no such roses see I in her cheeks,
And in some perfumes is there more delight
8 Than in the breath that from my mistress reeks.
I love to hear her speak, yet well I know
That music hath a far more pleasing sound.
I grant I never saw a goddess go;
12 My mistress when she walks treads on the ground.
    And yet, by heaven, I think my love as rare
    As any she belied with false compare.

5 **damasked** mingled red and white 8 **reeks** emanates 11 **go** walk 14 **she** woman 14 **compare** comparison

131

Thou art as tyrannous, so as thou art,
As those whose beauties proudly make them cruel;
For well thou know'st to my dear doting heart
Thou art the fairest and most precious jewel.   *4*
Yet, in good faith, some say that thee behold,
Thy face hath not the power to make love groan;
To say they err I dare not be so bold,
Although I swear it to myself alone.   *8*
And, to be sure that is not false I swear,
A thousand groans, but thinking on thy face,
One on another's neck, do witness bear
Thy black is fairest in my judgment's place.   *12*
    In nothing art thou black save in thy deeds,
        And thence this slander, as I think, proceeds.

1 **so as thou art** i.e., even though you are black and not beautiful 3 **dear** loving 10 **but thinking on** when I but think of 11 **One on another's neck** i.e., in quick succession 12 **in my judgment's place** in the place assigned it by my judgment 13 **black** foul

132

Thine eyes I love, and they, as pitying me,
Knowing thy heart torment me with disdain,
Have put on black and loving mourners be,
4   Looking with pretty ruth upon my pain.
And truly not the morning sun of heaven
Better becomes the gray cheeks of the east,
Nor that full star that ushers in the even
8   Doth half that glory to the sober west
As those two mourning eyes become thy face.
O, let it then as well beseem thy heart
To mourn for me, since mourning doth thee grace,
12   And suit thy pity like in every part.
    Then will I swear beauty herself is black,
    And all they foul that thy complexion lack.

2 **torment** to torment   4 **ruth** pity   7 **even** evening   9 **mourn-ing** (with a pun on "morning")   12 **suit thy pity like** clothe thy pity alike   14 **foul** ugly

133

Beshrew that heart that makes my heart to groan
For that deep wound it gives my friend and me.
Is't not enough to torture me alone,
But slave to slavery my sweet'st friend must be?   *4*
Me from myself thy cruel eye hath taken,
And my next self thou harder hast engrossed.
Of him, myself, and thee, I am forsaken;
A torment thrice threefold thus to be crossed.   *8*
Prison my heart in thy steel bosom's ward,
But then my friend's heart let my poor heart bail;
Whoe'er keeps me, let my heart be his guard;
Thou canst not then use rigor in my jail.   *12*
    And yet thou wilt, for I, being pent in thee,
    Perforce am thine, and all that is in me.

1 **Beshrew** curse (mild imprecation)   2 **For** because of   6 **my next self** i.e., my friend   6 **engrossed** captured   8 **crossed** thwarted   9 **ward** cell   10 **bail** go bail for, i.e., free   11 **keeps** guards   11 **guard** guardhouse   12 **rigor** cruelty   12 **my jail** i.e., my heart

134

So, now I have confessed that he is thine
And I myself am mortgaged to thy will,
Myself I'll forfeit, so that other mine
4   Thou wilt restore to be my comfort still.
But thou wilt not, nor he will not be free,
For thou art covetous, and he is kind;
He learned but surety-like to write for me
8   Under that bond that him as fast doth bind.
The statute of thy beauty thou wilt take,
Thou usurer that put'st forth all to use,
And sue a friend came debtor for my sake;
12   So him I lose through my unkind abuse.
　　　Him have I lost, thou hast both him and me;
　　　He pays the whole, and yet am I not free.

2 **will** (1) purpose (2) carnal desire (perhaps with puns on Shake-
speare's name and the name of the friend)   3 **so** provided that
3 **other mine** i.e., my friend   4 **still** always   7–8 **He learned . . .
bind** (perhaps the idea is that the friend, as proxy, wooed the woman
for the poet but is now in her bondage)   9 **statute** security   10 **use**
usury   11 **came** who became (?)   12 **my unkind abuse** unkind de-
ception of me

135

Whoever hath her wish, thou hast thy *Will*,
And *Will* to boot, and *Will* in overplus;
More than enough am I that vex thee still,
To thy sweet will making addition thus.   *4*
Wilt thou, whose will is large and spacious,
Not once vouchsafe to hide my will in thine?
Shall will in others seem right gracious,
And in my will no fair acceptance shine?   *8*
The sea, all water, yet receives rain still
And in abundance addeth to his store;
So thou being rich in *Will* add to thy *Will*
One will of mine, to make thy large *Will* more.   *12*
    Let no unkind, no fair beseechers kill;
    Think all but one, and me in that one *Will*.

1 *Will* (1) a person named Will (perhaps the poet, perhaps the friend, perhaps the woman's husband, perhaps all; *Will* is capitalized and italicized in this and in the next sonnet wherever it so appears in the quarto) (2) desire, volition   3,9 **still** always   4 **making addition thus** i.e., by adding myself   5,7 (rhyming words are trisyllabic)   6 **vouchsafe** consent   10 **his** its   13 **no unkind** no unkind act, word, or person   13 **no fair beseechers** i.e., any applicants for your favors (?)   14 **Think all . . . *Will*** think all Wills as one and include me in that one

13 So in Q and a perfectly possible reading. Personally, however, I am inclined to accept Malone's emendation, *Let no unkind No fair beseechers kill*, which makes *No* a noun and *fair beseechers* the object of the verb *kill*. W.H.A.

136

If thy soul check thee that I come so near,
Swear to thy blind soul that I was thy *Will*,
And will, thy soul knows, is admitted there;
4 Thus far for love my love-suit, sweet, fulfill.
Will will fulfill the treasure of thy love,
Ay, fill it full with wills, and my will one.
In things of great receipt with ease we prove
8 Among a number one is reckoned none.
Then in the number let me pass untold,
Though in thy store's account I one must be;
For nothing hold me, so it please thee hold
12 That nothing me, a something, sweet, to thee.
　Make but my name thy love, and love that still,
　And then thou lovest me for my name is *Will*.

1 **check** rebuke 1 **come so near** (1) touch to the quick (2) come so
near to your bed 5 **fulfill the treasure** fill the treasury 6 **one** one
of them 7 **things of great receipt** i.e., large matters 8 **Among...
none** ("one is no number" was an Elizabethan saying) 9 **untold** un-
counted 10 **thy store's account** i.e., the inventory of your supply
(of lovers) 13 **my name** i.e., will, carnal desire (?) 13 **still** always

137

Thou blind fool, Love, what dost thou to mine eyes
That they behold and see not what they see?
They know what beauty is, see where it lies,
Yet what the best is take the worst to be.   *4*
If eyes, corrupt by overpartial looks,
Be anchored in the bay where all men ride,
Why of eyes' falsehood has thou forgèd hooks,
Whereto the judgment of my heart is tied?   *8*
Why should my heart think that a several plot,
Which my heart knows the wide world's common place?
Or mine eyes seeing this, say this is not,
To put fair truth upon so foul a face?   *12*
    In things right true my heart and eyes have erred,
    And to this false plague are they now transferred.

---

3 **lies** inhabits   5 **corrupt** corrupted   6 **ride** (pun on the sense "to mount sexually")   9 **that a several plot** that place a private field   10 **common place** open field (with a pun on *common* = promiscuous)   12 **To** so as to   14 **plague** (1) plague of falseness (2) mistress

138

When my love swears that she is made of truth,
I do believe her though I know she lies,
That she might think me some untutored youth,
4   Unlearnèd in the world's false subtleties.
Thus vainly thinking that she thinks me young,
Although she knows my days are past the best,
Simply I credit her false-speaking tongue;
8   On both sides thus is simple truth suppressed.
But wherefore says she not she is unjust?
And wherefore say not I that I am old?
O, love's best habit is in seeming trust,
12   And age in love loves not to have years told.
        Therefore I lie with her, and she with me,
        And in our faults by lies we flattered be.

1 **truth** fidelity   3 **That** so that   7 **Simply** (1) foolishly (2) pre-
tending to be simple   7 **credit** believe   9 **unjust** unfaithful
11 **habit** appearance   11 **seeming trust** the appearance of truth
12 **told** counted   13 **lie with** (1) lie to (2) sleep with

139

O, call not me to justify the wrong
That thy unkindness lays upon my heart;
Wound me not with thine eye but with thy tongue;
Use power with power and slay me not by art.   *4*
Tell me thou lov'st elsewhere; but in my sight,
Dear heart, forbear to glance thine eye aside;
What need'st thou wound with cunning when thy might
Is more than my o'erpressed defense can bide?   *8*
Let me excuse thee; ah, my love well knows
Her pretty looks have been mine enemies,
And therefore from my face she turns my foes,
That they elsewhere might dart their injuries.   *12*
    Yet do not so; but since I am near slain,
    Kill me outright with looks and rid my pain.

---

4 **with power** i.e., openly, directly   4 **art** artful means   8 **o'er-
pressed** overpowered   11 **my foes** i.e., her looks

140

Be wise as thou art cruel; do not press
My tongue-tied patience with too much disdain,
Lest sorrow lend me words, and words express
4   The manner of my pity-wanting pain.
If I might teach thee wit, better it were,
Though not to love, yet love, to tell me so;
As testy sick men, when their deaths be near,
8   No news but health from their physicians know.
For if I should despair, I should grow mad,
And in my madness might speak ill of thee.
Now this ill-wresting world is grown so bad
12   Mad slanderers by mad ears believèd be.
    That I may not be so, nor thou belied,
      Bear thine eyes straight, though thy proud heart go wide.

1 **press** oppress 4 **manner** nature 4 **pity-wanting** unpitied
5 **wit** wisdom 6 **so** i.e., that you love me 7 **testy** fretful 11 **ill-wresting** i.e., misinterpreting everything for the worse 13 **so** (1) a "mad slanderer" (2) so believed 14 **wide** wide of the mark

141

In faith I do not love thee with mine eyes,
For they in thee a thousand errors note;
But 'tis my heart that loves what they despise,
Who in despite of view is pleased to dote. 4
Nor are mine ears with thy tongue's tune delighted,
Nor tender feeling to base touches prone,
Nor taste, nor smell, desire to be invited
To any sensual feast with thee alone. 8
But my five wits nor my five senses can
Dissuade one foolish heart from serving thee,
Who leaves unswayed the likeness of a man,
Thy proud heart's slave and vassal wretch to be. 12
    Only my plague thus far I count my gain,
    That she that makes me sin awards me pain.

4 **Who in despite of view** which in spite of what they see   6 **base touches** sexual contact   9 **But** but neither   9 **five wits** common wit, imagination, fantasy, estimation, memory   10 **serving** loving 11 **Who . . . man** i.e., which ceases to rule and so leaves me what is only the semblance of a man

142

Love is my sin, and thy dear virtue hate,
Hate of my sin, grounded on sinful loving.
O, but with mine compare thou thine own state,
4   And thou shalt find it merits not reproving,
Or if it do, not from those lips of thine,
That have profaned their scarlet ornaments
And sealed false bonds of love as oft as mine,
8   Robbed others' beds' revenues of their rents.
Be it lawful I love thee as thou lov'st those
Whom thine eyes woo as mine importune thee.
Root pity in thy heart, that, when it grows,
12   Thy pity may deserve to pitied be.
    If thou dost seek to have what thou dost hide,
    By self-example mayst thou be denied.

1 **dear** inmost   4 **it** i.e., my state   6 **scarlet ornaments** i.e., lips
(compared to scarlet wax that seals documents)   8 **Robbed ...
rents** i.e., has robbed wives of what their husbands owed them   9 **Be
it** let it be   13 **what** that which, i.e., pity

143

Lo, as a careful housewife runs to catch
One of her feathered creatures broke away,
Sets down her babe, and makes all swift dispatch
In pursuit of the thing she would have stay;   *4*
Whilst her neglected child holds her in chase,
Cries to catch her whose busy care is bent
To follow that which flies before her face,
Not prizing her poor infant's discontent: *8*
So run'st thou after that which flies from thee,
Whilst I, thy babe, chase thee afar behind;
But if thou catch thy hope, turn back to me
And play the mother's part, kiss me, be kind.   *12*
    So will I pray that thou mayst have thy *Will*,
    If thou turn back and my loud crying still.

---

5 **holds her in chase** chases her   8 **prizing** regarding

13–14 Some scholarly follies are so extraordinary that they deserve
to be immortalized. Gregor Sarrazin, a German-Swiss, emended these
lines as follows:
So will I pray that thou may'est have thy *Hen*, (short for Henry)
If thou turn back and my loud crying pen.
                              W.H.A.

144

Two loves I have, of comfort and despair,
Which like two spirits do suggest me still;
The better angel is a man right fair,
4   The worser spirit a woman colored ill.
To win me soon to hell, my female evil
Tempteth my better angel from my side,
And would corrupt my saint to be a devil,
8   Wooing his purity with her foul pride.
And whether that my angel be turned fiend
Suspect I may, yet not directly tell;
But being both from me, both to each friend,
12   I guess one angel in another's hell.
     Yet this shall I ne'er know, but live in doubt,
     Till my bad angel fire my good one out.

1 **of comfort and despair** i.e., one offering heavenly mercy, the other offering hellish despair   2 **suggest me still** always urge me   4 **colored ill** i.e., dark   10 **directly** precisely   11 **from** away from   11 **each** each other   12 **in another's hell** (with an allusion to the female sexual organ)   14 **fire my good one out** i.e., communicate venereal disease

145

Those lips that Love's own hand did make
Breathed forth the sound that said, "I hate"
To me that languished for her sake.
But when she saw my woeful state,   *4*
Straight in her heart did mercy come,
Chiding that tongue that ever sweet
Was used in giving gentle doom,
And taught it thus anew to greet: *8*
"I hate," she altered with an end
That followed it as gentle day
Doth follow night, who, like a fiend,
From heaven to hell is flown away.   *12*
    "I hate" from hate away she threw,
        And saved my life, saying, "not you."

7 **doom** judgment 9 **end** ending 13 **hate away** Hathaway,
Shakespeare's wife's surname

146

Poor soul, the center of my sinful earth,
My sinful earth these rebel pow'rs that thee array,
Why dost thou pine within and suffer dearth,
4 Painting thy outward walls so costly gay?
Why so large cost, having so short a lease,
Dost thou upon thy fading mansion spend?
Shall worms, inheritors of this excess,
8 Eat up thy charge? Is this thy body's end?
Then, soul, live thou upon thy servant's loss,
And let that pine to aggravate thy store;
Buy terms divine in selling hours of dross;
12 Within be fed, without be rich no more:
    So shalt thou feed on Death, that feeds on men,
    And Death once dead, there's no more dying then.

1 **sinful earth** i.e., body   2 **My sinful earth** (obviously the printer mistakenly repeated here words of the previous line. Among suggested emendations are: "Feeding," "Thrall to," "Fooled by," "Rebuke," and "Leagued with")   4 **Painting** i.e., adorning   5 **cost** expense   7 **excess** extravagant expenditure   8 **charge** (1) expense (2) burden, i.e., the body   10 **that** i.e., the body   10 **aggravate** increase 11 **terms divine** ages of immortality

147

My love is as a fever, longing still
For that which longer nurseth the disease,
Feeding on that which doth preserve the ill,
Th' uncertain sickly appetite to please.　　　　　4
My reason, the physician to my love,
Angry that his prescriptions are not kept,
Hath left me, and I desperate now approve
Desire is death, which physic did except.　　　　8
Past cure I am, now reason is past care,
And frantic-mad with evermore unrest;
My thoughts and my discourse as madmen's are,
At random from the truth vainly expressed:　　　12
　　For I have sworn thee fair, and thought thee bright,
　　Who art as black as hell, as dark as night.

1 **still** always　3 **preserve the ill** prolong the illness　7–8 **approve . . . except** find by experience that Desire, which refused medicine, is death (?)

148

O me, what eyes hath Love put in my head,
Which have no correspondence with true sight!
Or, if they have, where is my judgment fled,
4   That censures falsely what they see aright?
If that be fair whereon my false eyes dote,
What means the world to say it is not so?
If it be not, then love doth well denote
8   Love's eye is not so true as all men's no.
How can it? O, how can Love's eye be true,
That is so vexed with watching and with tears?
No marvel then though I mistake my view;
12   The sun itself sees not till heaven clears.
       O cunning Love, with tears thou keep'st me blind,
       Lest eyes well-seeing thy foul faults should find.

4 **censures** judges   8 **eye** (with a pun on "aye" in contrast with "all men's no")   10 **watching** wakefulness   11 **mistake my view** err in what I see

149

Canst thou, O cruel, say I love thee not,
When I against myself with thee partake?
Do I not think on thee when I forgot
Am of myself, all tyrant for thy sake?   *4*
Who hateth thee that I do call my friend?
On whom frown'st thou that I do fawn upon?
Nay, if thou lour'st on me, do I not spend
Revenge upon myself with present moan?   *8*
What merit do I in myself respect
That is so proud thy service to despise,
When all my best doth worship thy defect,
Commanded by the motion of thine eyes?   *12*
   But, love, hate on, for now I know thy mind;
   Those that can see thou lov'st, and I am blind.

2 **partake** unite   3–4 **forgot/Am of** forget   4 **all tyrant** i.e., having become altogether a tyrant   8 **present moan** immediate grief
11 **defect** lack of good qualities

150

O, from what pow'r hast thou this pow'rful might
With insufficiency my heart to sway?
To make me give the lie to my true sight
4   And swear that brightness doth not grace the day?
Whence hast thou this becoming of things ill
That in the very refuse of thy deeds
There is such strength and warrantize of skill
8   That in my mind thy worst all best exceeds?
Who taught thee how to make me love thee more,
The more I hear and see just cause of hate?
O, though I love what others do abhor,
12   With others thou shouldst not abhor my state:
      If thy unworthiness raised love in me,
      More worthy I to be beloved of thee.

2 **insufficiency** unworthiness   2 **sway** rule   3 **give the lie to my true sight** accuse my true sight of lying   5 **becoming of things ill** i.e., power to make evil look attractive   7 **warrantize of skill** guarantee of mental power   13 **raised** (sexual innuendo?)

151

Love is too young to know what conscience is,
Yet who knows not conscience is born of love?
Then, gentle cheater, urge not my amiss,
Lest guilty of my faults thy sweet self prove.   4
For, thou betraying me, I do betray
My nobler part to my gross body's treason;
My soul doth tell my body that he may
Triumph in love; flesh stays no farther reason,   8
But, rising at thy name, doth point out thee,
As his triumphant prize. Proud of this pride,
He is contented thy poor drudge to be,
To stand in thy affairs, fall by thy side.   12
　　No want of conscience hold it that I call
　　Her "love" for whose dear love I rise and fall.

---

3 **urge not my amiss** stress not my sinfulness   8 **flesh** the pe-
nis   8 **stays** awaits   8 **reason** talk   9 **rising** rebelling (with a
sexual pun, as in "point," line 9; "stand" and "fall," line 12; and "rise
and fall," line 14)   10 **Proud of** swelling with

152

In loving thee thou know'st I am forsworn,
But thou art twice forsworn, to me love swearing;
In act thy bed-vow broke, and new faith torn
4 In vowing new hate after new love bearing.
But why of two oaths' breach do I accuse thee,
When I break twenty? I am perjured most,
For all my vows are oaths but to misuse thee,
8 And all my honest faith in thee is lost;
For I have sworn deep oaths of thy deep kindness,
Oaths of thy love, thy truth, thy constancy;
And, to enlighten thee, gave eyes to blindness,
12 Or made them swear against the thing they see;
    For I have sworn thee fair; more perjured eye,
    To swear against the truth so foul a lie.

1 **am forsworn** i.e., have broken (my marriage) vows   7 **but to misuse** merely to misrepresent   11 **enlighten thee** make you shine   11 **gave eyes to blindness** i.e., caused my eyes not to see the truth   13 **eye** eyes (with a pun on "I")

153

Cupid laid by his brand and fell asleep.
A maid of Dian's this advantage found,
And his love-kindling fire did quickly steep
In a cold valley-fountain of that ground;   *4*
Which borrowed from this holy fire of Love
A dateless lively heat, still to endure,
And grew a seething bath, which yet men prove
Against strange maladies a sovereign cure.   *8*
But at my mistress' eye Love's brand new-fired,
The boy for trial needs would touch my breast;
I, sick withal, the help of bath desired,
And thither hied, a sad distempered guest,   *12*
    But found no cure; the bath for my help lies
    Where Cupid got new fire—my mistress' eyes.

1 **brand** torch   2 **Dian** Diana, goddess of chastity   2 **advantage**
opportunity   6 **dateless lively** eternal living   6 **still** always
7 **seething** boiling   7 **prove** find by experience   8 **sovereign** po-
tent   10 **for trial needs would** as a test had to   11 **withal** with
it   11 **bath** (possibly an allusion to the city of Bath, famous for its
curative waters)   12 **distempered** diseased

154

The little Love-god lying once asleep
Laid by his side his heart-inflaming brand,
Whilst many nymphs that vowed chaste life to keep
4   Came tripping by, but in her maiden hand
The fairest votary took up that fire,
Which many legions of true hearts had warmed;
And so the general of hot desire
8   Was, sleeping, by a virgin hand disarmed.
This brand she quenchèd in a cool well by,
Which from Love's fire took heart perpetual,
Growing a bath and healthful remedy
12   For men diseased; but I, my mistress' thrall,
    Came there for cure, and this by that I prove:
    Love's fire heats water, water cools not love.

FINIS

1 **Love-god** Cupid   2 **brand** torch   5 **votary** one vowed to chastity
7 **general** leader, i.e., Cupid   12 **thrall** slave

Commentaries

HALLETT SMITH

From Elizabethan Poetry

Some of the most impressive and eloquent of the sonnets are those which depend less upon a reflective situation for their framework than upon an apparent display of the poet's moods directly. It is especially true that, of these sonnets, those expressing a mood of despair or disillusion, of melancholy over the failure of the world or of the human personality, remind us of passages in the tragedies. The ideas are sometimes bitter in the manner of a Hamlet or a Lear. The motivation seems to be partly the same motivation that lies behind the satire of the 1590s, partly a more profound sense of the inevitable corruption of man in a world which is beyond his managing or even his understanding. Hamlet's awareness of the reasons for rejecting the world is reflected in No. 66, "Tir'd with all these, for restful death I cry." Yet the main burden of these sonnets of despondency is not that the fault lies in a corrupting world; they throw the principal emphasis upon the truant disposition of the speaker himself; that is to say, on the face of it they seem more psychological than satirical. Two of the most effective of these sonnets of mood are Nos. 29 and 30, "When in disgrace with fortune and men's eyes" and "When to the sessions of sweet silent thought."

Shakespeare's method in these sonnets may best be observed in No. 73. Here the professed subject is the poet's age, which is contrasted with the youth of the young man addressed

From *Elizabethan Poetry: A Study in Conventions, Meaning, and Expression* by Hallett Smith (Cambridge, Mass.: Harvard University Press, Copyright, 1952, by the President and Fellows of Harvard College). Reprinted by permission of the publisher.

in several other sonnets. But the resultant mood is the same mood of despair as that of the sonnets we have mentioned. The utility of that mood, some of its origins, and the way in which it unifies and makes effective the sonnet are worth analysis.

> That time of year thou mayst in me behold
> When yellow leaves, or none, or few, do hang
> Upon those boughs which shake against the cold,
> Bare ruin'd choirs, where late the sweet birds sang.
> In me thou see'st the twilight of such day
> As after sunset fadeth in the west,
> Which by and by black night doth take away,
> Death's second self, that seals up all in rest.
> In me thou see'st the glowing of such fire,
> That on the ashes of his youth doth lie,
> As the death-bed whereon it must expire
> Consum'd with that which it was nourish'd by.
>   This thou perceiv'st, which makes thy love more strong,
>   To love that well which thou must leave ere long.*

The quatrains here are clearly divided, the first devoting itself to an image of trees in early winter or late fall, the second to an image of twilight and the beginning of night, and the third to the image of a dying fire. The relationship of these to the professed subject of the poem, old age, is fairly obvious, and it might be said that the sonnet is merely an application of these images to the idea. However, Shakespeare's method is not quite so simple as this, and the way in which the images are worked out and the way in which they influence each other are worth notice.

The indirectness of Shakespeare's method could hardly better be exemplified than in the first quatrain. Here the picture of the trees in winter is used to project a situation of the feelings, rather than the external attributes of age. "When yellow leaves, or none, or few": the uncertainty here is clearly deliberate. Yellow leaves as a symbol of age are obvious enough, even if we do not recall Macbeth's "My way of life is fall'n into the sere, the yellow leaf," but the curious effect produced here is by the alternatives of "yellow leaves," "none," and "few." Then the purely descriptive part of the image is extended, with "Upon

*Brooke, *Shakespeare's Sonnets*, p. 163.

those boughs which shake against the cold" carrying us farther into the picture of winter and away from the relationship between the speaker and the image. If we stop at this point and ask of the first line, In what respect may this time of year be seen "in me," there is no answer, for the figure has left the speaker behind and developed in a purely descriptive direction. But then in line 4 the boughs themselves are made the subject of further metaphor, "bare ruin'd choirs," and then returned immediately to their first existence as boughs by the "explanation" of the choir figure, "where late the sweet birds sang."

The problem here is one of deciding just what the nature of this figure is. To what degree does the image of the speaker remain in the reader's eye: are those boughs which shake against the cold supposed to cause us to picture an old man's arms? When the boughs are momentarily transformed by the "bare ruin'd choirs," are we to evoke very fully the picture of the decayed monastery churches with their ruined choirs and, as William Empson suggests,* the choirboys themselves, and associate this with the feeling of the poet toward the young man addressed? The control of the associations is very difficult. In general, it seems safest to say that the picture, doubly metaphorical, of the winter boughs is only atmospherically and symbolically connected with "in me." There is nothing of an allegorical correspondence or even a conceit. It is this reticence about the application of the description to the subject that allows for further development in the following quatrains.

The image of twilight fading and being taken away by night brings the imagery closer to the subject, for the night is called "Death's second self," and the ambiguous "that seals up all in rest" applies to both night and death, the two selves. "Seals up" is another of those rural terms common in Shakespeare's figurative language; it applies to putting cattle away for the night.†

The third quatrain uses the image of a dying fire, and here

Seven Types of Ambiguity (London, 1930), p. 3.
†See T. G. Tucker, *The Sonnets of Shakespeare* (Cambridge, England, 1924), p. 149. In some ways Tucker's edition is the most useful of all editions of the sonnets, especially for the kind of analysis which I have been attempting here. He is, however, insufficiently sensitive to ambiguities in meaning, and his comment will often dogmatize on a single meaning when two or more exist at once.

there is a genuine conceit. The fire still burns, but on the ashes of what has been already burnt. This is like old age, which rests on the youth which has produced it. But an additional idea is that this is a deathbed, relating our associations to the night-death image of the preceding quatrain, and the idea of a bed of ashes inevitably suggests repentance and humiliation. Moreover, the ashes tend to choke the fire, though they represent former fire, former fuel. Therefore, we get a formulation of a favorite idea of Shakespeare's: "Consum'd with that which it was nourish'd by." The irony of process, as it might be called, has many expressions in these sonnets; it is an indication of the antique cast of Shakespeare's mind: "And time that gave doth now his gift confound."*

Sonnet 73 is clear in its general design. The three quatrains have a relationship to each other and a natural development. They proceed from the declining of the year to the declining of the day to a declining of the fire, bringing the metaphorical point closer to the subject as the poem progresses. But the relationship of the figures to each other is also a metaphorical one: the year and the day are both metaphors for a lifetime; the fire has to do both with the heat and life of summer and noonday as well as with the vital essence of life. The richness of the sonnet derives more from its metaphorical involutions than it does from the clarity of its structure.†

*Sonnet 60.
†R. M. Alden (*The Sonnets of Shakespeare* [Boston, 1916], p. 183) called this "the finest example of the Shakespearian mode," presumably because of its structure, for Alden is so resistant to the metaphors in Shakespeare that he recoiled with horror at some of the more obvious images in sonnet 60, preferring to pretend that they are not there. John Crowe Ransom's essay "Shakespeare at Sonnets," *Southern Review* 3 (1937–38): 531–53, republished in *The World's Body* (New York, 1938), comments on and praises the three-quatrain sonnets above the others. Arthur Mizener's reply to Ransom in *Southern Review* 5 (1939–40): 730–47, deals with the structure of Shakespeare's figurative language. The line in sonnet 73 which I discussed only briefly, "Bare ruin'd choirs, where late the sweet birds sang," offers an example of the difficulties of critics: Ransom says he deplores the coexistence of the images of the boughs shaking against the cold and of the bare ruin'd choirs; not only this but he also says, "I believe everybody will deprecate *sweet*" ("Shakespeare at Sonnets," p. 550). Tucker, on the other hand, does not deprecate it. He says, "The epithet is not idle; the choirs formerly rang with 'sweet' singing. The implication is 'I was a summer poet once' " (*The Sonnets of Shakespeare*, p. 149).

WINIFRED M. T. NOWOTTNY

Formal Elements in Shakespeare's Sonnets: Sonnets 1–6

Despite Shakespeare's own description of his sonnets as being "far from variation or quick change," they have proved to be remarkably resistant to generalizations. It is, however, the purpose of this article to suggest that there is one generalization that can be made about them; one, moreover, that affords a point of view from which it is always helpful to regard them: namely, that the *Sonnets* reveal Shakespeare's strong sense of form, and that it is with respect to their form that the peculiar features or striking effects of individual sonnets may best be understood. There are in the *Sonnets* so many experiments with form that it would be difficult to lay down at the outset a definition of "form" at once comprehensive and precise, but the meaning of the term as it is used here will be sufficiently indicated by describing "form" as "that in virtue of which the parts are related one to another," or indeed as "that which manifests itself in the relationships of the parts." What is important for the purposes of this article is not the precise definition of form, but rather the indication of elements which commonly contribute to the manifestation of form. At the present day, the most illuminating criticism of individual sonnets is characterized by its concentration on imagery, and though it is true that imagery in the *Sonnets* is of great importance, it is not of exclusive or even of paramount importance. In this article I shall try to show that in Shakespeare's sonnets imagery is subordinated to the creation of the form of the whole and that imagery itself is at its most effective when it supports or is supported by the action of formal elements of a different kind.

From *Essays in Criticism* 2 (January 1952): 76–84. Reprinted by permission of Basil Blackwell, publisher.

Sonnets 1–6 of the 1609 Quarto afford illustration. Shakespeare is often praised for his power of using imagery as an integrating element, yet in these sonnets it is evident that he has sacrificed the integration of the imagery of the individual sonnet to larger considerations of form; this sacrifice has features which show that it is in fact a sacrifice and not the ineptitude of a novice in sonnet-writing. In Sonnet 1, the degree to which the images assist the organization of the poem is slight indeed. Almost every line has a separate image, and these images are heterogeneous (for instance: "Beauty's rose"—"heir"—"contracted"—"flame"—"famine"—"foe"—"herald"—"buriest"—"glutton"). The relation between the images is, for the most part, a relation via the subject they illustrate; it is not by their relations to one another that the poem is organized. This, however, is not ineptitude. The separateness, the repetitiveness (in that there is no increasing penetration of the object, but only an ever-renewed allegorization), and the regularity (a single new image in each of the first twelve lines) give this sonnet the character of a litany. If Sonnet 1 is indeed in its rightful place, there would seem to be here a recognizable decorum of form in the poet's electing to open by a litany of images* a sonnet sequence which makes extended use of each. Further, the hypothesis that in Sonnet 1 there is a decorum of form which to the poet seemed more important than the congruity of images within the individual sonnet is borne out by some features of Sonnets 2–4. The imagery of Sonnet 2 falls into two distinct parts connected by a modulation. In the first quatrain there is a group of images all referring to the beauty of the face; in the third quatrain a very different group, not visual like the first, but moral or prudential, relating to beauty considered as treasure, inheritance, and a matter for the rendering of accounts; the intervening quatrain is entirely devoted to a modulation from one type to the other:

> Then, being ask'd where all thy beauty lies,
> Where all the treasure of thy lusty days,
> To say, within thine own deep-sunken eyes,
> Were an all-eating shame and thriftless praise.

---

*The litany of images is at the same time a litany of considerations or arguments, for in these sonnets the image is often an emblem of an argument.

(In this modulation the visual and the prudential—"beauty" and "treasure"—are formally balanced, and the "deep-sunken" unites the eyes and the treasure in a single imaging epithet.) This careful four-line modulation suggests that Shakespeare was well aware of the virtue of relating images one to another as well as to the object they convey; yet the very necessity for a modulation here derives from the remoteness from one another of the two types of imagery. Here again the discrepancy finds its justification in larger considerations of form: namely, in the relation of Sonnet 2 to Sonnets 3 and 4. Sonnet 3 takes up and expands the first quatrain of Sonnet 2, turning as it does upon the beauty of the face ("Look in thy glass, and tell the face thou viewest . . ."), and Sonnet 4 takes up and expands the third quatrain of Sonnet 2, turning as it does entirely upon the beauty as treasure, inheritance, and a matter for the rendering of accounts. It is further to be observed that Sonnets 5 and 6 repeat this pattern, 5 dealing with visual beauty in visual terms, and 6 dealing with "beauty's treasure" in a long-sustained conceit drawn from usury. Would it be fanciful to suggest that the infelicity of the usury conceit in Sonnet 6 reflects the difficulty the poet found in bringing this little sequence to a formally symmetrical conclusion?

In each of these six sonnets, features of the individual sonnet are illuminated by a consideration of the design of the whole group. But since we have no external warrant of the correctness of the 1609 order, the case for Shakespeare's sense of form must further be argued on grounds affording independent corroboration. This is found in Sonnet 4 where, though the imagery chosen relates the sonnet to its fellows, the development of that imagery within the sonnet is a self-contained exercise in abstract form. The sonnet must be quoted and discussed in full.

> Unthrifty loveliness, why dost thou spend
> Upon thyself thy beauty's legacy?
> Nature's bequest gives nothing, but doth lend,
> And, being frank, she lends to those are free.
> Then, beauteous niggard, why dost thou abuse
> The bounteous largess given thee to give?
> Profitless usurer, why dost thou use
> So great a sum of sums, yet canst not live?
> For, having traffic with thyself alone,

> Thou of thyself thy sweet self dost deceive.
> Then how when nature calls thee to be gone?
> What acceptable audit canst thou leave?
> Thy unus'd beauty must be tomb'd with thee,
> Which, used, lives, th'executor to be.

Here we have a sonnet in which, patently, there is a high degree of organization. Firstly, the imagery of financial matters is sustained throughout. Secondly, there is within this integrated scheme a number of strongly marked subsidiary systems. The most immediately striking, which may therefore be cited first, is the ringing of the changes in lines 5–8 on "abuse"— "usurer"—"use," which is taken up in the couplet by "unus'd," "used." Another marked system is that of the reflexive constructions associated with "thee": "spend upon thyself"— "traffic with thyself"—"thou of thyself thy sweet self dost deceive," taken up in the couplet by "thy . . . beauty . . . tomb'd with thee." That these are deliberate systems, not inept repetitions, is proved by the way in which they interlock in the couplet: "unus'd" is, in the first line of the couplet, linked with "thy beauty . . . tomb'd with thee," and this contrasts with the second line of the couplet, where there is a linking of "used," "executor," and "lives," to produce the complete formal balance in thought, diction and syntax, of

> Thy unus'd beauty must be tomb'd with thee,
> Which, used, lives, th'executor to be.

This formal balance is of course closely related to the thought of the sonnet: Nature, which lends beauty in order that it may be given, is contrasted with the youth, whose self-regarding results in a usurious living on capital alone, which is a negation of Nature and of life; these paradoxes of the thought make possible the correspondences and contrasts of the verbal systems. What is remarkable is the way in which the poet evolves from this material an intricate and beautiful form which is very close to the art of fugue. Like the fugue, its effect resides in the interaction of the parts; critical analysis, which cannot reproduce the simultaneousness of the original, must labor heavily behind, discussing first the development of each part and then their interaction. We may note, then, that "Unthrifty loveliness," with which the sonnet opens, is, as it were, a first blending of those two distinct voices, "why dost thou spend upon thyself" and "Nature's bequest." The second quatrain blends them again in "beauteous niggard," which is itself an inversion, formally complete, of "unthrifty loveliness," and moreover an inversion which leads on to the extreme of "profitless usurer"; further, the movement toward the judgment represented by "profitless usurer" has all the while been less obtrusively going on in the verbs as well as in the vocatives ("spend"—"abuse"—"yet canst not live"). Then, with "yet canst not live," the sonnet brings out the second voice, that reflexive (and self-destructive) action announced in "spend upon thyself," but kept low in the first eight lines, maintaining itself there only by the formal parallels of "why dost thou spend"— "why dost thou abuse"—"why dost thou use." This voice now emerges predominant in "For, having traffic with thyself alone," and this voice in turn reaches its extreme of formal development in the line "Thou of thyself thy sweet self dost deceive." The remaining lines bring the two voices to a sharp contrast with "nature calls thee to be gone" (where "nature" and "thee" achieve a syntactical nearness embodying a conflict of opposed concepts, and this conflict-in-nearness is fully stated in the complete formal balance of the couplet). In this rough analysis of the blending of the voices in this sonnet, much has had to be passed over, but now we may go back and point to the incidental contrast and harmony of "beauteous niggard" with "bounteous largess"; to the transition, in the pun of "canst not live," from usury to death (which leads on to the contrast in the couplet); to the felicity of "audit" in line 12, which is relevant not only to all the financial imagery that has gone before, but also to the rendering of an account when life is at an end; to the subtle conceptual sequence of "unthrifty loveliness" (the fact of beauty), "beauteous niggard" (the poet's reproof), "profitless usurer" (the youth's own loss), and finally, "unus'd beauty" (the whole tragedy—of beauty, of the poet, and of the youth—in the hour of death). Thus this sonnet, which in its absence of visual imagery has little attraction for the hasty reader, reveals itself to analysis as having an intricate beauty of form to which it would be hard to find a parallel in the work of any other poet.

Though Sonnet 4 is a *tour de force* in the handling of form, Sonnet 5 is even more important to the critic who would make much of formal elements, in that it has a quality which sets it apart from the preceding four: a quality the average reader might call seriousness or sincerity. Here Shakespeare deals with Time and Beauty (and for the application of these to the particular case of the youth requires Sonnet 6, linked to 5 by "Then let not . . ."). The evident artifice of Sonnets 1–4 (emblematic imagery, conceits, punning and patterned word play) gives place in Sonnet 5 to language which, though it is of course figurative, derives its figures from that realm of common experience in which processes conceived philosophically by the mind have in fact their manifestations to the senses: from the seasons which figure Time, from the flower and its fragrance which figure Beauty and Evanescence. In short, the poem appeals to us in that realm of experience where we are all, already, half poets. Yet despite this change from the "artificial" to the "sincere," this poem too derives much of its strength from its formal design. This design is simple but perfect. The easy continuous process of Time is stated in lines themselves easy and continuous:

> Those hours that with gentle work did frame
> The lovely gaze where every eye doth dwell,

and in the next two lines, which suggest that this process implies a coming reversal, the reversal is still a thing of the future and is indicated not by any change in the movement but only by the verbal contrasts between "gentle" and "will play the tyrant" and between "fairly" and "unfair." So the continuous movement flows uninterrupted through these lines and on into the fifth:

> For never-resting time leads summer on

but in the sixth line,

> To hideous winter and confounds him there

the reversal so casually foretold in the first quatrain becomes, by the violence of "hideous winter" and "confounds" and by the change of tense, a present catastrophe, and the movement of the fifth and sixth lines taken together perfectly corresponds to the sense: the running-on movement of summer is checked by "hideous winter" and again by the heavy pause at "there."

The next two lines embody perfectly, by sound and imagery as well as by sense, this checking and reversal:

> Sap check'd with frost and lusty leaves quite gone,
> Beauty o'ersnow'd and bareness everywhere.

(Particularly subtle is the way in which the alliteration of "lusty leaves" gives place to that of "beauty" with "bareness.") Now in the remaining six lines the poet in his turn attempts a reversal, and the beauty of the form is to be seen in the way in which he now uses the two kinds of movement already laid down in the sonnet (the one of flowing, the other of checking). What he does is to *transfer to Beauty* the flowing movement of Time, and then to *arrest* Beauty in a state of permanent *perfection*; this he does by the long flowing movement, ending in arrest and permanence, of the line,

> Then, were not summer's distillation left . . .

This triumphant transfer to Beauty of the movement formerly associated with Time, is of a piece with the imagery of the next line ("A liquid prisoner pent in walls of glass"), where Beauty's distillation is at once arrested ("prisoner," "pent") yet free ("liquid") and visible ("glass"); this image of course reverses the implications of the earlier images of winter, where the sap was checked with frost and beauty was o'ersnow'd. Thus the movement of the first eight lines proves to have been designed not merely to make the sound repeat the sense, but rather to lay down formal elements whose reversal enables the poet to reverse the reversal implicit in Time. Similarly, the image of distillation is seen to be not merely an illustration of the concept of preserving Beauty, but also an answer to the image of winter's freezing of the sap and obliteration of Beauty. Clearly, the formal elements of Sonnet 5 are part of the poetic logic: the movement, as much as the imagery, is a means of poetic power. It is because of this that the study of formal elements in the *Sonnets* is not an arid academic exercise. Such a study can help one to arrive at a fuller understanding of Shakespeare's means of communication and a fuller possession of those poetic experiences with which the *Sonnets* deal.

This article has dealt only with the first six sonnets of the 1609 Quarto. These six sonnets are not exceptional in their successful handling of form; from the whole range of the *Sonnets* many examples more subtle and more striking might have been chosen but it seemed to me best, in order to argue the case for Shakespeare's interest in form, to make no arbitrary selection, but simply to begin at the beginning and scrutinize what is to be found there. The findings warrant a much greater attention to formal aspects of the *Sonnets* than is at present customary. The result of such an attentiveness to Shakespeare's handling of form is the discovery that the greater the immediate effect of a sonnet, the more surely does it prove, upon examination, that the effects rest no less upon the form than upon the appeal of the sentiments or of the imagery (as, for instance, in the famous Sonnet 116, "Let me not to the marriage of true minds . . ."). Again, it will be found that many of the sonnets which are not commonly held to be of the finest, reveal an unsuspected depth and strength when they are, after scrutiny of their form, revalued. It is upon this last point that particular stress may well be laid, for it is here that one becomes aware of new possibilities for the interpretation of Shakespeare's language, not only in the poems but also in the plays. A close study of the language of the *Sonnets* makes it clear that, great as was Shakespeare's ability to use imagery not only for its beauty but also for its integrating power, he possessed in even greater measure the power to make the formal elements of language express the nature of the experience with which the language deals. No doubt a knowledge of rhetoric, which must direct attention to verbal patterns, did something to develop this power. Of the early plays it may be true to say that sometimes the rhetorical forms are empty, that they have little virtue beyond that of providing a ready-made mold for the flow of what is thought and felt. But Shakespeare's rejection of rhetorical forms of the overelaborate and merely self-regarding type was coupled with an increasing awareness of the expressiveness of those forms he did retain. Thus in the language of the great plays the recurrence of a marked form is not fortuitous, nor is it, in cases where a recurring form is associated with a particular speaker, merely a device for adding body to a character; that is to say, these features of the style are rarely, if ever, designed to contribute merely to the creation of a "character part"; they are almost always an expression of something essential in the speaker himself considered in his relation to the play as a whole. Pope in his preface to his edition of Shakespeare commented on the highly individualized styles of the characters. It still remains for the interpreters of Shakespeare in our own time to discover to what extent these styles are expressive as well as characteristic. And further it may be said that the expressiveness of formal organizations in Shakespeare's language is matched by the expressiveness of form in all his dramatic structures. Every age rediscovers the genius of Shakespeare. It is open to ours to discover and to show the working of his genius in the realm of forms.

HELEN VENDLER

Shakespeare's Sonnets:
The Uses of Synecdoche

In his sonnets, Shakespeare takes up very large themes—
love, jealousy, death. We could say that the very first aesthetic
problem such themes present is their unmanageability. Unless
they can be reduced to manageable size, the poet cannot create
a believable poem. In finding an almost infinite variety of man-
ageable structures, Shakespeare exercised his best ingenuity;
and the example of success in this mode that I want to take up
here is an apparently playful sonnet depending on synecdoche,
the trope *par excellence* of reduction, which usually takes the
form of substituting the part for the whole, for example "roof"
for "house," or "hands" for "workers." The sonnet finds in synec-
doche a solution to the aesthetic problem of how one represents
sexual jealousy in other than tragic or satiric terms. By under-
standing that a problem is being solved, we can understand the
aesthetic gaiety of the comic solution, and we end by conceiv-
ing of this sonnet not as a frigid triviality (as the more solemn
commentators would have it) but rather as a triumphant *jeu
d'esprit* on the dangerous subject of sexual infidelity.

The sonnet I take up is 128:

> How oft, when thou, my music, music play'st
> Upon that blessèd wood whose motion sounds
> With thy sweet fingers when thou gently sway'st
> The wiry concord that mine ear confounds,
> Do I envy those jacks that nimble leap
> To kiss the tender inward of thy hand,
> Whilst my poor lips, which should that harvest reap,
> At the wood's boldness by thee blushing stand.

This essay has been written especially for the Signet Classics edition of
Shakespeare's poems.

To be so tickled, they would change their state
And situation with those dancing chips,
O'er whom thy fingers walk with gentle gait,
Making dead wood more blest than living lips.
    Since saucy jacks so happy are in this,
    Give them thy fingers, me thy lips to kiss.

We recall Romeo's wish that he could be a glove upon the hand of Juliet so that he might touch her cheek. Here, the speaker's wish to be a musical "jack" or key touched by his mistress's hand, is not taken literally, any more than Romeo's wish to be a glove. Readers can become impatient with such a conceit (a figurative expression); they feel they are being asked to concur in language inappropriate to a grown man. But in fact there is no such "real" wish; the object in the conceit serves as a miniature surrogate actor playing on an invented stage the drama of physical touch that the lover wishes to act out in "real life." The absurdity of the drama of reduction (in which a glove or keyboard plays the role desired by the lover) lends the fantasy its aesthetic interest. Shakespeare prolongs his conceit for fourteen lines, and uses it to deflect feelings of sexual competition too painful for direct utterance.

When Shakespeare's playlet opens, the lover is standing by his mistress as she plays the virginals, wishing that he could be the "blessèd wood" that resounds under the touch of her "sweet fingers." The conceit of the poem is apparently so brief—"I envy the wood that kisses your hand"—that one principal aesthetic project here must simply be to keep invention going. In the first quatrain, only tender words are addressed to the mistress. She is herself her lover's music, her fingers are sweet, her playing gentle, and her touch a blessing. Scarcely a line passes without the interjection of some melting word of praise. (In fact, the whole poem, before the couplet, is bracketed by the two words "blest" and "gentle": the "blessèd wood" becomes "wood more blest," and the concord "gently" swayed engenders the "gentle" gait near the close.)

To reinforce the apparent semantic tenderness, a mimic conjunction of lover and lady is played out in the poem by antiphonal pronominal kisses—my music, thy fingers; mine ear, thy hand; my lips, thy fingers; thy fingers, me, thy lips—thereby exhibiting the private, but frustrated, desire for union which has engendered the speaker's mock jealousy of the instrument's "saucy jacks." The bracketing of the drama early and late by "blest" and "gentle" and "fingers" tells us that the fictional situation does not change between lines one and twelve: the wood is still *blest* because of the continued *gentle* playing of the lady's *fingers* upon it. The central project of invention, then, is to modify, during twelve lines, the lover's response to an unchanging situation. It is a project so fragile that too heavy a hand will wreck it.

Shakespeare schematizes the scene, as I have said, by reduction through synecdoche. He reduces the lady, seated, into a hand and fingers; he reduces the lover, standing beside her, into an eye, an ear, and lips. The courting-concert has been a rich subject for genre-paintings; if we think of the amount of decorative incident possible given a room, a lady, a gentleman, and a musical instrument, we become keenly aware of Shakespeare's drastic reduction of the scene to bodily synecdoche. At first, as I have said, the speaker is an ear, an implied eye watching the lady, a self referred to as "I," and a pair of lips; his ear, he tells us, is confounded, his eye watches the nimble jacks as they leap, he envies the wood, and his lips blush at the wood's boldness. The first eight lines of the sonnet are a sketch, then, in which a complex human scene is reduced to its very few active elements. We might conceive of such a poem as a drawing in which an image has been reduced to the minimum number of barely descriptive strokes.

But there is even a reduction of this reduction. In the third quatrain the lover is further reduced to nothing but a pair of lips, the lady to nothing but a set of fingers. Here, the lover also abandons the first person, and speaks of his lips in the third person, thereby affecting an impartial "outside" judgment on her fingers and his lips alike. This third-quatrain narrowing and reconceiving of the conceit, done of course in the service of erotic argument (so that the lover and the lady can equally be spectators of the poor disenfranchised lips), turns the poem from present-time habitual retrospect ("How oft") to conditional-mood hopeful prospect ("To be so tickled, [my lips] would change their state / And situation with those dancing chips").

Finally, in the couplet, the continuing synecdoche for the lady (her fingers) is suddenly and winningly changed to an element (lips) that the lover has already been said to own, but which the lady has not yet been mentioned as possessing. And the lover (who in the couplet resumes his first-person account) has so recently been represented by his lips alone that the plea "Give . . . me thy lips" is itself, by the conjunction of "me" and "thy lips," that desired kiss of lips to lips toward which the poem has been aspiring and on which it ends. The poem is a kiss deferred and, finally, a kiss verbally enacted; one aesthetic problem of the sonnet is that of finding a way to enact the lover's yearning to kiss, and its final implied success.

I have neglected till now the introductory metaphor of the sonnet, the metaphor of music. The tonic note is sounded in the opening sigh, "How oft, when thou, my music, music play'st." The rest of the poem exists to amplify the sense in which, by synecdoche, the lady can be called the lover's music. What is emphasized about music here is the erotic reciprocity between player and instrument (one of the countless images of reciprocity in the sonnets, reciprocity being one of their directing metaphors). This reciprocity at first opposes a conventional female gentleness to an equally conventional male bold leap to kiss; but it later adds, we should notice, a female provocative tickling and a male responsive dancing, suggesting the lady's deliberate unchastity. "Music" as we see it here is an affair of a body that both initiates and responds, offering concord and confusion at once.

In the throes of his mock jealousy of the jacks, the lover will refer self-deprecatingly to "my poor lips"; but as he prepares to argue his own case, he calls the jacks "dead wood," while he, by contrast, possesses "living lips." Until this moment, he had ostensibly hoped only that the lady's *fingers* might stray away from the nimble jacks and toward his lips; but now his mock envy turns to a mock largesse, as he invents a more fitting cessation to the drama. Let the music continue, he suggests, thereby satisfying the jacks and granting the lady her desire to continue "tickling" them; but let a kiss be offered in the lover's direction: "Since saucy jacks so happy are in this, / Give them thy fingers, me thy lips to kiss." The jacks are allocated the fingers as their portion (in the quarto, the line reads "give them *their* fingers"); to the lover are allocated the surprising lips (which until this moment the lady did not verbally possess). The distribution of benefits is announced, it would seem, with a happiness which is delighted that all concerned can be satisfied at once.

But behind the mock envy, the mock largesse, and the

animated fiction of the jacks that leap across the line break to kiss; behind the self-deprecation of mock modesty as the timid lover stands blushing at the sexual audacity of the jacks, there lies the recollection—ironic of course but touching—of the hyperbolic treasuring in adolescence of all proximity to the beloved. Doting is an emotion not much described in verse: adults are ashamed to dote. But this is a poem content to be abject in doting—longing to blush, to be tickled, to dance, to kiss, to worship every motion of the beloved, even at the price of sharing her with other lovers.

The metamorphosis proposed by the lover—that his lips should themselves change state and situation and become dancing chips in order to receive the favors of the lady—never has to take place, but it serves to enact the hopeless intensities of sexual jealousy on a comically reduced plane. The jacks reap the harvest that rightfully belongs to the lover. The lady shows no disposition to give up the kisses of the jacks—on the contrary, she deliberately tickles the jacks into their responsive leaps. The first thirteen lines of the poem are, we realize at the end, an elaborate pretext to justify the prayer of the fourteenth; and the fourteenth rings as conclusively as it does because it is a phonetic re-inscription. It inscribes over "leap / To kiss" (the action of the jacks) the homonymic phrase "lips to kiss" (the hope of the lover).

In Shakespeare's reduction, the erogenous zones (including here the ear and the fingers, as well as the palm and the lips) eventually take on such importance that the other parts of the body, and all surrounding items, pale into insignificance. In the final totalization of the original synecdoche, she is all fingers and lips, he entirely a yearning pair of living lips. And only one action is permitted to exist—the touch of one element to another, the kiss of fingers to wood, or lips to lips.

The problem of conveying, in a comic mode, the eroticized and tormented state of the sensibility of the lover has been solved both economically and elegantly, with a leavening of bitter humor that permits sexual suggestiveness while aestheticizing it in the convention of courtship by music. The terrors of infidelity, jealousy, promiscuity, and sexual mistress-sharing are brought down to manageable proportions. Shakespeare's brilliant verbal solution has the tact to remain at the playful level of the set problem—the "correct" distribution of the lady's erotic energies. The final verbal kiss satisfies both the lady's free will (she can still give her fingers to the jacks) and the lover's yearning. It is probably no accident that this displacement of jealousy into comedy is followed, in sonnets 129 (on lust) and 131 (on the lady's "black" deeds), by the furious return of the repressed.

The usefulness of the figure of synecdoche lies not only in its reducing to manageability the agonies of love. It lies as well in what this trope manages to exclude. Fixing, as it does, on one or two elements—here, fingers and lips—it succeeds in excluding the whole world of other objects, competing essences. It suggests, in miniature, what the aesthetic of the sonnet sequence itself must be, as it reduces the world to a very few personages—the lover, his beloved, his rivals. To those accustomed to the wide social sweep of fiction this reduction may seem a defect. But it is a mistake to think of the lyric as acting in a world smaller than that of other literary fictions. On the contrary, it acts in the only world there is—the world extending vertically from the Trinity (105) to hell (129), and horizontally from East to West (132). Lyric enlarges its personae to fill that cosmic space: the personages in lyric are so great that the world can contain only two or three of them at once. They usurp all available space. The speaker says of his love that it fears not policy, "but all alone stands hugely politic" (124). Shakespeare's need to reduce suggests the anterior daunting immensity of his theme; his frequent turn from reduction to hyperbole implies that the innate grandeur of love will make itself felt, even when reduced to a set of eyes, lips, or fingers. What is implicit, in this raising of the human figure to the scale of all that exists, is the vastness, to human consideration, of the self and its immediate concerns.

The sonnet sequence asserts that human relations are worthy of an (almost) infinite number of poems devoted to aspects of love. We can draw a parallel between the value Shakespeare accords to love and the value he accords to the sonnet form: the form cannot be exhausted, any more than its topic can. In the sequence, the sonnet form tirelessly re-inscribes itself as if in scorn of all other lyric forms; the topic of love re-inscribes itself as if in scorn of any other interest proffered by the larger world. The sonnets, in their exploration, ever deeper and deeper, of a single poetic form and a single topic, suggest that the centripetal aspect of consciousness cannot be adequately embodied in the linearity of the novel or the dialectic of drama, but can find itself only in a poetry of lyric intensity, in which a single sensibility sounds the expressive potential of a single topic in the ultimate service of the depth of our inner life.

Shakespeare's use of consciously maintained tropes suggests his sustained interest in the fictions of the mind. We see in the sonnets his continued analysis of the power of the mind to greatly restrict or greatly expand the scale of its perceptions, to change its opinions, to clarify the obscure by reinspection, to fantasize, to adjust its fictions to an uncooperative reality, to luxuriate in its own inventions, and above all—as he writes his argument of love—to deepen its investigations of a profound idea while deepening at the same time its power over a flexible and inexhaustible poetic form.

Narrative
Poems

Introduction

The poems of Shakespeare have great ability and moments of genius, but we need not labor to praise them, since we must rejoice that he went back to the theater—recognizing perhaps that they were in some way inadequate for him. Nonetheless, they saved his career at the one crucial time, and they record (though mainly in the *Sonnets*) an experience so formative that the plays echo it for the rest of his life. No other playwright known to us worked regularly for the public theaters both before and after their long shutdown because of the plague in 1592–94, after which new companies of actors had to be formed; to survive it was an achievement. At this time a patron was essential for him, whereas afterwards (apart from one graceful kindness) he seems to avoid writing for patrons. His early life is obscure but two facts stand out like rocks: he dedicated to the Earl of Southampton (b. October, 1573) both *Venus and Adonis* (1593) and *The Rape of Lucrece* (1594), sounding much more intimate on the second occasion. Our first record of Shakespeare as a member of the Lord Chamberlain's Company, in which he stayed for the rest of his working life—indeed our first record of it performing at a London theater—is dated just after the Earl's coming of age. The Earl became liable to a heavy fine for rejecting a marriage arranged during his minority, so perhaps did not pay very much, but would help to get the company launched. By writing for a patron, Shakespeare met the crisis in an accepted manner, as a modern author might apply for "relief"; the playwright Marlowe, born in the same year, was also at this time writing a mythological narrative poem, though it happened to be interrupted by his murder; maybe they pretended to one another that this was a tiresome chore. Shakespeare's meter had been made the fashionable one for the purpose by Lodge in 1589; and may I at once refer anybody who wants further information of this scholarly kind to the excellent New Cambridge edition of the *Poems* by J. C. Maxwell (1966). I want in this essay to concentrate on what may be called the human or experiential reality of the poems, presenting such evidence as I have about that with decent care.

Taking this line of approach, it is a startling initial fact that *Venus and Adonis,* his first publication, appears in the Stationers' Register as licensed by the Archbishop of Canterbury in person. The poem soon made its impact, and libidinous undergraduates are said to have slept with it under their pillows. To have bearded and won over the "little black husband" of Elizabeth, a particularly grim member of her Court, argues that the Bard was in great nerve and good spirits. Shakespeare was not yet thirty, and few of the people who had enjoyed his plays would remember his name, but that is a time when authors need to make contacts. One can glean a little from the Register itself about the conditions of his problem. The *Dictionary of National Biography* reports that John Whitgift (1530–1604) accepted the theories of Calvin throughout his career, sometimes to the annoyance of the Queen, but denied their application to Church Government, so that he was free to persecute Calvinists as well as Papists, bringing them ruin by repeated fines; at this work he showed "brutal insolence in examining prisoners, and invariably argued for the severest penalties." Having a private fortune, he maintained a troop in his own livery, and this was what arrested Essex and his followers during their attempt at rebellion. Soon after his appointment in 1583 he secured a tightening-up of the licensing system: for example, the ballads on separate sheets had now to be approved; and, unlike his predecessor, he would license a few books under his own name every year. Nearly all of them were pamphlets on current theological controversies, for which his decision would anyway be needed, but he also showed a creditable interest in the advancement of learning; for example, he licensed books purporting to teach the Welsh language and the history of China. The Bishop of London, who was another established licensing authority, also adopted the custom of giving his own name to a few books each year; most of them dealt with political news from Western Europe. He worked closely with the Archbishop but seems to have had no literary leanings, though he had of course social ones.

Thus in February, 1591, the Archbishop and the Bishop together licensed the rather perfunctory translation of the *Orlando Furioso* by Sir John Harrington. The Queen (so people said at the time) had found her maids of honor giggling over his translation of a sexy canto, and had ordered him to go and stay in his country house till he had translated the whole epic. Both his parents had been with her during her imprisonment in the Tower, when she was almost without hope, and she had made him her godson. It was agreed that the English badly needed raising to the cultural level of the Italians somehow, and yet admittedly, on the moral side, such a poem needed thorough sanctification by the Church of England. Thus the occasion had every claim upon the assistance of the hierarchy. I count about 180 entries in the Register for 1590, 40 of them by the Bishop and 8 by the Archbishop; these proportions are fairly steady for the next few years. In 1592 the Archbishop licenses a book of love poems, though in Latin—the *Amintae Gaudia* of Thomas Watson (1557?–1592). Watson was a classical scholar of good family, and he had just died; he had assisted the poverty of better poets, and his verses were sure not to excite desire. The Archbishop entered the fatal year 1593 by licensing Hooker's *Ecclesiastical Polity* and on April 9 he licensed Churchyard's *Challenge.* The book is a final miscellany by a sturdy, loyal old chap, then about seventy-three, who died soon after; it calls the Queen a phoenix on several occasions. Nobody could blame the Archbishop, but he was perhaps starting to go a little out of his way, as Churchyard had no social claims. Within three weeks he had licensed the indecent *Venus and Adonis.* There is no immediate sign of trouble; it is the only year he reaches double figures, ending in September with Nashe—*Christ's Tears over Jerusalem* and *The Unfortunate Traveler* (Nashe had defended the Anglican hierarchy in comic pamphlets, and the first of these books is a work of penitence). But in the following year, 1594, only one publication is licensed by the Archbishop himself: "The Table of Ten Commandments, with the Pictures of Moses and Aaron." A poster, no doubt, for display in all churches; the Queen felt she had to let him keep up appearances so far. In the following year he appears to be forgiven, signing for works of theological controversy at a merry pace, but never again does he license anything even appearing to be a work of literature.

When the poem became notorious, somebody would look it up in the Register hoping to find an irregularity; and, when the truth got about, the Queen evidently told the Archbishop that he must stop making a fool of himself for at least a year. We may be sure he said, as a number of modern critics would say, that these randy students were the ones who had got the poem wrong; probably he could also claim that the author had told him so. A letter from Southampton would be needed for Shakespeare to get an interview, but it would cut little ice with the Archbishop, and Shakespeare would then have to rely on his own eloquence. The apology of Chettle shows that he was socially adroit.* He would be found to share the anxieties of the Archbishop about the petulant Earl, regarding him with grave pity. His own little poem, designed as a warning for the young man, carried a peculiarly high and severe moral allegory; and might he perhaps illustrate the point by quotation? (He would read from the final curse of Venus, saying that all loves on earth will in future be upset by parents arranging marriages and suchlike.) Whitgift had almost certainly ruined Shakespeare's father, whether the father was a Papist or a Puritan; it gives a welcome feeling of reality to see an author of revenge plays actually taking a quiet civil revenge. I doubt whether he felt this as a duty, but it might seem an excuse for letting himself be pushed forward by the giggling Southampton. He would enjoy the scene chiefly as a test of skill.

C. S. Lewis found the poem disgusting, mainly because Venus sweats, and J. C. Maxwell writes very sensibly here (his edition, p. xii): Shakespeare, he finds, is "exploiting . . . the sheer comedy of sexuality" in lines 230–40, where we meet the "sweet bottom-grass" of the erotic landscape. This explanation is rather too disinfectant; there is a joke, sure enough, based on evasion of a censorship, but a young man who felt prepared to take this Venus on would find the description positively exciting. We recognize Venus as divine because she is free not merely from bodily shame but even from social precaution;

---

*Chettle had published the dying pamphlet of Greene, which contained various libels on authors—some of them justified, says Chettle (December, 1592); but he has now met Shakespeare and found "his demeanour no less excellent than the quality he professes. Besides, divers of worship have reported his uprightness of dealing, which argues his honesty, and his facetious grace in writing, which approves his art."

that Adonis is snubbing her just cannot enter her mind. But also the modern conventions about sweat are sharply different from the Elizabethan ones. Many love poems of the time regard the sweat of a lady as somehow a proof of her elegance and refinement; the smell is not recommended as an excitement for our lower nature, the only way it could be praised in a modern novel. In this book we find the sweat of the chaste Lucrece while she is peacefully asleep singled out for praise; one hand is

> On the green coverlet; whose perfect white
> Showed like an April daisy on the grass,
> With pearly sweat resembling dew of night. (394–96)

I do not know that any poet before Andrew Marvell praised the smell of the sweat of male farmhands, but I expect someone did. Spenser would have blamed Lewis here for being "nice," meaning squeamish and proud of it, an unsoldierly trait. And indeed the impressiveness, the final solidity, of *Venus and Adonis* does turn upon not being "nice," partly from its firm show of acquaintance with country sport, partly from not even caring whether you find the details funny or not. And then, in his own mind, the story would have some bearing on his marriage to a woman of twenty-six when he was eighteen. No doubt it all took a bit of nerve.

At the end of the poem (1166) the corpse of Adonis is "melted like a vapor" and a flower springs up from his blood; Venus plucks it, saying that it smells like Adonis, though not as nice, and that the sap dripping from the break is like the tears that he shed too readily:

> . . . this was thy father's guise—
>
> . . .
>
> For every little grief to wet his eyes;
> To grow unto himself was his desire,
>   And so 'tis thine; but know, it is as good
>   To wither in my breast as in his blood.
>
> (1177–82)

The earlier Sonnets frequently blame the man addressed for trying to live to himself like a flower, and for resisting a marriage; the personal application was easy enough to recognize. But people in the know were meant to regard this as only incidental to the structure. The poem recounts a Myth of Origin, like "how the Elephant got its Trunk," a form that scholars, both in Shakespeare's time and our own, revere to a rather surprising degree. (The genuinely ancient examples are believed to have been designed to support the practice of some already existing ritual or custom.) Shakespeare meant his poem to be classically respectable, unlike the plays which he could make a living from, and the motto on his title page boasts of it; but he is not hampered by the form, spurred by it rather. The terrible prophecy of Venus, at the end, at least seems to tell a general truth and thereby give the poem a universal "significance." Also, I have come to think, he extracted from the Myth of Origin a new literary device, very important in the seventeenth century, though hardly ever employed by himself in its pure form except for *The Phoenix and the Turtle.*

The central trope of John Donne, the only bit of metaphysics in Metaphysical Poetry, runs as follows: A ruler or mistress or saint is being praised, for Justice, Beauty, Holiness, or what not, and this is done by saying "You are the Platonic Idea, in person, of Justice or what not"; in the same way, Venus had always been Love walking about in person. Elizabeth Drury has to hold this position in the *Anniversaries,* or they are mere nonsense. Only Jesus Christ (an individual who was also the Logos) had ever deserved such praise, but the literary acceptance of classical deities meant that it could be used without feeling blasphemous. It has become an arid formula when Donne writes to the Countess of Bedford:

> Your (or You) Virtue two vast uses serves;
> It ransoms one sex, and one Court preserves.

The two words in parenthesis have to mean "or perhaps Virtue *is* you," but probably poor Donne is just hammering out the formula to try and get some of his wife's grocery bills paid. When I was a student, people thought that he had imported this trick from Spain, but Professor Edward Wilson kindly tells me that there is at least no prominent use of it in sixteenth-century Spanish poetry. Some recent critic has named the trick "inverted

Platonism," and it certainly needs to be distinguished from Platonism. It is rather silly, though there were some splendid uses of it, so perhaps I will not seem too patriotic when claiming it as a home product.

No one will be surprised that Shakespeare could see the dramatic or "quibbling" possibilities of his story, as when saying of Venus:

> She's Love, she loves, and yet she is not loved.   (610)

or when the irritated Adonis, like C. S. Lewis, says that what she calls love is really "sweating Lust" (794). But Venus at line 12 is already saying it about Adonis, who is merely human—at any rate, till after he is dead. In the full "metaphysical" trope, it is standard to say that the death of the individual entails a universal absence of the abstraction—after Punctuality Smith has died, nobody can ever catch a train again. But why should this be true of Adonis, unless because Venus will go off in a huff? Her presentiment of his death, she says, cannot be true because the consequences of it would be too awful:

> "O Jove," quoth she, "how much a fool was I
> To be of such a weak and silly mind
> To wail his death who lives, and must not die
> Till mutual overthrow of mortal kind!
>   For he being dead, with him is beauty slain,
>   And, beauty dead, black chaos comes again."
>
> (1015–20)

She already expects the race of man to destroy itself; and the last two hundred lines of the poem, after she has found him dead, are loaded with her despairing insistence that there is no love left in the world. The conception is not a minor decoration in the poem.

Shakespeare did not need to invent it here because he had already used it superbly in *Titus Andronicus* (5.2), published in 1594 to help launch the company but probably written about 1590. The Empress Tamora, who has done great wrong to Titus, believes him to be in consequence so mad that he can be tricked into facilitating the murder of his surviving son Lucius. She therefore visits him disguised as Revenge-in-Person, bringing her two sons disguised as Rape and Murder. An Elizabethan spectator was of course thoroughly accustomed to allegorical pageants and charades; he too could if necessary have disguised himself as Revenge. Titus cannot help behaving queerly, but uses this weakness to further his revenge, like Hieronymo in *The Spanish Tragedy* of Kyd, and the eventual Hamlet of Shakespeare. He plays up to her with eerie glee and magnificent rhetoric:

> (To Demetrius) Look round about the wicked streets of
> Rome,
> And when thou find'st a man that's like
> thyself,
> Good Murder, stab him; he's a murderer.

After a good deal of this, she is so certain he is mad that he can easily deceive her into eating her two sons, disguised as a pie. It is wild but not irrelevant, indeed flatly true, because the practical trouble with revenge is that it does not finish, but produces blood feuds. Shakespeare is always prepared to think, "Why are we interested in the story?" and then say the reason why on the stage. The poem about Venus offered a very different opportunity for the technique, but one can see that his mind would take to it readily. I do not know that anybody else was already using it so early.

We need not doubt that Shakespeare considered the end of the poem dignified, and half believed what he told the Archbishop. But the dedication of it already envisages that a "graver labor" will come next, so there was no change of plan before setting out on *The Rape of Lucrece*. This too is a Myth of Origin; to insist upon it, the death of Lucrece causes an absurd change in human blood (1750). A hero did not need to be a god before such things could happen; one could easily have a historical Myth of Origin (for example, *Macbeth* is about how the Scots, thanks to the Stuarts, took to civilized hereditary rule instead of tribal warfare). The story of Lucrece was an exciting and dangerous example because it explained how Rome threw off her kings and thus acquired an almost superhuman virtue; though somewhat obscurely, this gave its justifying importance to the heroine's choice of suicide. Both the Bible (I Sam. 12:12–25) and the classics (in practice, Plutarch) disapproved of royalty; the institution could only be defended as a necessity for our fallen natures. Also Brutus had a mysterious importance for a patriot and a dramatist. No other great period of drama, anywhere in the world, had so much interest in madmen as the Elizabethan one. This apparently derived from the Hamlet of Kyd, whose story came from a twelfth-century historian of Denmark, "the Saxon who knew Latin." But the story had classical authority from Livy's brief remarks on Lucius Junius Brutus, who pretended imbecility in order to be safe till he could take revenge; indeed, Saxo has been suspected of imitating Livy to provide elegance for his savage material, so that Hamlet, whose basic trouble in the fairy tale was that he could not tell a lie, was truthful as ever when he said "I am more an antique Roman than a Dane." The Brutus who killed Caesar was his bastard, as Shakespeare remarks in *Henry VI, Part Two* (4.1), though he kept it out of *Caesar*; and a more antique Brutus, a parricide as usual, had been the first to civilize Britain; hence the name. Now, it was Brutus who plucked the dagger from Lucrece's body and championed the expulsion of the kings. He had pretended imbecility up to that very moment . . .

> Burying in Lucrece' wound his folly's show.
> He with the Romans was esteemèd so
> As seely jeering idiots are with kings,
> For sportive words and utt'ring foolish things;
>
> But now he lays that shallow habit by
> Wherein deep policy did him disguise. . . . (1810–15)

The Romans take an oath, and the last line of the poem says that the Tarquins were banished forever.

J. C. Maxwell says in his note:

> It is curious that Shakespeare makes no mention here (though the Argument concludes with it) of the historical importance of this, as involving the abolition of the monarchy (unless "everlasting" glances at it); this tells heavily against the view . . . that the popularity of the poem owed much to its bearing on political issues.

It is curious that the scholars of our age, though geared up as never before, are unable to imagine living under a censorship or making an effort to avoid trouble with Thought Police; these unpleasant features of current experience were also familiar in most historical periods, so that the disability must regularly prevent scholars from understanding what they read.

Southampton, who seemed fated to irritate the Queen, might well be inclined to cool thoughts about royalty; and Shakespeare would be wise to hesitate as to how far one might go. Though never very republican, you would think, he was certainly interested in Brutus; he had already, in *Titus Andronicus,* written better than any other Elizabethan the part of the half-genuine madman. Yet both themes are subdued to the decorum of his poem.

The resulting work is hard to read straight through, but one should realize that Shakespeare has made it static by deliberate choice. Mr. Francis Berry pointed out in *The Shakespeare Inset* that, although both these poems contain a high proportion of dialogue, the reader does not remember them so, because all the harangues might just as well be soliloquies. Indeed the silent colloquy between Lucrece and the low-class messenger, blushing together at cross-purposes (1339), stands out because it is as near as we get to any contact between two minds. In a play the audience wants the story to go forward, but here the Bard could practice rhetoric like five-finger exercises on the piano. Also, the rhetoric works mainly by calling up parallel cases, so that here again the figure of myth becomes a sort of generalization. Even this perhaps hardly excuses the long stretch of looking at tapestries of the Fall of Troy, which one may suspect was written later as a substitute for dangerous thoughts about royalty; Lucrece when appealing to Tarquin flatters his assumptions by recalling the virtues of royalty, and the highly formal structure of the work demands that she should recognize the inadequacy of such ideals after her appeal has failed. It would be sensible to have an unpublished version suited to the patron, who contributed a great deal more than the buyers would; and besides, it would give the welcome feeling of conspiracy. But anyhow the poem needs here a feeling of grim delay—she has already decided upon suicide, but has to wait for the arrival of the proper witnesses.

Whether she was right to kill herself has been long discussed, and Shakespeare was probably not so absurd as we think to let her review the Christian objection to suicide—its origins are hard to trace. St. Augustine, caddish as usual, had written "if adulterous, why praised? if chaste, why killed?"; and one might suspect that the romantic rhetoric of Shakespeare is used only to evade this old dilemma. But he is interested in the details of the case, and probably had in mind a solution, though he did not care to express it grossly. Livy already has Tarquin force her by an inherently social threat; if she rejects him, he will stab both her and a male servant in the same bed and claim afterwards that he had been righteously indignant at finding them there (670). It is assumed that her reputation has a political importance for her aristocratic family, which she puts before everything else; he gags her with her bedclothes, but not because she is expected to resist. Immediately after the rape, and till her death, she speaks of herself as guilty, and Shakespeare concurs. However, just before she stabs herself the assembled lords protest that she is still innocent, and she does not deny this, but brushes it aside as unimportant beside a social consequence:

> "No, no!" quoth she, "no dame hereafter living
> By my excuse shall claim excuse's giving."   (1714–15)

Coleridge in a famous passage derided Beaumont and Fletcher because the ladies in their plays regard chastity as a costly trinket which they are liable to mislay, and it is not obvious why Shakespeare is different here. When Tarquin slinks from her bed, he says, "She bears the load of lust he left behind"; "She desperate with her nails her flesh doth tear"; she "there remains a hopeless castaway" (734, 739, 744). Perhaps, he reflects, the instability of women is an excuse for her: they have "waxen minds . . . Then call them not the authors of their ill" (1240–44). Just before killing herself, she speaks to her husband and the assembled lords of her "gross blood" and its "accessary yieldings" (1655, 1658); one could hardly ask her to be much plainer. She was no virgin, having several children; and it is a basic fact about the young Shakespeare that he considers young men in general overwhelmingly desirable to women, let alone brave young lords. Thus she took an involuntary pleasure in the rape, though she would have resisted it in any way possible; that is why she felt guilty, and why some of her blood turned black, making a precedent for all future corrupted blood (1750). The reader perhaps is also guilty, having taken a sexual pleasure in these descriptions of sexual wrong—as much at least as the "homely villain" who wondered how she was making him blush. But we are not told that she would have killed herself for this private shame; she considers the suicide useful for public reasons. St. Augustine would conclude that she deserved death for enjoying the rape and Hell for her suicide afterwards; but the dramatist is sure that all her reactions, in this tricky situation, do her the greatest credit and are enough to explain the permanent majesty of Rome.

The Passionate Pilgrim (1599) is a cheat, by a pirate who is very appreciative of the work of Shakespeare. It starts with two genuine sonnets (138 and 144 in *Sonnets*) each of them implying plenty of story and giving a smart crack at the end; and the third item, a sonnet extracted from *Love's Labor's Lost,* follows quite naturally. Paging ahead in the bookshop, one found poems that might easily be Shakespeare's, though most of them are now generally considered not to be; it would be sensible to buy at once. What we learn from this is that Shakespeare had become news, a personality exciting curiosity, and there are other signs of it. In the previous year, for the first time, a play had been printed with his name on the title page ("*Love's Labor's Lost,* as it was presented before her Highness this last Christmas"), and the absurd *Palladis Tamia* by Meres had at least treated his work as deserving scholarly attention. The *Shakespeare Allusion Book* finds many more references to Falstaff than to any other character (Hamlet comes second, with the others far behind him). Thus in 1598 his reputation so to speak came to the boil; this was why his public was willing to trust him through his tragic period, though they did not like it so much.

The editor would have printed more sonnets if he could, and yet the ones chosen are well suited to his purpose—how could that happen? Dr. Dover Wilson in his *Introduction to the Sonnets of Shakespeare* thought that the Dark Woman (he will not call her a lady) had allowed a publisher two specimens with a view to raising the price of her whole collection. But this ignores the state of the market; she would have succeeded in publishing her collection and would not have needed to offer bait. I think that a visitor was left to wait in a room where a cabinet had been left unlocked—rather carelessly, but the secret poems were about five years old; he saw at once that they would sell, but did not know how much time was available. Thumbing through the notebook (the poems cannot have been on separate sheets, or he could have taken more without being noticed), he chose two with saucy last couplets for hurried copying. In one of the variants, the 1609 edition has a simple misprint, but as a rule it has slightly the better text—either because the thief miscopied or because Shakespeare had second thoughts. I think that one of these cases allows us to decide the alternative:

> I smiling credit her false-speaking tongue,
> Outfacing faults in love with love's ill rest.

In 1609 the second line has become:

> On both sides thus is simple truth supprest.

J. C. Maxwell gives an admirable gloss for the pirate version: "With (the help of) the ill-grounded sense of security that is characteristic of love," and plainly this is more like Shakespeare. But it is rather out of place; the poem has very little to do with his private experience or sensibility, commenting with sad good-humor on almost universal departures from truth. The duller line is more good-mannered in a way, and he would not give his first draft of a sonnet to his "private friends" (as Meres wrote), or even, one would think, to the Dark Lady. Poets of our own time have been known to add in the desired obscurity when they rewrite, but Shakespeare is more likely to have removed it. So probably he was the one who left the cabinet unlocked.

This publication also refutes the Herbert Theory of the Sonnets, for a reason that its supporters have been too high-minded to observe. William Herbert, later Earl of Pembroke, became eighteen in April, 1598, and was hardly allowed to come to London earlier, as he was a sickly lad, addicted to headaches (Dover Wilson, op. cit., p. 66); though later, I don't deny, an honest man and a useful patron, who deserved to have the First Folio dedicated to him in 1623. But this would mean that the sonnet about letting Shakespeare's boy patron borrow his mistress, when the pirate got it into print, would be hot news. The Elizabethans would call the incident thorough toad-eating, and it would be sure to get mentioned in some of the letters of gossip. I am not saying that Shakespeare would not have done it, though I think it was outside his mode of life at this date, but that he could not have hushed it up, in these circumstances. Consider what moral Ben Jonson would find to say (whereas, in 1594, moral Ben Jonson had not yet poked his nose above the boards). The first soliloquy of Prince Hal, assuring the audience that he will betray Falstaff, has close verbal echoes of the first of the pathetic sonnets ("Full many a glorious morning") trying to defend the patron for a betrayal of Shakespeare. But this does not mean that they were written at the same time; the implications would be horrible. The joke of Falstaff largely turns on the repeated bite of his self-defense, and Shakespeare may well be drawing a good deal upon his own humiliations when the servant of a patron, in his twenties. But he would need to use these memories in the assurance of secrecy, feeling them distant, feeling that they could be laughed over.

The reader should be warned of a slight change of idiom in the couplet:

> The truth I shall not know, but live in doubt
> Till my bad angel fire my good one out.

The Variorum edition gives a list of references to periodicals, mainly Victorian, and till I looked them up I imagined they proved that the Dark Lady is accused of having gonorrhea. They merely show that the phrase *fire out* was then used as we use *fire*, to mean "dismiss a person from a job"; it did not then, as now, inevitably suggest firing something from a gun. Shakespeare need only be saying: "I will not know whether the Dark Lady has seduced the Patron till she gets bored and dismisses him; then no doubt both will come round to me with indignant stories." We may be sure he did realize that an explosive insult was in the background, because he had a complex verbal awareness, as when he left his wife his second-best bed; but if the Dark Lady had really caught the disease we would hear more about it in his personal poems. A labored epigram by Edward Guilpin, published in 1598, is I think simply a crude imitation of Shakespeare's joke here; he must have been one of the "private friends" who were allowed (says Meres) to read some of the "sugared Sonnets." It would be pretty sad to believe that Shakespeare copied the merry thought from Guilpin as soon as he read his book, and had it stolen at once.

One has to try to make sense of these dates; it is fundamental to the understanding of Shakespeare's development, I think, that the relations with a patron come in 1592–95, when a patron was needed. Mr. Leslie Hotson, indeed, has put the *Sonnets* five years earlier, in an entertaining recent book that proposed a new addressee for them (*Mr. W. H.,* 1964); he laughs at the scholars for viewing Shakespeare as Little Dopey, shambling along in the rear of Marlowe and the rest, "a remarkably late developer." But his development really is unusual; usually the lyrical power comes earlier than the constructive one. Reading through the plays in the generally accepted order—*The Comedy of Errors,* the three parts of *Henry VI, The Taming of the Shrew, Titus Andronicus*—you get hardly a breath of poetry so far, though plenty of vigorous rhetoric, and a clear mind at work making the best of the plots. A little poetry comes in with *Richard III,* so that he was just beginning to be a poet, aged twenty-seven or so, when the plague forced him to rely on it for survival. After two years, when the theaters open again, he seems essentially a poetic dramatist. Another contrast, though more trivial, is perhaps more striking. Bernard Shaw remarked that Shakespeare must have suffered torture if he ever read over his comedies after he had grown up—assuming, I think, that any adult feels an obscure personal shame when he hears another man boast of being a gentleman. Probably the boasting of lads together is much the same in all classes, but it is true that an entry of three young lords, swanking by making jokes that are assumed to be top-class, occurs in all his comedies between 1594 and 1598, whereas the characters in the early comedies are mostly traders, and the lords in *Henry VI* simply murderers.

One might perhaps blame Shakespeare for choosing to write
about aristocrats, but not, having chosen to, for doing some
fieldwork on how they actually talked. It is not what is now
called snobbery, because he could not pretend to be anything
but the servant of his Earl. Probably he would be allowed to
hand around drinks at a party given by the Earl for young men
of standing—listening with all his ears, though, as one gathers
from the plays, much more free to make jokes himself than a
modern servant is. In private he seems to have scolded his lord
unreasonably, as privileged servants often do. C. S. Lewis, in
English Literature in the Sixteenth Century (1954), spoke of
"the self-abnegation, the 'naughting,' " of the sonnets, more
like a parent than a lover: "In certain senses of the word 'love,'
Shakespeare is not so much our best as our only love-poet" (p.
505). This is noble, but it is perhaps only the other side of a
feeling that the gratitude is over-strained. And yet, a number of
the sonnets thank the patron because

> thou . . .dost advance
> As far as learning my rude ignorance.   (Sonnet 78)

The actual teaching of the Earl can hardly have been more than
a few social tips, but as a window upon the great world Shake-
speare had been feeling the need of him badly. The feelings
seem better grounded if you realize that the childish patron was
giving far more than he knew. And, unless you redate the plays
as a whole, remembering that the evidence is quite an elaborate
structure, there is only one plausible time for fitting in this bit
of education.

A Lover's Complaint was printed at the end of the sonnets in
1609, but many critics have denied that Shakespeare wrote it—
chiefly on grounds of vocabulary and imagery, but also by call-
ing lines bad when they are simply dramatic, imagined as by
another speaker (e.g., 106–11). Much of it, he would consider,
had needed correcting before it was published, as indeed do
many of the sonnets themselves; he forces the words into his
rhyme scheme and general intention so hurriedly that our tex-
tual notes sometimes only amount to lame excuses (e.g., around
235). But at least Professor Kenneth Muir has now proved
Shakespeare's authorship, by "clusters" (*William Shakespeare
1564–1964*, ed. E. A. Bloom); the principle is that if an author

happens to use one word of a cluster his mind drags in most of the others soon after, and this process is not conscious or noticeable enough for an admirer to imitate it, nor is it affected, as imagery in general can be, by a change of subject matter or recent experience. I think the poem is evidently by Shakespeare on psychological grounds, and a kind of echo of the sonnets (this of course is why they were kept together, and eventually pirated together); but I am confronted by an agreement among the scholars (Maxwell's edition, p. xxxv) that it must have been written after 1600. Similar arguments have been used to maintain that the sonnets themselves were written late; the explanation, I think, is that Shakespeare often first tried out a novelty of style in his private poetry. I only ask for two years; the poem was written in 1598, with tranquillity, looking back with tender humor at his relations with Southampton, and just after killing off Falstaff. There would be no intention of publication; perhaps he wrote it in the evenings of a solitary journey. It would at any rate be a change, after seeing himself as Falstaff, to become the traditional forsaken damsel (forsaken, because by 1596 the Earl had become absorbed in his dangerous life; we need not look for a specific ground of quarrel, though we may expect that Shakespeare did, at the time). Shakespeare, like other authors, often used poetry to scold himself out of a bad state of mind, and took for granted that no one would realize he was doing it. He knew it was a delusion that the Earl had betrayed him, and writing about Falstaff had aggravated the sentiment, so he wrote a parody. Or perhaps he merely felt it was delightful to carry the belief to a wild extreme. These conjectures have the merit of explaining why the poem was written at all, though (fairly clearly) not intended for publication. Most people find that working for a repertory company is exhausting in itself, especially if they have part responsibility for the management; a man who also gives the company two masterpieces a year, as regular as clockwork, with a good deal of reading behind them, is not looking around for something to do. It is thus in order to suppose an internal reason for undertaking this quite lengthy bit of work, since there is no external one.

The first ten verses set the scene, and the rest is all spoken by the ruined girl; as many critics have remarked, the best and most Shakespearean lines express reproach:

> Thus merely with the garment of a Grace,
> The naked and concealèd fiend he covered.... (316–17)

> O father, what a hell of witchcraft lies
> In the small orb of one particular tear!   (288–89)

All the same, the girl firmly asserts in the last words of the
poem that she would have him ruin her again if she got the
chance:

> O, all that borrowed motion, seeming owed,
> Would yet again betray the fore-betrayed
> And new-pervert a reconcilèd maid!   (327–30)

No other author would do this; one man would bewail the
seduction and another treat it jovially, but not both at once.
Indeed, rather few male poets seem convinced that young
men in general are irresistible to women. A reader of novels
will rightly feel baffled at not knowing the social arrange-
ments of this village, where many people write sonnets ex-
pounding the suitability of the rich jewels that they are
presenting to the young man (210); is it in Arcadia or War-
wickshire? is he the son of a laborer, or the heir to a hundred
acres, say?

> He had the dialect and different skill,
> Catching all passions in his craft of will,
>
> That he did in the general bosom reign
> Of young, of old, and sexes both enchanted,
> To dwell with him in thoughts, or to remain
> In personal duty, following where he haunted. (125–30)

The magical picture only applies to one person, who had been
already an Earl when still a child; no wonder, after puzzling
their heads, they decided that he was the one who was clever,
and not just his horse (114–19). In all the undramatic poems
Shakespeare is deliberately holding back the power to be
funny, which was considered when he wrote *A Lover's Com-
plaint* to be much his greatest power; but he knew a joke when
he saw one, even if he had just written it down himself. But

perhaps when I say "funny" I would be more intelligible to young people (who have such grim ideas now of what makes a joke) if I said "charming." The chief merit of Dr. Rowse's account, on the other hand (*William Shakespeare*, 1964), was in its powerful presentation of Southampton as a typical neurotic invert, intolerably disagreeable, who could only regard the Queen as a personal rival. Under James, after he had unexpectedly won back his life, he played a considerable part in founding the English colonies in America, and the only picture that conveys his charm shows him as an elder statesman. (It is in C. C. Stopes's *Life*, p. 449.) But we have a glimpse of him when twenty in the Valentine of the *Two Gentlemen of Verona*. This figure is bustling along, with a rope ladder hidden under his cloak, to abduct the daughter of the Duke of Milan, but the Duke accosts him and asks his advice—how is one to abduct a lady who is kept locked up in a high bedroom? Why, with a rope ladder, of course, equipped with grappling irons but light enough to carry under one's cloak; Valentine feels he is cleverly secret because he just manages to restrain himself from offering to share the use of his rope ladder with the outraged father, but so far from that, he and his cloak are farcically transparent. The brash informative practicality of this does not feel to me neurotic at all, and I expect that many of his servants were in love with him when he was twenty, not only Shakespeare. Plainly he seemed very young to Shakespeare, who was not only ten years older but had had a harder time. The Bard could not be considered low; as heir to an ex-mayor of Stratford he would become entitled to gentility. But the social ladder was long and steep, and the expense of the clothes the Earl wore all the time would alone be enough to make him seem legendary—though he did not seem another breed from common men, the title being a recent creation.

A grave change in the whole tone of Shakespeare's writing arrives at the time of *Hamlet* (1600), the first major tragedy, and here it would be fussy to suppose that he was even remembering his relations with the patron. Critics since A. C. Bradley have pretty well agreed that "sex-horror" is prominent all through the tragic period (perhaps burning itself out in the unfinished *Timon of Athens*, before *Antony and Cleopatra*). I do not understand this change, though I expect there is a simple answer if we knew it. The reason why *The Lover's Complaint* must have been written before it is simply that otherwise it would have been much grimmer. The change I think is prominent even in the parallels to *Hamlet* which give Professor Muir his main evidence; *The Lover's Complaint* is regularly less fierce than the echoes of it which convey the doom of Ophelia. We have no nondramatic poems to guide us after the tragic period has set in.

Only one remains to be considered, and it is short; but it has come to seem the only very good poem in the book, exquisite, baffling, and exalted: *The Phoenix and the Turtle.** It is much better, I think, if viewed less portentously than has become usual. The occasion for Shakespeare's agreeing to write this bit of praise, in late 1598 or early 1599, was a humane and domestic one, though socially rather smart. I have no impulse to deny that vast and fundamental meanings derive or arise from the poem, such as were adumbrated when C. S. Lewis said that reading it was like entering the secret origins of creation, or at least of the creation of the heroines of Shakespeare's plays. But it does not tell Queen Elizabeth to produce an heir by the Earl of Essex, nor even mutter about the marital secrets of the

---

*There has been a recent move in favor of saying *The Phoenix and Turtle* instead of *The Phoenix and the Turtle*. It is true that the title pages of Chester speak of "The Phoenix and Turtle," and Shakespeare's poem as first printed has no title. But his way of regarding this pair has long been recognized as slightly different from Chester's. A social column will report the presence at a party of "The Earl and Countess of X" because they are expected to go together, and that is how Chester feels about his Phoenix and Turtle, but Shakespeare, whatever else he feels, always regards their co-presence with a touch of surprise. A critic may write about a poem: "The familiar lion and unicorn serve to emphasize the wholly conventional character of the imagery," but they become "the lion and *the* unicorn" when they are fighting for the crown. Shakespeare's poem really is a bit like "The Walrus and the Carpenter," and cannot be properly appreciated unless that is seen. Looking now for evidence to support the traditional preference (though it is apparently no older than a Boston edition of 1805), I find the poem grants it repeatedly:

> Phoenix and *the* turtle fled . . . *this* turtle and his queen . . . *the* turtle saw his right . . . it made this threne, To the phoenix and *the* dove . . . And *the* turtle's loyal breast To eternity doth rest.

In effect, *The Phoenix and the Turtle* emerges as a habitual rhythm of Shakespeare's poem, and an illogical pedantry ought not to be allowed to destroy so natural a title.

Countess of Bedford. If Shakespeare had been prone to say things like that, he would not have stayed afloat for at all long upon the smoking waters of the Court. It may be hoped that such theories are going out of fashion, but what we are regularly told now, though it sounds more modest, is quite as damaging to the poem. J. C. Maxwell takes it for granted when he remarks that Shakespeare's poem "contradicts the personal allegory of Chester's poem," so that "our interpretation must be from within the poem itself." He seems to feel that this makes it pure. But Shakespeare would have been abominably rude if he had behaved like that, after agreeing to take part in the social event of offering a volume of congratulation to Sir John Salisbury. The whole book was about the birth of a new phoenix from the ashes of the old one, a story that every reader had been taught at school, and here it was somehow in praise of Salisbury's marriage; but Shakespeare is presumed to say: "No, of course the new Phoenix wasn't born. When you burned the old one you simply killed it, as anybody could have told you you would." But, even if he had tried to offer this rudeness, it would not get printed. The immense indulgences nowadays offered to the avant-garde are not in question here. Salisbury was a forthright and decisive man, brought up to advance the glory of his house, and we know he made Ben Jonson rewrite one of the poems for his book; he would no more have allowed Shakespeare to palm off on him a subjective poem than a seditious one.

Verses by Shakespeare, Marston, Chapman, and Jonson, and also by an anonymous poet who seems to be Jonson again (probably one of his team had backed out from fear of ridicule) are added at the end of a long allegorical poem, *Love's Martyr,* by Robert Chester (unregistered, 1601); a separate title page assures us that these too are "never before extant, and (now first) consecrated to the love and merit of the thrice-noble knight, Sir John Salisbury." The book appeared at the height of the War of the Theaters, when several of the contributors were quarreling, and soon after the execution of Essex, when it was very dangerous to print a riddle that might arouse the suspicions of the Queen. Surely it is natural to expect that the poems were written earlier.

The introduction to an edition by Carleton Brown (1914) of *Poems by Sir John Salusbury and Robert Chester* (Early

English Text Society, 113) is a mine of information and entertainment about these characters, and ought I think to have settled the question. Salisbury (we may use the ordinary spelling because Chester's book does) was squire of Lleweny in north Wales, and had married in 1586 at the age of twenty an illegitimate but recognized daughter of the King of Man (or Earl of Derby); some verses written for the wedding already call her a royal bird. In 1595 he came to London as a law student and was made squire of the body to the Queen; he was her cousin, and a determined Anglican (having got the estate when his Papist brother was executed for the Babington Plot), and had a standing quarrel in Denbighshire with supporters of the Essex faction. This last would be no help until the execution of Essex, early in 1601, but in June of that year he was knighted by the Queen herself. By October he is back home being elected to Parliament as Knight of the Shire, with scandalous disorders, so he must have moved fast. Clearly, the poem was hurried out to celebrate the knighthood, unregistered to save time and because the Queen would not suspect a man she was rewarding for his loyalty; but the writing would have been done beforehand, to wait for the occasion. A line from Jonson's "Epode" here is quoted in *England's Parnassus* (1600) showing that at least some of these poems were ready about two years before publication. Also an autograph copy of Jonson's "Enthusiastic Ode" survives, inscribed to the Countess of Bedford. The squire would show round all the poems at Court, as soon as they were ready; and the ever-helpful Countess might be expected to want her own copy of Jonson's contribution, as it was not yet to be available in print. In this poem he was evidently struggling to be as jolly about the Phoenix as the Turtle demanded. Clumsy as Jonson was, he would not have given it to the Countess as direct praise of her own charms; or at least, she would not have kept it, if he had.

In 1597 the squire had printed some poems at the end of *Sinetes Passion* by Robert Parry, who calls him "the Patron"; they make very elaborate anagrams (in easy singing lines) on the names of three adored ladies, one of them his wife's sister. While very pugnacious, he was what a later age called "a martyr to the fair," attentive to the ladies, so it had seemed all right at the time of the wedding to make him a sacrifice as Turtle beside the semiroyal bride as Phoenix. In 1598 he would be a very useful patron for the young Ben Jonson, who was in desperate need of one, and he seems to have told Jonson to whip up a chorus of London poets. Shakespeare's company was giving Jonson a production, and it would be consistent to help him here too—assuming that Shakespeare had no objections to the general plan. So far from that, Shakespeare was amused or charmed both by the squire and his poet—as is clear once you admit that he wrote his tribute, not while Hamlet was saying he couldn't bear to think what his mum did in bed, but while Henry the Fifth was saying:

> Though it appear a little out of fashion
> There is much care and valor in this Welshman.

Shakespeare made it part of his business to keep an eye on these pushful Welsh cousins of the Queen, and he recommended them to his audiences without hiding their absurdity.

Chester, says Brown, was probably the resident chaplain in the big house at Lleweny, anyway a dependent who praised the family by an allegory at the time of the grand wedding. Later he was induced to add a lot of tedious padding (Nature takes the Phoenix on a grand tour), but the basic allegory is quite short and readable, though radically absurd. A marriage does indeed require mutual accommodation, and love may genuinely receive "a mystical reinforcement" on the birth of a child; but to praise a grand marriage by calling it a martyrdom is a gaffe, all the more absurd because sure to be suspected of being true. Chester evidently came to feel this during the years while he was adding the encyclopedia verses, and when at last he had to tell the London poets what the whole thing meant, so that they could reinforce it, he said it meant "married chastity." This idea had not been prominent when he began, though the intention was already high and pure. When Nature at last leads the Phoenix to the Turtle, she asks whether he has been chaste, and, on being reassured, explains that for her to produce issue requires burning alive; both birds at once collect twigs, so there is no long period of married chastity. (This of course is *why* you sometimes see birds carrying about twigs.) The main poem by Ben Jonson puzzles about his set theme, in a plain-man way; it seems a new idea to him. Trying to isolate the ideal, he appears to describe a man who spares his wife the act of sex in order not to offend her delicacy. We should welcome any sign of readiness among men of that age to treat their wives more considerately, especially if it meant spacing out the childbirths; but the refined thoughts expressed by Jonson here are remote from his tastes and convictions as otherwise known. He is not a hypocrite, because he is writing to a set theme; but his modern admirers should not praise him for his nobility. Rather out of the side of his mouth, he lets drop that one need not praise a husband who chose this course merely to hide impotence:

> We do not number here
> Such spirits as are only continent
> Because lust's means are spent.

Oddly enough Shakespeare manages to work the same reflection into his mood of total praise; the reproduction of the Phoenix, he surmises, has only failed because of the married chastity of the couple:

> 'Twas not their infirmity.

Various modern critics have explained that Shakespeare could not bear the thought of reproduction when he wrote the poem; but nobody has yet ascribed quite so much delicacy to Ben Jonson.

The Mutual Flame by Professor G. Wilson Knight (1955) shows that the Phoenix legend had often been used to symbolize a love denied bodily consummation, because that would be adulterous or homosexual or politically disruptive, so that the love is driven to more spiritual courses. He suggests that the poem may be about the squire's love for his wife's sister, which would at least avoid absurdity. One should remember here an epigram of C. S. Lewis, that Spenser was the first poet to have the nerve to say it is convenient for a man to be in love with his own wife. There had been a change of feeling since the Middle Ages, a thing so general that poor Chester, in the backwoods, around 1587, was running Spenser close for the priority. Salisbury of course really did consider himself ready for heroic self-sacrifice whenever that became necessary; the idea was basic to his status, and had to be expressed firmly in his book; but otherwise he wanted the book to be as jolly as possible, and his pride in his wife had better be expressed in a firmly sexy manner—that was a point where he could take over from his chaplain. His marriage had produced four children in the first four years, six in the next ten (no twins), and one of his bastards had been baptized in the parish church in 1597. No wonder Jonson argued about what Chester could have meant. The Phoenix herself will not have come to London, with all those ailing children, but a few vigorous comments survive from her and she apparently lived to be seventy-five.* Shakespeare might genuinely have supposed it to be an ideal though perhaps barbaric marriage.

The Wilson Knight thesis does have a secondary truth; what keeps the long absurd poem sweet is Chester's love for his master. This kind of love was avowable and not usually tormented, but when Chester comes to present himself as the Pelican, who gazes upon the burning, he positively claims a share in the honors of sacrifice; both the Phoenix and the Turtle become the "young ones" of this Pelican and feed their "hungry fancies" on her breast. He has been underrated, I think; so long as he is praising his dear lion (the coat-of-arms of Salisbury was a white lion) he has any amount of limpid depth. And why should not his absurdity (though he fears it) express something profound? If anything seems wrong with his poem, he says as he lumbers toward the end, abandoning for a moment the disguise of the Pelican,

> tis lameness of the mind
> That had no better skill; yet let it pass,
> For burdenous loads are set upon an ass.

This is the royal generosity of the Shakespearean clown, and Shakespeare was quite right to salute it.

Once the general tone has been grasped, of slightly fuddled

---

*Brown, op. cit., p. xxvi. Chester's poem says that the Phoenix had been anxious before meeting the Turtle, being of ripe age and fearing to have no offspring. No doubt it was often a tricky business to find a good enough marriage for the bastard daughter of an Earl. I expect she was twenty-five when the elder brother of young John was hanged, so that he inherited the estate and became free to marry her in what would be considered the nick of time. It does not mean that she was the Queen, who would be sixty-five.

good humor, the dramatic placing of the piece by Shakespeare can be seen as reasonably good. The two first additional poems are subscribed "Vatum Chorus" (all the poets) and praise the virtues of Salisbury only, not his wife or family; then two poems subscribed "Ignoto" (Unknown, by the starving but invincible Ben Jonson again of course), without pretending not to know the Phoenix legend (which would be too absurd), manage to direct our attention onto the sacrifice of the old Phoenix, not presenting it as repaid by the birth of a new one. Such is the purpose of the phrasing:

> One Phoenix born, another Phoenix burn.

The buildup is only rough, but it is an intentional preparation for what Shakespeare is going to do. Shakespeare then presents himself as one of the spectators after the burning, among the non-predatory birds who are the voice of Reason, and they fall into despair because the result of the experiment is delayed. I gather from J. C. Maxwell's edition that it was traditional to allow a period of dramatic suspense. Shakespeare ingeniously fits in the set theme of "married chastity" as an excuse for the failure of the experiment. But what follows his noble resignation, what holds the opposite page, is the astonishment of a birth from the ashes. It begins:

> O twas a moving epicidium!
> Can Fire? Can Time? Can blackest Fate consume
> So rare Creation? No, tis thwart to sense;
> Corruption quakes to touch such excellence.

The recent scholarly edition of Marston's *Poems* (1961, ed. Davenport) says firmly that this word *epicidium* (poem about death) means the poem by Shakespeare just concluded. Marston snatches a moment to compliment Shakespeare, as he bounds onto the stage to describe the event in an entirely different literary style; and his only objection is that the forecast in Shakespeare's poem has, astoundingly, turned out wrong:

> Let me stand numbed with wonder; never came
> So strong amazement on astonished eye
> As this, this measureless pure rarity.

I consider that very good poetry. The subsequent poems all deal with Salisbury's domestic life, wife or child being mentioned every time, so that Shakespeare's poem acts as a watershed. Anyhow, he could not have intended to spoil the show because of his neuroses; that would be quite outside his habits and training. He was acting as a good trouper when he left the climax to Marston, and he seems to have remembered Marston's bit long afterwards for the last scene of *The Winter's Tale*.

Having thus restored the poem to decency, one may consider its use of "inverted Platonism." It says that, because these two ideal lovers are dead, there will never be real lovers again, anywhere:

> Truth may seem, but cannot be;
> Beauty brag, but 'tis not she;
> Truth and Beauty buried be.

However, the next and final verse abandons this high extremity of nonsense:

> To this urn let those repair
> That are either true or fair;
> For these dead birds sigh a prayer.

I suppose the reason why Shakespeare can afford to be lax about it in this curious way, which allows him a graceful ending to the poem, is that he is working in an accepted mode. All the poets in the book seem in command of the trick, even Robert Chester; he uses it when the Pelican rejoices that the Turtle chose to burn alive, though the Phoenix tried to spare him (the experience turned out to be a pleasure, according to the Pelican's eye-witness account). Otherwise, he says:

> Love had been murdered in the infancy;
> Without these two, no love at all can be.

It is clear then that Chester was writing another Myth of Origin. But can he have had the whole machine ready in 1587, a homely author, remotely secluded? This seemed to me a great puzzle, and I am glad to have it removed by W. H. Matchett's

recent book on the poem (1965). He explains that Chester
added the Pelican section, at the end of his first draft, when the
squire took him to London to negotiate with the poets (the
squire would not himself have demanded to be praised for mar-
ried chastity). In a way, Chester must have known the idea
from the start because it is inherent in this use of myth, but he
had become uneasy about the absurdity of his whole plan; so
that it would be a great relief when the smart poets, though they
did laugh at him as he had expected, told him that his absurdity
had become the height of fashion. He was inspired to add what
is the most eloquent and personal section of the whole work.

Mr. Matchett has a very welcome energy of logic and re-
search; what other critics limply assume, he follows up.* I
hope his book will drive out of people's minds the main idea
which he champions, that Shakespeare was writing about the
loves of Elizabeth and Essex; when he says that Shakespeare
refers to the Queen as already dead in order to rebuke her for
not having followed his previous advice, whereas in fact the
exasperated and appalling old woman had become dangerous
to anybody who had to approach her, surely this is enough to
act as a purge. But I think he is right (for instance) in saying
that Jonson became frightened on hearing that the poems
would appear during 1601, when they were likely to be sup-
posed to be about Essex; he made some baffling remarks in his
plays of that year, hoping to offset the publication. Mr. Match-
ett also gets his teeth into "inverted Platonism," as one might
expect, and it is a great comfort to find a critic who is prepared
to attend to the words. Somehow he contrives to denounce
Marston and not Shakespeare for using this trope:

> Against Shakespeare's materialistic basis for negative judg-
> ment, he asserts a pseudo-Platonic basis for positive judg-
> ment. As an exposition of Platonic abstractions, Marston's
> poem is an awkward melange; as a compliment to an allego-
> rized individual—claiming that this person is himself the
> Idea upon which all else depends—his poem further degrades
> the very idealism it pretends to express.

---

*He remarks that a scribe may write the name of the author after copying
a poem without intending a signature, and this would destroy a good deal of
the edifice of Carleton Brown. But if you wrote a name with set formal
flourishes, surely that implied it was your signature.

Marston says he had been wondering why all the young girls were so ugly and stupid nowadays till he saw the new Phoenix, and then he realized that Nature had just been saving up, so as to give her everything. The eldest Salisbury child, a daughter, would be about twelve when this was written for her, and it seems well enough calculated for her age group; she would think it rather fun. If anything, I should call it Science Fiction, not Platonism; it does not deserve to be rebuked as false philosophy, because it scarcely even pretends to be philosophy. But somebody else deserves the rebuke; why do modern critics invariably write down that the trope is neoplatonic? Its effects, very various, are nearly always broader and more imaginative than would be gathered from this docketing.

Elizabethan jokes are notoriously confusing, but it would be wrong to think that the Welsh squire was being fooled by the city slickers. He wanted his book as jolly as was compatible with having it sustain the glory of his house, and he rejected the first draft of Ben Jonson's "Invocation"; at least, there is no other reason why this much more solemn version in Jonson's handwriting should have got kept among the Salisbury papers. And he must rather have strained the goodwill of his chaplain when he inserted his own "Cantos" at the end of the allegory, celebrating his delight in the beauty of the Phoenix in a very unsacrificial manner (only the first is announced as written by the Turtle, but they all have his very recognizable facility and ingenuity, and the printer might well get confused among the stage directions and acknowledgments). The celebration of his knighthood positively required family jollity; indeed, one can understand that Shakespeare, though willing to assist, felt he would avoid strain if he joined them only in their darkest hour. Even so, what he was joining was a kind of domestic game.

An important idea is at work in such love poetry, though admittedly one that was ridiculous in the eyes of the world; it forbade a husband to claim marital rights through his legal superiority, and such is the point of Shakespeare's ninth verse. We know that Chapman thought the affair funny, though in a grave pedantic manner, because he headed his piece (which praised the knight who has learned his virtues by serving his lady) "Peristeros, or the male Turtle." He has had to invent a masculine form for the word, since the Greeks considered all

doves female; however monogamous they may be, the crea-
tures do not know which sex they are, but try out the alterna-
tives (Sir Julian Huxley, in *Essays of a Biologist,* reports this
of various water birds). A female Phoenix had been invented
by the Renaissance to gratify a taste for Amazons—till then its
secret sex had been "known to God alone"; but a Turtle wear-
ing the trousers does seem to have been a real novelty, not only
for a classicist. It proved the grandeur of the Lion, as his poet
almost says in the *Epistle Dedicatory,* that he was safe from
ridicule even when presented as a Turtle. The Latin "Tur tur"
no doubt gave to the cooing of the pets of Venus, in the minds
of the poets, a deeper note of sultry passion; to make them into
symbols of chastity thus put an extra strain upon the gravity of
the reader—it had been the charm of the silly creatures that
no frustration attended their single-minded desires. Shake-
speare's poem is a wide valley brimful of an unspecified sor-
row, but one should also feel, before hearing any explanation,
the gaiety inherent in its effects of sound. As the anthem of the
birds reaches its severest exultation their tweeting modulates
into the arch baby-talk of a dandling nurse; as we soar heaven-
ward between the Co-supremes, we mysteriously almost graze
the Cow that jumped over the Moon;

> To themselves yet either neither,
> Simple were so well compounded.

It does seem rather odd, in a way, that he went straight on from
this to his great tragic period.

—William Empson
Sheffield University

Afterthought

A footnote by Professor F. T. Prince at line 1020 of *Venus
and Adonis* in his New Arden edition of *The Poems* may seem
all that is needed to destroy my position there. It is true that
T. W. Baldwin, in *On the Literary Genetics of Shakspere's
Poems and Sonnets* (pages 39–52), claims to find the sources
of such phrases in recent Latin poetry; and he may well be
right. But he seems unable to tell the difference between
making the general remark: "Without beauty, there would be

chaos," and saying: "Because this individual man is dead, all human love affairs will in future be chaotic." He offers no quotation of this second type. Nor can any be extracted from the *Four Hymns* of Spenser, mentioned by Professor F. T. Prince.

VENVS
AND ADONIS

Villa miretur vulgus: mihi flauus Apollo
Pocula Castalia plena ministret aqua.

LONDON

Imprinted by Richard Field, and are to be sold at
the signe of the white Greyhound in
Paules Church-yard.
1593.

Title page of *Venus and Adonis* (1593).

VENUS AND ADONIS

Vilia miretur vulgus: mihi flavus Apollo
Pocula Castalia plena ministret aqua.

To the Right Honorable
Henry Wriothesley
Earl of Southampton and Baron of Titchfield

Right Honorable,

I know not how I shall offend in dedicating my un-   5
polished lines to your Lordship, nor how the world will
censure me for choosing so strong a prop to support so
weak a burden; only, if your Honor seem but pleased,
I account myself highly praised, and vow to take
advantage of all idle hours, till I have honored you   10
with some graver labor. But if the first heir of my
invention prove deformed, I shall be sorry it had so
noble a godfather, and never after ear so barren a
land, for fear it yield me still so bad a harvest. I leave
it to your honorable survey, and your Honor to your   15
heart's content; which I wish may always answer your
own wish and the world's hopeful expectation.

Your Honor's in all duty,

William Shakespeare.

Vilia . . . aqua (from Ovid, *Amores*, I.xv.35–36: Let the mob admire base
things; may golden Apollo serve me full cups from the Castalian spring)
2 **Henry Wriothesley** third Earl of Southampton, 1573–1624, thought to
be Shakespeare's patron   11–12 **the first heir of my invention** my first
work brought to publication (a number of plays had already been written
and produced but were unpublished; and plays were usually considered not
worth publishing)   13 **ear** plow, till

Venus and Adonis

Even as the sun with purple-colored face
Had ta'en his last leave of the weeping morn,
Rose-cheeked Adonis hied him to the chase;
Hunting he loved, but love he laughed to scorn.
    Sick-thoughted Venus makes amain unto him,   *5*
    And like a bold-faced suitor 'gins to woo him.

"Thrice fairer than myself," thus she began,
"The field's chief flower, sweet above compare,
Stain to all nymphs, more lovely than a man,
More white and red than doves or roses are;   *10*
    Nature that made thee, with herself at strife,
    Saith that the world hath ending with thy life.

"Vouchsafe, thou wonder, to alight thy steed,
And rein his proud head to the saddlebow.
If thou wilt deign this favor, for thy meed   *15*
A thousand honey secrets shalt thou know.
    Here come and sit, where never serpent hisses,
    And being set, I'll smother thee with kisses.

"And yet not cloy thy lips with loathed satiety,
But rather famish them amid their plenty,   *20*
Making them red and pale with fresh variety:
Ten kisses short as one, one long as twenty.
    A summer's day will seem an hour but short,
    Being wasted in such time-beguiling sport."

1 **purple-colored** crimson   5 **Sick-thoughted** lovesick   5 **amain** swiftly, strongly   9 **Stain to all nymphs** i.e., by his surpassing beauty he eclipses them   15 **meed** reward   16 **honey** sweet   24 **wasted** spent

25 With this she seizeth on his sweating palm,
    The precedent of pith and livelihood,
    And trembling in her passion, calls it balm,
    Earth's sovereign salve to do a goddess good:
        Being so enraged, desire doth lend her force
30   Courageously to pluck him from his horse.

    Over one arm the lusty courser's rein,
    Under her other was the tender boy,
    Who blushed and pouted in a dull disdain,
    With leaden appetite, unapt to toy;
35   She red and hot as coals of glowing fire,
        He red for shame, but frosty in desire.

    The studded bridle on a ragged bough
    Nimbly she fastens. O, how quick is love!
    The steed is stallèd up, and even now
40 To tie the rider she begins to prove.
        Backward she pushed him, as she would be thrust,
        And governed him in strength, though not in lust.

    So soon was she along as he was down,
    Each leaning on their elbows and their hips.
45 Now doth she stroke his cheek, now doth he frown
    And 'gins to chide, but soon she stops his lips,
        And kissing speaks, with lustful language broken,
        "If thou wilt chide, thy lips shall never open."

    He burns with bashful shame; she with her tears
50 Doth quench the maiden burning of his cheeks;
    Then with her windy sighs and golden hairs
    To fan and blow them dry again she seeks.
        He saith she is immodest, blames her miss;
        What follows more, she murders with a kiss.

26 **precedent . . . livelihood** sign of strength and energy   29 **en-
raged** aroused   34 **unapt to toy** not ready for love's play
40 **prove** try   43 **along** stretched out   53 **miss** misbehavior

Even as an empty eagle, sharp by fast,   55
Tires with her beak on feathers, flesh, and bone,
Shaking her wings, devouring all in haste,
Till either gorge be stuffed or prey be gone—
    Even so she kissed his brow, his cheek, his chin,
    And where she ends she doth anew begin.   60

Forced to content, but never to obey,
Panting he lies and breatheth in her face.
She feedeth on the steam as on a prey
And calls it heavenly moisture, air of grace,
    Wishing her cheeks were gardens full of flowers,   65
    So they were dewed with such distilling showers.

Look how a bird lies tangled in a net,
So fastened in her arms Adonis lies.
Pure shame and awed resistance made him fret,
Which bred more beauty in his angry eyes: 70
    Rain added to a river that is rank
    Perforce will force it overflow the bank.

Still she entreats, and prettily entreats,
For to a pretty ear she tunes her tale.
Still is he sullen, still he low'rs and frets,   75
'Twixt crimson shame and anger ashy-pale.
    Being red, she loves him best; and being white,
    Her best is bettered with a more delight.

Look how he can, she cannot choose but love;
And by her fair immortal hand she swears   80
From his soft bosom never to remove
Till he take truce with her contending tears,
    Which long have rained, making her cheeks all wet;
    And one sweet kiss shall pay this comptless debt.

55 **sharp by fast** hungry from fasting   56 **Tires** tears   61 **content**
endure   67 **Look how** just as   69 **awed** intimidated   71 **rank**
full   74 **ear** (pun on "air")   78 **more** greater   84 **comptless**
countless

Upon this promise did he raise his chin,
Like a divedapper peering through a wave,
Who, being looked on, ducks as quickly in:
So offers he to give what she did crave,
    But when her lips were ready for his pay,
90   He winks, and turns his lips another way.

Never did passenger in summer's heat
More thirst for drink than she for this good turn.
Her help she sees, but help she cannot get;
She bathes in water, yet her fire must burn.
95   "O, pity," 'gan she cry, "flint-hearted boy!
    'Tis but a kiss I beg—why art thou coy?

"I have been wooed as I entreat thee now,
Even by the stern and direful god of war,
Whose sinewy neck in battle ne'er did bow,
100 Who conquers where he comes in every jar;
    Yet hath he been my captive and my slave,
    And begged for that which thou unasked shalt have.

"Over my altars hath he hung his lance,
His batt'red shield, his uncontrollèd crest,
105 And for my sake hath learned to sport and dance,
To toy, to wanton, dally, smile, and jest,
    Scorning his churlish drum and ensign red,
    Making my arms his field, his tent my bed.

"Thus he that overruled I overswayèd,
110 Leading him prisoner in a red-rose chain.
Strong-tempered steel his stronger strength obeyèd;
Yet was he servile to my coy disdain.
    O, be not proud, nor brag not of thy might,
    For mast'ring her that foiled the god of fight!

86 **divedapper** small waterbird   90 **winks** (1) winces (2) shuts his
eyes   91 **passenger** traveler   100 **jar** fight   104 **uncontrollèd
crest** unbowed helmet

"Touch but my lips with those fair lips of thine— 115
Though mine be not so fair, yet are they red—
The kiss shall be thine own as well as mine.
What seest thou in the ground? Hold up thy head,
　　Look in mine eyeballs, there thy beauty lies,
　　Then why not lips on lips, since eyes in eyes? 120

"Art thou ashamed to kiss? Then wink again,
And I will wink; so shall the day seem night.
Love keeps his revels where there are but twain.
Be bold to play; our sport is not in sight.
　　These blue-veined violets whereon we lean 125
　　Never can blab, nor know not what we mean.

"The tender spring upon thy tempting lip
Shows thee unripe; yet mayst thou well be tasted.
Make use of time, let not advantage slip;
Beauty within itself should not be wasted. 130
　　Fair flowers that are not gath'red in their prime
　　Rot and consume themselves in little time.

"Were I hard-favored, foul, or wrinkled old,
Ill-nurtured, crooked, churlish, harsh in voice,
O'erworn, despisèd, rheumatic, and cold, 135
Thick-sighted, barren, lean, and lacking juice,
　　Then mightst thou pause, for then I were not for
　　　　thee;
　　But having no defects, why dost abhor me?

"Thou canst not see one wrinkle in my brow;
Mine eyes are gray and bright and quick in turning. 140
My beauty as the spring doth yearly grow,
My flesh is soft and plump, my marrow burning;
　　My smooth moist hand, were it with thy hand felt,
　　Would in thy palm dissolve, or seem to melt.

121 **wink** close your eyes　127 **tender spring** young growth (that
will become a beard)　136 **Thick-sighted** with poor eyesight

145 "Bid me discourse, I will enchant thine ear,
      Or like a fairy trip upon the green,
      Or like a nymph with long dishevelled hair,
      Dance on the sands, and yet no footing seen.
          Love is a spirit all compact of fire,
150   Not gross to sink, but light, and will aspire.

"Witness this primrose bank whereon I lie;
These forceless flowers like sturdy trees support me.
Two strengthless doves will draw me through the sky
From morn till night, even where I list to sport me.
155   Is love so light, sweet boy, and may it be
        That thou should think it heavy unto thee?

"Is thine own heart to thine own face affected?
Can thy right hand seize love upon thy left?
Then woo thyself, be of thyself rejected;
160 Steal thine own freedom, and complain on theft.
        Narcissus so himself himself forsook,
        And died to kiss his shadow in the brook.

"Torches are made to light, jewels to wear,
Dainties to taste, fresh beauty for the use,
165 Herbs for their smell, and sappy plants to bear.
Things growing to themselves are growth's abuse.
        Seeds spring from seeds, and beauty breedeth
            beauty.
        Thou wast begot; to get it is thy duty.

"Upon the earth's increase why shouldst thou feed
170 Unless the earth with thy increase be fed?
By law of nature thou art bound to breed,
That thine may live when thou thyself art dead;
        And so in spite of death thou dost survive,
        In that thy likeness still is left alive."

---

149 **compact** composed   150 **aspire** rise up, float   151 **Witness . . .
lie** let this bank whereon I lie bear witness   152 **forceless** frail, with-
out strength   157 **to . . . affected** in love with thine own face
161 **Narcissus** a beautiful youth who fell in love with his own reflec-
tion   169 **increase** produce

By this the lovesick queen began to sweat,   175
For where they lay the shadow had forsook them,
And Titan, tirèd in the midday heat,
With burning eye did hotly overlook them,
    Wishing Adonis had his team to guide,
    So he were like him, and by Venus' side.   180

And now Adonis, with a lazy sprite,
And with a heavy, dark, disliking eye,
His low'ring brows o'erwhelming his fair sight,
Like misty vapors when they blot the sky,
    Souring his cheeks, cries, "Fie, no more of love!   185
    The sun doth burn my face—I must remove."

"Ay me," quoth Venus, "young, and so unkind?
What bare excuses mak'st thou to be gone!
I'll sigh celestial breath, whose gentle wind
Shall cool the heat of this descending sun.   190
    I'll make a shadow for thee of my hairs;
    If they burn too, I'll quench them with my tears.

"The sun that shines from heaven shines but warm,
And, lo, I lie between that sun and thee:
The heat I have from thence doth little harm,   195
Thine eye darts forth the fire that burneth me;
    And were I not immortal, life were done
    Between this heavenly and earthly sun.

"Art thou obdurate, flinty, hard as steel?
Nay, more than flint, for stone at rain relenteth.   200
Art thou a woman's son, and canst not feel
What 'tis to love? how want of love tormenteth?
    O, had thy mother borne so hard a mind,
    She had not brought forth thee, but died unkind.

175 **By this** by this time, now   177 **Titan** the sun-god   181 **lazy
sprite** dull spirit   188 **bare** inadequate   200 **relenteth** i.e., is worn
away

205 "What am I that thou shouldst contemn me this?
Or what great danger dwells upon my suit?
What were thy lips the worse for one poor kiss?
Speak, fair, but speak fair words or else be mute.
    Give me one kiss, I'll give it thee again,
210   And one for int'rest, if thou wilt have twain.

"Fie, lifeless picture, cold and senseless stone,
Well-painted idol, image dull and dead,
Statue contenting but the eye alone,
Thing like a man, but of no woman bred!
215   Thou art no man, though of a man's complexion,
    For men will kiss even by their own direction."

This said, impatience chokes her pleading tongue,
And swelling passion doth provoke a pause.
Red cheeks and fiery eyes blaze forth her wrong;
220 Being judge in love, she cannot right her cause.
    And now she weeps, and now she fain would speak,
    And now her sobs do her intendments break.

Sometime she shakes her head, and then his hand,
Now gazeth she on him, now on the ground.
225 Sometime her arms infold him like a band:
She would, he will not in her arms be bound.
    And when from thence he struggles to be gone,
    She locks her lily fingers one in one.

"Fondling," she saith, "since I have hemmed thee here
230 Within the circuit of this ivory pale,
I'll be a park, and thou shalt be my deer:
Feed where thou wilt, on mountain or in dale;
    Graze on my lips; and if those hills be dry,
    Stray lower, where the pleasant fountains lie.

205 **this** thus   208 **fair** fair one   215 **complexion** external appearance   216 **direction** volition   220 **Being judge … cause** i.e., though Venus is the judge in all disputes of love, she cannot obtain justice for herself   221 **fain** gladly   222 **intendments break** intentions (i.e., what she was going to say) interrupt   229 **Fondling** little fool (affectionate)   230 **pale** fence (here, her arms)

"Within this limit is relief enough,   235
Sweet bottom-grass, and high delightful plain,
Round rising hillocks, brakes obscure and rough,
To shelter thee from tempest and from rain.
    Then be my deer since I am such a park;
    No dog shall rouse thee though a thousand bark."   240

At this Adonis smiles as in disdain,
That in each cheek appears a pretty dimple;
Love made those hollows, if himself were slain,
He might be buried in a tomb so simple,
    Foreknowing well, if there he came to lie,   245
    Why, there Love lived, and there he could not die.

These lovely caves, these round enchanting pits,
Opened their mouths to swallow Venus' liking.
Being mad before, how doth she now for wits?
Struck dead at first, what needs a second striking?   250
    Poor queen of love, in thine own law forlorn,
    To love a cheek that smiles at thee in scorn!

Now which way shall she turn? What shall she say?
Her words are done, her woes the more increasing;
The time is spent, her object will away,   255
And from her twining arms doth urge releasing.
    "Pity!" she cries, "some favor, some remorse!"
    Away he springs and hasteth to his horse.

But, lo, from forth a copse that neighbors by
A breeding jennet, lusty, young, and proud,   260
Adonis' trampling courser doth espy,
And forth she rushes, snorts, and neighs aloud.
    The strong-necked steed, being tied unto a tree,
    Breaketh his rein, and to her straight goes he.

235 **relief** (1) topography, as on a relief-map (2) (sexual) satisfaction
236 **bottom-grass** valley-grass   237 **brakes** thickets   240 **rouse**
drive from cover   242 **That** so that   243 **if** so that if he   248 **lik-
ing** desire   257 **remorse** mercy   260 **jennet** small Spanish horse

265 Imperiously he leaps, he neighs, he bounds,
   And now his woven girths he breaks asunder;
   The bearing earth with his hard hoof he wounds,
   Whose hollow womb resounds like heaven's thunder;
     The iron bit he crusheth 'tween his teeth,
270   Controlling what he was controllèd with.

His ears up-pricked, his braided hanging mane
   Upon his compassed crest now stand on end;
   His nostrils drink the air, and forth again,
   As from a furnace, vapors doth he send;
275   His eye, which scornfully glisters like fire,
     Shows his hot courage and his high desire.

Sometime he trots, as if he told the steps,
   With gentle majesty and modest pride;
   Anon he rears upright, curvets, and leaps,
280 As who should say, "Lo, thus my strength is tried,
    And this I do to captivate the eye
    Of the fair breeder that is standing by."

What recketh he his rider's angry stir,
   His flattering "Holla" or his "Stand, I say"?
285 What cares he now for curb or pricking spur,
   For rich caparisons or trappings gay?
    He sees his love, and nothing else he sees,
    For nothing else with his proud sight agrees.

Look when a painter would surpass the life
290 In limning out a well-proportioned steed,
   His art with nature's workmanship at strife,
   As if the dead the living should exceed—
    So did this horse excel a common one
    In shape, in courage, color, pace, and bone.

267 **bearing** receiving   272 **compassed** arched   276 **courage** lust   277 **told** counted   279 **curvets** hops   283 **stir** excitement   284 **flattering** calming   289 **Look when** just as   290 **limning out** drawing   294 **bone** frame

Round-hoofed, short-jointed, fetlocks shag and long,   295
Broad breast, full eye, small head, and nostril wide,
High crest, short ears, straight legs and passing strong,
Thin mane, thick tail, broad buttock, tender hide:
    Look what a horse should have he did not lack,
    Save a proud rider on so proud a back.   300

Sometime he scuds far off, and there he stares;
Anon he starts at stirring of a feather.
To bid the wind a base he now prepares,
And whe'r he run or fly they know not whether,
    For through his mane and tail the high wind sings,   305
    Fanning the hairs, who wave like feath'red wings.

He looks upon his love and neighs unto her;
She answers him, as if she knew his mind.
Being proud, as females are, to see him woo her,
She puts on outward strangeness, seems unkind,   310
    Spurns at his love and scorns the heat he feels,
    Beating his kind embracements with her heels.

Then, like a melancholy malcontent,
He vails his tail, that, like a falling plume,
Cool shadow to his melting buttock lent;   315
He stamps, and bites the poor flies in his fume.
    His love, perceiving how he was enraged,
    Grew kinder, and his fury was assuaged.

His testy master goeth about to take him,
When, lo, the unbacked breeder, full of fear,   320
Jealous of catching, swiftly doth forsake him,
With her the horse, and left Adonis there.
    As they were mad unto the wood they hie them,
    Outstripping crows that strive to overfly them.

297 **crest** ridge of the neck   299 **Look what** whatever   303 **bid
the wind a base** challenge the wind to a chase   304 **whe'r** whether
310 **outward strangeness** show of indifference   314 **vails** lowers
316 **fume** rage   320 **unbacked** unbroken   321 **Jealous of catch-
ing** afraid of being caught   322 **horse** i.e., stallion

325 All swol'n with chafing, down Adonis sits,
    Banning his boist'rous and unruly beast;
    And now the happy season once more fits
    That lovesick Love by pleading may be blest;
        For lovers say the heart hath treble wrong
330   When it is barred the aidance of the tongue.

    An oven that is stopped, or river stayed,
    Burneth more hotly, swelleth with more rage;
    So of concealèd sorrow may be said
    Free vent of words love's fire doth assuage;
335   But when the heart's attorney once is mute,
        The client breaks, as desperate in his suit.

    He sees her coming and begins to glow,
    Even as a dying coal revives with wind,
    And with his bonnet hides his angry brow,
340 Looks on the dull earth with disturbèd mind,
        Taking no notice that she is so nigh,
        For all askance he holds her in his eye.

    O, what a sight it was, wistly to view
    How she came stealing to the wayward boy!
345 To note the fighting conflict of her hue,
    How white and red each other did destroy!
        But now her cheek was pale, and by and by
        It flashed forth fire, as lightning from the sky.

    Now was she just before him as he sat,
350 And like a lowly lover down she kneels;
    With one fair hand she heaveth up his hat,
    Her other tender hand his fair cheek feels.
        His tend'rer cheek receives her soft hand's print
        As apt as new-fall'n snow takes any dint.

326 **Banning** cursing   328 **Love** i.e., Venus   335 **the heart's at-
torney** i.e., the tongue   336 **breaks** goes bankrupt   343 **wistly** at-
tentively   344 **wayward** willful   347 **by and by** quickly   354
dint impression

O, what a war of looks was then between them,   355
Her eyes petitioners to his eyes suing!
His eyes saw her eyes as they had not seen them;
Her eyes wooed still, his eyes disdained the wooing;
    And all this dumb play had his acts made plain
    With tears which choruslike her eyes did rain.   360

Full gently now she takes him by the hand,
A lily prisoned in a jail of snow,
Or ivory in an alabaster band:
So white a friend engirts so white a foe.
    This beauteous combat, willful and unwilling,   365
    Showed like two silver doves that sit a-billing.

Once more the engine of her thoughts began:
"O fairest mover on this mortal round,
Would thou wert as I am, and I a man,
My heart all whole as thine, thy heart my wound!   370
    For one sweet look thy help I would assure thee,
    Though nothing but my body's bane would cure
      thee."

"Give me my hand," saith he. "Why dost thou feel it?"
"Give me my heart," saith she, "and thou shalt have it.
O, give it me lest thy hard heart do steel it,   375
And being steeled, soft sighs can never grave it.
    Then love's deep groans I never shall regard,
    Because Adonis' heart hath made mine hard."

"For shame!" he cries. "Let go, and let me go:
My day's delight is past, my horse is gone,   380
And 'tis your fault I am bereft him so.
I pray you hence, and leave me here alone;
    For all my mind, my thought, my busy care
    Is how to get my palfrey from the mare."

357 **as** as if   359 **dumb play** dumb show, pantomime   359 **his** its
360 **choruslike** i.e., served as a commentator   367 **engine of her
thoughts** i.e., her tongue   368 **mover . . . mortal round** living crea-
ture on earth   370 **my wound** i.e., wounded like mine   372 **bane**
ruin   375 **steel** turn to steel   376 **grave** engrave

385 Thus she replies: "Thy palfrey, as he should,
Welcomes the warm approach of sweet desire.
Affection is a coal that must be cooled;
Else, suffered, it will set the heart on fire.
    The sea hath bounds, but deep desire hath none;
390   Therefore no marvel though thy horse be gone.

"How like a jade he stood, tied to the tree,
Servilely mastered with a leathern rein;
But when he saw his love, his youth's fair fee,
He held such petty bondage in disdain,
395   Throwing the base thong from his bending crest,
    Enfranchising his mouth, his back, his breast.

"Who sees his true-love in her naked bed,
Teaching the sheets a whiter hue than white,
But, when his glutton eye so full hath fed,
400 His other agents aim at like delight?
    Who is so faint that dares not be so bold
    To touch the fire, the weather being cold?

"Let me excuse thy courser, gentle boy;
And learn of him, I heartily beseech thee,
405 To take advantage on presented joy.
Though I were dumb, yet his proceedings teach thee.
    O, learn to love! The lesson is but plain,
    And once made perfect, never lost again."

"I know not love," quoth he, "nor will not know it,
410 Unless it be a boar, and then I chase it.
'Tis much to borrow, and I will not owe it:
My love to love is love but to disgrace it;
    For I have heard it is a life in death,
    That laughs and weeps, and all but with a breath.

---

387 **Affection** passion 388 **suffered** tolerated 391 **jade** con-
temptuous term for horse 393 **fair fee** due reward 396 **Enfran-
chising** setting free 397 **naked** (modifies "true-love," not "bed")
400 **agents** organs 405 **on** of 411 **owe** own 412 **My love . . .
disgrace it** my only attitude toward love is a desire to discredit it
414 **but with a** in the same

"Who wears a garment shapeless and unfinished? 415
Who plucks the bud before one leaf put forth?
If springing things be any jot diminished,
They wither in their prime, prove nothing worth.
　　The colt that's backed and burdened being young
　　Loseth his pride, and never waxeth strong. 420

"You hurt my hand with wringing; let us part,
And leave this idle theme, this bootless chat;
Remove your siege from my unyielding heart;
To love's alarms it will not ope the gate.
　　Dismiss your vows, your feignèd tears, your flatt'ry; 425
　　For where a heart is hard they make no batt'ry."

"What! canst thou talk?" quoth she. "Hast thou a
　　　　tongue?
O, would thou hadst not, or I had no hearing!
Thy mermaid's voice hath done me double wrong;
I had my load before, now pressed with bearing: 430
　　Melodious discord, heavenly tune harsh sounding,
　　Ear's deep-sweet music, and heart's deep-sore
　　　　wounding.

"Had I no eyes but ears, my ears would love
That inward beauty and invisible;
Or were I deaf, thy outward parts would move 435
Each part in me that were but sensible.
　　Though neither eyes nor ears, to hear nor see,
　　Yet should I be in love by touching thee.

"Say that the sense of feeling were bereft me,
And that I could not see, nor hear, nor touch, 440
And nothing but the very smell were left me,
Yet would my love to thee be still as much;
　　For from the stillitory of thy face excelling
　　Comes breath perfumed that breedeth love by
　　　　smelling.

419 **backed** broken in　422 **bootless** useless　424 **alarms** attacks
426 **batt'ry** successful entry　429 **mermaid's** siren's　430 **pressed**
oppressed　436 **sensible** able to receive any other sensations
443 **stillitory** distilling plant

445　"But, O, what banquet wert thou to the taste,
　　　Being nurse and feeder of the other four!
　　　Would they not wish the feast might ever last
　　　And bid Suspicion double-lock the door,
　　　　　Lest Jealousy, that sour unwelcome guest,
450　　　Should by his stealing in disturb the feast?"

　　　Once more the ruby-colored portal opened
　　　Which to his speech did honey passage yield;
　　　Like a red morn that ever yet betokened
　　　Wrack to the seaman, tempest to the field,
455　　　Sorrow to shepherds, woe unto the birds,
　　　　　Gusts and foul flaws to herdmen and to herds.

　　　This ill presage advisedly she marketh.
　　　Even as the wind is hushed before it raineth,
　　　Or as the wolf doth grin before he barketh,
460　Or as the berry breaks before it staineth,
　　　　　Or like the deadly bullet of a gun,
　　　　　His meaning struck her ere his words begun.

　　　And at his look she flatly falleth down,
　　　For looks kill love, and love by looks reviveth;
465　A smile recures the wounding of a frown.
　　　But blessèd bankrout that by love so thriveth!
　　　　　The silly boy, believing she is dead,
　　　　　Claps her pale cheek, till clapping makes it red,

　　　And all amazed brake off his late intent,
470　For sharply he did think to reprehend her,
　　　Which cunning love did wittily prevent.
　　　Fair fall the wit that can so well defend her!
　　　　　For on the grass she lies as she were slain
　　　　　Till his breath breatheth life in her again.

454 **Wrack** wreck　456 **flaws** blasts of wind　459 **grin** bare its
fangs　465 **recures** heals　466 **bankrout** bankrupt　467 **silly** in-
nocent　471 **wittily** cleverly　472 **Fair fall** prosperity befall

He wrings her nose, he strikes her on the cheeks, 475
He bends her fingers, holds her pulses hard,
He chafes her lips; a thousand ways he seeks
To mend the hurt that his unkindness marred.
   He kisses her; and she, by her good will,
   Will never rise, so he will kiss her still. 480

The night of sorrow now is turned to day:
Her two blue windows faintly she upheaveth,
Like the fair sun when in his fresh array
He cheers the morn and all the earth relieveth;
   And as the bright sun glorifies the sky, 485
   So is her face illumined with her eye;

Whose beams upon his hairless face are fixed,
As if from thence they borrowed all their shine.
Were never four such lamps together mixed,
Had not his clouded with his brow's repine; 490
   But hers, which through the crystal tears gave light,
   Shone like the moon in water seen by night.

"O, where am I?" quoth she, "in earth or heaven,
Or in the ocean drenched, or in the fire?
What hour is this? or morn or weary even? 495
Do I delight to die, or life desire?
   But now I lived, and life was death's annoy;
   But now I died, and death was lively joy.

"O, thou didst kill me, kill me once again!
Thy eyes' shrewd tutor, that hard heart of thine, 500
Hath taught them scornful tricks, and such disdain
That they have murd'red this poor heart of mine;
   And these mine eyes, true leaders to their queen,
   But for thy piteous lips no more had seen.

478 **marred** inflicted 479 **by her good will** willingly 482 **blue windows** i.e., her eyelids 490 **repine** vexation 495 **or . . . or** either . . . or 497 **annoy** torment 500 **shrewd** harsh 503 **their queen** i.e., the heart

505 "Long may they kiss each other, for this cure!
     O, never let their crimson liveries wear;
     And as they last, their verdure still endure,
     To drive infection from the dangerous year;
         That the stargazers, having writ on death,
510   May say the plague is banished by thy breath.

     "Pure lips, sweet seals in my soft lips imprinted,
     What bargains may I make, still to be sealing?
     To sell myself I can be well contented,
     So thou wilt buy, and pay, and use good dealing;
515   Which purchase if thou make, for fear of slips
         Set thy seal manual on my wax-red lips.

     "A thousand kisses buys my heart from me;
     And pay them at thy leisure, one by one.
     What is ten hundred touches unto thee?
520 Are they not quickly told and quickly gone?
         Say for nonpayment that the debt should double,
         Is twenty hundred kisses such a trouble?"

     "Fair queen," quoth he, "if any love you owe me,
     Measure my strangeness with my unripe years.
525 Before I know myself, seek not to know me:
     No fisher but the ungrown fry forbears;
         The mellow plum doth fall, the green sticks fast,
         Or being early plucked is sour to taste.

     "Look, the world's comforter, with weary gait,
530 His day's hot task hath ended in the west;
     The owl, night's herald, shrieks; 'tis very late;
     The sheep are gone to fold, birds to their nest,
         And coal-black clouds that shadow heaven's light
         Do summon us to part, and bid good night.

506 **crimson liveries wear** red colors wear out   507 **verdure**
freshness   509 **stargazers . . . death** astrologers, who have pre-
dicted an epidemic   512 **still** always   512 **sealing** i.e., kissing
515 **slips** errors   516 **seal manual** signet ring (i.e., lips)   519
touches i.e., kisses   520 **told** counted   523 **owe** bear   524 **Mea-
sure . . . unripe years** account for my shyness by my youth   526 **fry**
young fish

"Now let me say good night, and so say you.   535
If you will say so, you shall have a kiss."
"Good night," quoth she; and, ere he says "Adieu,"
The honey fee of parting tend'red is:
    Her arms do lend his neck a sweet embrace;
    Incorporate then they seem; face grows to face;   540

Till breathless he disjoined, and backward drew
The heavenly moisture, that sweet coral mouth,
Whose precious taste her thirsty lips well knew,
Whereon they surfeit, yet complain on drouth.
    He with her plenty pressed, she faint with dearth,   545
    Their lips together glued, fall to the earth.

Now quick desire hath caught the yielding prey,
And gluttonlike she feeds, yet never filleth.
Her lips are conquerors, his lips obey,
Paying what ransom the insulter willeth;   550
    Whose vulture thought doth pitch the price so high
    That she will draw his lips' rich treasure dry.

And having felt the sweetness of the spoil,
With blindfold fury she begins to forage;
Her face doth reek and smoke, her blood doth boil,   555
And careless lust stirs up a desperate courage,
    Planting oblivion, beating reason back,
    Forgetting shame's pure blush and honor's wrack.

Hot, faint, and weary with her hard embracing,
Like a wild bird being tamed with too much handling,   560
Or as the fleet-foot roe that's tired with chasing,
Or like the froward infant stilled with dandling,
    He now obeys and now no more resisteth,
    While she takes all she can, not all she listeth.

540 **Incorporate** joined into one body   545 **pressed** oppressed
550 **insulter** exultant winner   555 **reek** i.e., steam   562 **froward**
fretful   564 **listeth** wants

565 What wax so frozen but dissolves with temp'ring
And yields at last to every light impression?
Things out of hope are compassed oft with vent'ring,
Chiefly in love, whose leave exceeds commission.
    Affection faints not like a pale-faced coward,
570   But then woos best when most his choice is froward.

When he did frown, O, had she then gave over,
Such nectar from his lips she had not sucked.
Foul words and frowns must not repel a lover.
What though the rose have prickles, yet 'tis plucked.
575   Were beauty under twenty locks kept fast,
    Yet love breaks through and picks them all at last.

For pity now she can no more detain him;
The poor fool prays her that he may depart.
She is resolved no longer to restrain him;
580 Bids him farewell, and look well to her heart,
    The which, by Cupid's bow she doth protest,
    He carries thence incagèd in his breast.

"Sweet boy," she says, "this night I'll waste in sorrow,
For my sick heart commands mine eyes to watch.
585 Tell me, love's master, shall we meet tomorrow?
Say, shall we? shall we? wilt thou make the match?"
    He tells her no; tomorrow he intends
    To hunt the boar with certain of his friends.

"The boar!" quoth she; whereat a sudden pale,
590 Like lawn being spread upon the blushing rose,
Usurps her cheek; she trembles at his tale,
And on his neck her yoking arms she throws.
    She sinketh down, still hanging by his neck,
    He on her belly falls, she on her back.

---

567 **out of** beyond 567 **compassed . . . vent'ring** achieved often
by venturing 568 **leave exceeds commission** liberty goes beyond
what was permitted 569 **Affection** passion, desire 570 **when
most his choice is froward** when the object of his passion is most ob-
stinate 573 **Foul** unpleasant 578 **poor fool** (expression of ten-
derness) 583 **waste** spend 584 **watch** stay open 589 **pale**
pallor 590 **lawn** a fine linen

Now is she in the very lists of love, 595
Her champion mounted for the hot encounter.
All is imaginary she doth prove,
He will not manage her, although he mount her;
    That worse than Tantalus' is her annoy,
    To clip Elysium and to lack her joy. 600

Even so poor birds, deceived with painted grapes,
Do surfeit by the eye and pine the maw;
Even so she languisheth in her mishaps
As those poor birds that helpless berries saw.
    The warm effects which she in him finds missing 605
    She seeks to kindle with continual kissing.

But all in vain; good queen, it will not be!
She hath assayed as much as may be proved:
Her pleading hath deserved a greater fee;
She's Love, she loves, and yet she is not loved. 610
    "Fie, fie!" he says. "You crush me; let me go!
    You have no reason to withhold me so."

"Thou hadst been gone," quoth she, "sweet boy, ere
        this,
But that thou told'st me thou wouldst hunt the boar.
O, be advised, thou know'st not what it is 615
With javelin's point a churlish swine to gore,
    Whose tushes never sheathed he whetteth still,
    Like to a mortal butcher bent to kill.

"On his bow-back he hath a battle set
Of bristly pikes that ever threat his foes; 620
His eyes like glowworms shine when he doth fret;
His snout digs sepulchers where'er he goes;
    Being moved, he strikes whate'er is in his way,
    And whom he strikes his crooked tushes slay.

595 **lists** field of combat   597 **prove** experience (i.e., all that she
experiences is in her imagination)   598 **manage** ride   599 **That
worse ... annoy** so that her torment is worse than that of Tantalus (in
Hades, Tantalus was surrounded by food and drink that he could never
touch)   600 **clip** embrace   602 **pine the maw** starve the stomach
605 **effects** consequences   608 **assayed** tried   608 **proved** tried
617 **tushes** tusks   618 **mortal** deadly   621 **fret** rage   623 **moved**
angered

625 "His brawny sides, with hairy bristles armèd,
Are better proof than thy spear's point can enter;
His short thick neck cannot be easily harmèd;
Being ireful, on the lion he will venter.
    The thorny brambles and embracing bushes,
630   As fearful of him, part; through whom he rushes.

"Alas, he naught esteems that face of thine,
To which Love's eyes pay tributary gazes;
Nor thy soft hands, sweet lips, and crystal eyne,
Whose full perfection all the world amazes;
635   But having thee at vantage (wondrous dread!)
    Would root these beauties as he roots the mead.

"O, let him keep his loathsome cabin still:
Beauty hath naught to do with such foul fiends.
Come not within his danger by thy will.
640 They that thrive well take counsel of their friends.
    When thou didst name the boar, not to dissemble,
    I feared thy fortune, and my joints did tremble.

"Didst thou not mark my face? Was it not white?
Saw'st thou not signs of fear lurk in mine eye?
645 Grew I not faint? and fell I not downright?
Within my bosom, whereon thou dost lie,
    My boding heart pants, beats, and takes no rest,
    But, like an earthquake, shakes thee on my breast.

"For where Love reigns, disturbing Jealousy
650 Doth call himself Affection's sentinel,
Gives false alarms, suggesteth mutiny,
And in a peaceful hour doth cry 'Kill, kill!'
    Distemp'ring gentle Love in his desire,
    As air and water do abate the fire.

626 **better proof** stronger armor   628 **venter** venture   633 **eyne**
eyes   636 **root** uproot   637 **cabin** i.e., sty   639 **within his dan-**
ger within distance of his power to harm   641 **not to dissemble** to
tell the truth   645 **downright** directly   649 **Jealousy** anxiety
651 **suggesteth** incites   653 **Distemp'ring** decreasing

"This sour informer, this bate-breeding spy,   655
This canker that eats up Love's tender spring,
This carry-tale, dissentious Jealousy,
That sometime true news, sometime false doth bring,
    Knocks at my heart, and whispers in mine ear
    That if I love thee, I thy death should fear.   660

"And more than so, presenteth to mine eye
The picture of an angry-chafing boar,
Under whose sharp fangs on his back doth lie
An image like thyself, all stained with gore;
    Whose blood upon the fresh flowers being shed   665
    Doth make them droop with grief and hang the
      head.

"What should I do, seeing thee so indeed,
That tremble at th' imagination?
The thought of it doth make my faint heart bleed,
And fear doth teach it divination.   670
    I prophesy thy death, my living sorrow,
    If thou encounter with the boar tomorrow.

"But if thou needs wilt hunt, be ruled by me:
Uncouple at the timorous flying hare,
Or at the fox which lives by subtlety,   675
Or at the roe which no encounter dare.
    Pursue these fearful creatures o'er the downs,
    And on thy well-breathed horse keep with thy
      hounds.

"And when thou hast on foot the purblind hare,
Mark the poor wretch, to overshoot his troubles,   680
How he outruns the wind, and with what care
He cranks and crosses with a thousand doubles.
    The many musits through the which he goes
    Are like a labyrinth to amaze his foes.

655 **bate-breeding** strife-creating   656 **canker** worm (that preys on
blossoms)   656 **spring** bud   674 **Uncouple at** loose your hounds
upon   677 **fearful** timid   678 **well-breathed** well-conditioned
679 **on foot** in chase   679 **purblind** weak-sighted   680 **over-
shoot** run beyond   682 **cranks** turns   683 **musits** gaps in a hedge
or fence   684 **amaze** confuse

685 "Sometime he runs among a flock of sheep,
     To make the cunning hounds mistake their smell,
     And sometime where earth-delving conies keep,
     To stop the loud pursuers in their yell;
         And sometime sorteth with a herd of deer.
690   Danger deviseth shifts, wit waits on fear;

     "For there his smell with others being mingled,
     The hot scent-snuffing hounds are driven to doubt,
     Ceasing their clamorous cry, till they have singled
     With much ado the cold fault cleanly out.
695   Then do they spend their mouths; echo replies,
         As if another chase were in the skies.

     "By this, poor Wat, far off upon a hill,
     Stands on his hinder legs with list'ning ear,
     To hearken if his foes pursue him still.
700 Anon their loud alarums he doth hear,
         And now his grief may be comparèd well
         To one sore sick that hears the passing bell.

     "Then shalt thou see the dew-bedabbled wretch
     Turn, and return, indenting with the way.
705 Each envious brier his weary legs do scratch;
     Each shadow makes him stop, each murmur stay;
         For misery is trodden on by many
         And, being low, never relieved by any.

     "Lie quietly and hear a little more.
710 Nay, do not struggle, for thou shalt not rise.
     To make thee hate the hunting of the boar,
     Unlike myself thou hear'st me moralize,
         Applying this to that, and so to so,
         For love can comment upon every woe.

687 **earth-delving conies keep** rabbits that dig burrows dwell   688
in their yell i.e., in full cry   689 **sorteth** mingles   690 **shifts** tricks
690 **waits on** goes with   694 **cold fault** lost scent   695 **spend
their mouths** yelp   697 **Wat** (traditional name for a hare)   702
passing funeral   704 **indenting** zigzagging   705 **envious** mali-
cious

"Where did I leave?" "No matter where," quoth he;   *715*
"Leave me, and then the story aptly ends.
The night is spent." "Why, what of that?" quoth she.
"I am," quoth he, "expected of my friends;
    And now 'tis dark, and going I shall fall."
    "In night," quoth she, "desire sees best of all.   *720*

"But if thou fall, O, then imagine this:
The earth, in love with thee, thy footing trips,
And all is but to rob thee of a kiss.
Rich preys make true men thieves. So do thy lips
    Make modest Dian cloudy and forlorn,   *725*
    Lest she should steal a kiss and die forsworn.

"Now of this dark night I perceive the reason:
Cynthia for shame obscures her silver shine,
Till forging Nature be condemned of treason
For stealing molds from heaven that were divine;   *730*
    Wherein she framed thee, in high heaven's despite,
    To shame the sun by day, and her by night.

"And therefore hath she bribed the Destinies
To cross the curious workmanship of Nature,
To mingle beauty with infirmities   *735*
And pure perfection with impure defeature,
    Making it subject to the tyranny
    Of mad mischances and much misery;

"As burning fevers, agues pale and faint,
Life-poisoning pestilence, and frenzies wood,   *740*
The marrow-eating sickness whose attaint
Disorder breeds by heating of the blood,
    Surfeits, imposthumes, grief, and damned despair
    Swear Nature's death for framing thee so fair.

---

724 **preys** booty   724 **true** honest   725 **Dian** Diana (goddess of
chastity and of the hunt)   725 **cloudy** gloomy   726 **forsworn** i.e.,
having broken her vow of chastity   728 **Cynthia** the moon, i.e., Di-
ana   729 **forging** counterfeiting   732 **her** i.e., the moon   734
cross thwart   734 **curious** elaborate   736 **defeature** disfigure-
ment   740 **wood** mad   741 **marrow-eating sickness** syphilis (?)
741 **attaint** infection   743 **imposthumes** abscesses

745 "And not the least of all these maladies
      But in one minute's fight brings beauty under;
      Both favor, savor, hue, and qualities,
      Whereat th' impartial gazer late did wonder,
        Are on the sudden wasted, thawed, and done,
750   As mountain snow melts with the midday sun.

      "Therefore, despite of fruitless chastity,
      Love-lacking vestals, and self-loving nuns,
      That on the earth would breed a scarcity
      And barren dearth of daughters and of sons,
755   Be prodigal; the lamp that burns by night
        Dries up his oil to lend the world his light.

      "What is thy body but a swallowing grave,
      Seeming to bury that posterity
      Which by the rights of time thou needs must have
760   If thou destroy them not in dark obscurity?
        If so, the world will hold thee in disdain,
        Sith in thy pride so fair a hope is slain.

      "So in thyself thyself art made away,
      A mischief worse than civil home-bred strife,
765   Or theirs whose desperate hands themselves do slay,
      Or butcher sire that reaves his son of life.
        Foul cank'ring rust the hidden treasure frets,
        But gold that's put to use more gold begets."

      "Nay, then," quoth Adon, "you will fall again
770   Into your idle overhandled theme.
      The kiss I gave you is bestowed in vain,
      And all in vain you strive against the stream;
        For by this black-faced night, desire's foul nurse,
        Your treatise makes me like you worse and worse.

745–46 **And . . . under** i.e., even the least of these maladies in one
minute can destroy beauty   747 **favor** features   747 **hue** com-
plexion   762 **Sith** since   766 **reaves** deprives   767 **frets** erodes
774 **treatise** discourse

"If love have lent you twenty thousand tongues,   775
And every tongue more moving than your own,
Bewitching like the wanton mermaid's songs,
Yet from mine ear the tempting tune is blown;
    For know, my heart stands armèd in mine ear
    And will not let a false sound enter there,   780

"Lest the deceiving harmony should run
Into the quiet closure of my breast;
And then my little heart were quite undone,
In his bedchamber to be barred of rest.
    No, lady, no; my heart longs not to groan,   785
    But soundly sleeps while now it sleeps alone.

"What have you urged that I cannot reprove?
The path is smooth that leadeth on to danger.
I hate not love, but your device in love,
That lends embracements unto every stranger.   790
    You do it for increase. O strange excuse,
    When reason is the bawd to lust's abuse!

"Call it not love, for Love to heaven is fled
Since sweating Lust on earth usurped his name;
Under whose simple semblance he hath fed   795
Upon fresh beauty, blotting it with blame;
    Which the hot tyrant stains and soon bereaves,
    As caterpillars do the tender leaves.

"Love comforteth like sunshine after rain,
But Lust's effect is tempest after sun.   800
Love's gentle spring doth always fresh remain;
Lust's winter comes ere summer half be done.
    Love surfeits not, Lust like a glutton dies;
    Love is all truth, Lust full of forgèd lies.

782 **closure** enclosure   787 **reprove** refute   789 **device** cunning
797 **hot tyrant** i.e., lust   797 **bereaves** spoils

805 "More I could tell, but more I dare not say:
The text is old, the orator too green.
Therefore in sadness now I will away.
My face is full of shame, my heart of teen;
    Mine ears, that to your wanton talk attended,
810   Do burn themselves for having so offended."

With this he breaketh from the sweet embrace
Of those fair arms which bound him to her breast
And homeward through the dark laund runs apace;
Leaves Love upon her back, deeply distressed.
815   Look how a bright star shooteth from the sky,
    So glides he in the night from Venus' eye;

Which after him she darts, as one on shore
Gazing upon a late-embarkèd friend
Till the wild waves will have him seen no more,
820 Whose ridges with the meeting clouds contend.
    So did the merciless and pitchy night
    Fold in the object that did feed her sight.

Whereat amazed, as one that unaware
Hath dropped a precious jewel in the flood,
825 Or 'stonished as night-wand'rers often are,
Their light blown out in some mistrustful wood,
    Even so confounded in the dark she lay,
    Having lost the fair discovery of her way.

And now she beats her heart, whereat it groans,
830 That all the neighbor caves, as seeming troubled,
Make verbal repetition of her moans.
Passion on passion deeply is redoubled;
    "Ay me!" she cries, and twenty times, "Woe, woe!"
    And twenty echoes twenty times cry so.

806 **green** young   807 **in sadness** in all seriousness   808 **teen** sorrow   813 **laund** open space in a forest   815 **Look how** just as 825 **'stonished** bewildered   826 **mistrustful** feared   832 **Passion** lamentation

She, marking them, begins a wailing note   835
And sings extemporally a woeful ditty:
How love makes young men thrall, and old men dote;
How love is wise in folly, foolish-witty.
    Her heavy anthem still concludes in woe,
    And still the choir of echoes answer so.   840

Her song was tedious and outwore the night,
For lovers' hours are long, though seeming short.
If pleased themselves, others, they think, delight
In such-like circumstance, with such-like sport.
    Their copious stories, oftentimes begun,   845
    End without audience, and are never done.

For who hath she to spend the night withal
But idle sounds resembling parasits,
Like shrill-tongued tapsters answering every call,
Soothing the humor of fantastic wits?   850
    She says " 'Tis so." They answer all, " 'Tis so,"
    And would say after her if she said "No."

Lo, here the gentle lark, weary of rest,
From his moist cabinet mounts up on high
And wakes the morning, from whose silver breast   855
The sun ariseth in his majesty;
    Who doth the world so gloriously behold
    That cedar tops and hills seem burnished gold.

Venus salutes him with this fair good-morrow:
"O thou clear god, and patron of all light,   860
From whom each lamp and shining star doth borrow
The beauteous influence that makes him bright;
    There lives a son that sucked an earthly mother
    May lend thee light, as thou dost lend to other."

837 **thrall** captive   848 **parasits** i.e., flatterers   854 **cabinet** i.e.,
nest

865 This said, she hasteth to a myrtle grove,
    Musing the morning is so much o'erworn,
    And yet she hears no tidings of her love.
    She hearkens for his hounds and for his horn.
        Anon she hears them chant it lustily,
870   And all in haste she coasteth to the cry.

    And as she runs, the bushes in the way
    Some catch her by the neck, some kiss her face,
    Some twine about her thigh to make her stay.
    She wildly breaketh from their strict embrace,
875   Like a milch doe, whose swelling dugs do ache,
        Hasting to feed her fawn, hid in some brake.

    By this she hears the hounds are at a bay;
    Whereat she starts, like one that spies an adder
    Wreathed up in fatal folds just in his way,
880 The fear whereof doth make him shake and shudder.
        Even so the timorous yelping of the hounds
        Appals her senses and her spirit confounds.

    For now she knows it is no gentle chase,
    But the blunt boar, rough bear, or lion proud,
885 Because the cry remaineth in one place,
    Where fearfully the dogs exclaim aloud;
        Finding their enemy to be so curst,
        They all strain court'sy who shall cope him first.

    This dismal cry rings sadly in her ear,
890 Through which it enters to surprise her heart,
    Who, overcome by doubt and bloodless fear,
    With cold-pale weakness numbs each feeling part:
        Like soldiers when their captain once doth yield,
        They basely fly, and dare not stay the field.

---

870 **coasteth** approaches   874 **strict** tight   876 **brake** thicket
877 **at a bay** (the moment during a hunt when an animal is forced to
turn against its pursuers)   884 **blunt** rough   887 **curst** savage
888 **They all strain court'sy** i.e., each holds back to allow the other
to go first

Thus stands she in a trembling ecstasy, 895
Till cheering up her senses all dismayed,
She tells them 'tis a causeless fantasy,
And childish error that they are afraid;
  Bids them leave quaking, bids them fear no more;
  And with that word she spied the hunted boar, 900

Whose frothy mouth, bepainted all with red,
Like milk and blood being mingled both togither,
A second fear through all her sinews spread,
Which madly hurries her she knows not whither.
  This way she runs, and now she will no further, 905
  But back retires, to rate the boar for murther.

A thousand spleens bear her a thousand ways;
She treads the path that she untreads again;
Her more than haste is mated with delays,
Like the proceedings of a drunken brain, 910
  Full of respects, yet naught at all respecting,
  In hand with all things, naught at all effecting.

Here kennelled in a brake she finds a hound
And asks the weary caitiff for his master;
And there another licking of his wound, 915
'Gainst venomed sores the only sovereign plaster;
  And here she meets another sadly scowling,
  To whom she speaks, and he replies with howling.

When he hath ceased his ill-resounding noise,
Another flap-mouthed mourner, black and grim, 920
Against the welkin volleys out his voice;
Another and another answer him,
  Clapping their proud tails to the ground below,
  Shaking their scratched ears, bleeding as they go.

895 **ecstasy** fit   907 **spleens** impulses   909 **mated with** checked
by   911 **respects** considerations   912 **In hand** occupied   914
caitiff wretch   920 **flap-mouthed** loose-lipped   921 **welkin** sky

925 Look how the world's poor people are amazèd
At apparitions, signs, and prodigies,
Whereon with fearful eyes they long have gazèd,
Infusing them with dreadful prophecies:
 So she at these sad signs draws up her breath
930 And sighing it again, exclaims on Death.

"Hard-favored tyrant, ugly, meager, lean,
Hateful divorce of love!" (thus chides she Death)
"Grim-grinning ghost, earth's worm, what dost thou
 mean,
To stifle beauty and to steal his breath
935 Who, when he lived, his breath and beauty set
 Gloss on the rose, smell to the violet?

"If he be dead—O no, it cannot be,
Seeing his beauty, thou shouldst strike at it!
O yes, it may; thou hast no eyes to see,
940 But hatefully at randon dost thou hit;
 Thy mark is feeble age, but thy false dart
 Mistakes that aim, and cleaves an infant's heart.

"Hadst thou but bid beware, then he had spoke,
And hearing him, thy power had lost his power.
945 The Destinies will curse thee for this stroke:
They bid thee crop a weed; thou pluck'st a flower.
 Love's golden arrow at him should have fled,
 And not Death's ebon dart to strike him dead.

"Dost thou drink tears, that thou provok'st such
 weeping?
950 What may a heavy groan advantage thee?
Why hast thou cast into eternal sleeping
Those eyes that taught all other eyes to see?
 Now Nature cares not for thy mortal vigor,
 Since her best work is ruined with thy rigor."

925 **amazèd** perplexed 930 **exclaims on** denounces 940 **ran-
don** random 944 **his** its 948 **ebon** black 950 **advantage** profit
953 **mortal vigor** deadly power

Here overcome, as one full of despair, 955
She vailed her eyelids, who like sluices stopped
The crystal tide that from her two cheeks fair
In the sweet channel of her bosom dropped;
  But through the floodgates breaks the silver rain
  And with his strong course opens them again. 960

O, how her eyes and tears did lend and borrow,
Her eye seen in the tears, tears in her eye,
Both crystals, where they viewed each other's sorrow—
Sorrow that friendly sighs sought still to dry;
  But like a stormy day, now wind, now rain, 965
  Sighs dry her cheeks, tears make them wet again.

Variable passions throng her constant woe,
As striving who should best become her grief.
All entertained, each passion labors so
That every present sorrow seemeth chief, 970
  But none is best; then join they all together
  Like many clouds consulting for foul weather.

By this far off she hears some huntsman halloa.
A nurse's song ne'er pleased her babe so well.
The dire imagination she did follow 975
This sound of hope doth labor to expel;
  For now reviving joy bids her rejoice
  And flatters her it is Adonis' voice.

Whereat her tears began to turn their tide,
Being prisoned in her eye like pearls in glass; 980
Yet sometimes falls an orient drop beside,
Which her cheek melts, as scorning it should pass
  To wash the foul face of the sluttish ground,
  Who is but drunken when she seemeth drowned.

956 **vailed** lowered   956 **who like sluices stopped** which, like floodgates, dammed   963 **crystals** i.e., mirrors   968 **striving who** competing which   969 **entertained** admitted   972 **consulting** plotting   979 **turn their tide** ebb   981 **orient** bright

985   O hard-believing love, how strange it seems
      Not to believe, and yet too credulous!
      Thy weal and woe are both of them extremes;
      Despair and hope makes thee ridiculous:
          The one doth flatter thee in thoughts unlikely,
990   In likely thoughts the other kills thee quickly.

      Now she unweaves the web that she hath wrought:
      Adonis lives, and Death is not to blame;
      It was not she that called him all to naught.
      Now she adds honors to his hateful name:
995   She clepes him king of graves, and grave for kings,
          Imperious supreme of all mortal things.

      "No, no," quoth she, "sweet Death, I did but jest;
      Yet pardon me I felt a kind of fear
      When as I met the boar, that bloody beast
1000 Which knows no pity but is still severe.
          Then, gentle shadow (truth I must confess),
          I railed on thee, fearing my love's decesse.

      " 'Tis not my fault the boar provoked my tongue;
      Be wreaked on him, invisible commander.
1005 'Tis he, foul creature, that hath done thee wrong;
      I did but act; he's author of thy slander.
          Grief hath two tongues, and never woman yet
          Could rule them both, without ten women's wit."

      Thus hoping that Adonis is alive,
1010 Her rash suspect she doth extenuate;
      And that his beauty may the better thrive,
      With Death she humbly doth insinuate;
          Tells him of trophies, statues, tombs; and stories
          His victories, his triumphs, and his glories.

---

985 **hard-believing** i.e., skeptical   993 **all to naught** worthless
995 **clepes** names   996 **Imperious supreme** imperial ruler   1001
shadow specter   1002 **decesse** decease   1004 **wreaked** revenged
1010 **suspect** suspicion   1012 **insinuate** ingratiate herself   1013
stories relates

"O Jove," quoth she, "how much a fool was I   1015
To be of such a weak and silly mind
To wail his death who lives, and must not die
Till mutual overthrow of mortal kind!
 For he being dead, with him is beauty slain,
 And, beauty dead, black chaos comes again.   1020

"Fie, fie, found love, thou art as full of fear
As one with treasure laden, hemmed with thieves.
Trifles, unwitnessèd with eye, or ear,
Thy coward heart with false bethinking grieves."
 Even at this word she hears a merry horn,   1025
 Whereat she leaps that was but late forlorn.

As falcons to the lure, away she flies;
The grass stoops not, she treads on it so light,
And in her haste unfortunately spies
The foul boar's conquest on her fair delight;   1030
 Which seen, her eyes, as murd'red with the view,
 Like stars ashamed of day, themselves withdrew;

Or as the snail, whose tender horns being hit,
Shrinks backward in his shelly cave with pain,
And there, all smoth'red up, in shade doth sit,   1035
Long after fearing to creep forth again;
 So, at his bloody view her eyes are fled
 Into the deep-dark cabins of her head;

Where they resign their office and their light
To the disposing of her troubled brain,   1040
Who bids them still consort with ugly night
And never wound the heart with looks again;
 Who, like a king perplexèd in his throne,
 By their suggestion gives a deadly groan,

1023 **unwitnessèd with** unperceived by 1032 **ashamed of** put to
shame by 1041 **still consort** always keep company 1043 **Who**
which

1045 Whereat each tributary subject quakes,
As when the wind, imprisoned in the ground,
Struggling for passage, earth's foundation shakes,
Which with cold terror doth men's minds confound.
    This mutiny each part doth so surprise
1050   That from their dark beds once more leap her eyes,

And, being opened, threw unwilling light
Upon the wide wound that the boar had trenched
In his soft flank, whose wonted lily white
With purple tears that his wound wept was drenched.
1055   No flow'r was nigh, no grass, herb, leaf, or weed,
    But stole his blood and seemed with him to bleed.

This solemn sympathy poor Venus noteth.
Over one shoulder doth she hang her head.
Dumbly she passions, franticly she doteth:
1060 She thinks he could not die, he is not dead;
    Her voice is stopped, her joints forget to bow;
    Her eyes are mad that they have wept till now.

Upon his hurt she looks so steadfastly
That her sight dazzling makes the wound seem three;
1065 And then she reprehends her mangling eye,
That makes more gashes where no breach should be.
    His face seems twain, each several limb is doubled;
    For oft the eye mistakes, the brain being troubled.

"My tongue cannot express my grief for one,
1070 And yet," quoth she, "behold two Adons dead!
My sighs are blown away, my salt tears gone,
Mine eyes are turned to fire, my heart to lead.
    Heavy heart's lead, melt at mine eyes' red fire!
    So shall I die by drops of hot desire.

1052 **trenched** cut   1059 **passions** grieves   1062 **mad** distracted
1062 **till** i.e., before

"Alas, poor world, what treasure hast thou lost!   *1075*
What face remains alive that's worth the viewing?
Whose tongue is music now? What canst thou boast
Of things long since, or any thing ensuing?
  The flowers are sweet, their colors fresh and trim,
  But true sweet beauty lived and died with him.   *1080*

"Bonnet nor veil henceforth no creature wear;
Nor sun nor wind will ever strive to kiss you.
Having no fair to lose, you need not fear:
The sun doth scorn you, and the wind doth hiss you.
  But when Adonis lived, sun and sharp air   *1085*
  Lurked like two thieves, to rob him of his fair;

"And therefore would he put his bonnet on,
Under whose brim the gaudy sun would peep;
The wind would blow it off, and being gone,
Play with his locks; then would Adonis weep;   *1090*
  And straight, in pity of his tender years,
  They both would strive who first should dry his
    tears.

"To see his face the lion walked along,
Behind some hedge, because he would not fear him.
To recreate himself when he hath song,   *1095*
The tiger would be tame, and gently hear him.
  If he had spoke, the wolf would leave his prey
  And never fright the silly lamb that day.

1083 **fair** beauty   1088 **gaudy** bright   1094 **fear** frighten   1098
silly innocent

"When he beheld his shadow in the brook,
1100 The fishes spread on it their golden gills;
When he was by, the birds such pleasure took
That some would sing, some other in their bills
    Would bring him mulberries and ripe-red cherries:
    He fed them with his sight, they him with berries.

1105 "But this foul, grim, and urchin-snouted boar,
Whose downward eye still looketh for a grave,
Ne'er saw the beauteous livery that he wore;
Witness the entertainment that he gave.
    If he did see his face, why then I know
1110   He thought to kiss him, and hath killed him so.

" 'Tis true, 'tis true! thus was Adonis slain:
He ran upon the boar with his sharp spear,
Who did not whet his teeth at him again,
But by a kiss thought to persuade him there;
1115   And nuzzling in his flank, the loving swine
    Sheathed unaware the tusk in his soft groin.

"Had I been toothed like him, I must confess,
With kissing him I should have killed him first;
But he is dead, and never did he bless
1120 My youth with his; the more am I accurst."
    With this she falleth in the place she stood
    And stains her face with his congealèd blood.

She looks upon his lips, and they are pale;
She takes him by the hand, and that is cold;
1125 She whispers in his ears a heavy tale,
As if they heard the woeful words she told.
    She lifts the coffer-lids that close his eyes,
    Where lo, two lamps burnt out in darkness lies;

1105 **urchin** hedgehog   1108 **entertainment** reception   1127
coffer-lids lids to treasure chests

Two glasses, where herself herself beheld
A thousand times, and now no more reflect; 1130
Their virtue lost wherein they late excelled,
And every beauty robbed of his effect.
    "Wonder of time," quoth she, "this is my spite,
      That thou being dead, the day should yet be light.

"Since thou art dead, lo here I prophesy, 1135
Sorrow on love hereafter shall attend.
It shall be waited on with jealousy,
Find sweet beginning, but unsavory end,
    Ne'er settled equally, but high or low,
      That all love's pleasure shall not match his woe. 1140

"It shall be fickle, false, and full of fraud;
Bud, and be blasted, in a breathing while;
The bottom poison, and the top o'erstrawed
With sweets that shall the truest sight beguile.
    The strongest body shall it make most weak, 1145
      Strike the wise dumb, and teach the fool to speak.

"It shall be sparing, and too full of riot,
Teaching decrepit age to tread the measures;
The staring ruffian shall it keep in quiet,
Pluck down the rich, enrich the poor with treasures; 1150
    It shall be raging mad, and silly mild,
      Make the young old, the old become a child.

"It shall suspect where is no cause of fear;
It shall not fear where it should most mistrust;
It shall be merciful, and too severe, 1155
And most deceiving when it seems most just;
    Perverse it shall be where it shows most toward;
      Put fear to valor, courage to the coward.

1133 **spite** grief 1142 **in a breathing while** in one breath 1143
o'erstrawed strewn docile

"It shall be cause of war and dire events
1160 And set dissension 'twixt the son and sire,
Subject and servile to all discontents,
As dry combustious matter is to fire.
    Sith in his prime death doth my love destroy,
    They that love best their loves shall not enjoy."

1165 By this the boy that by her side lay killed
Was melted like a vapor from her sight,
And in his blood, that on the ground lay spilled,
A purple flower sprung up, check'red with white,
    Resembling well his pale cheeks and the blood
1170   Which in round drops upon their whiteness stood.

She bows her head the new-sprung flower to smell,
Comparing it to her Adonis' breath,
And says within her bosom it shall dwell,
Since he himself is reft from her by death;
1175   She crops the stalk, and in the breach appears
    Green-dropping sap, which she compares to tears.

"Poor flow'r," quoth she, "this was thy father's
        guise—
Sweet issue of a more sweet-smelling sire—
For every little grief to wet his eyes;
1180 To grow unto himself was his desire,
    And so 'tis thine; but know, it is as good
    To wither in my breast as in his blood.

"Here was thy father's bed, here in my breast;
Thou art the next of blood, and 'tis thy right.
1185 Lo in this hollow cradle take thy rest;
My throbbing heart shall rock thee day and night:
    There shall not be one minute in an hour
    Wherein I will not kiss my sweet love's flow'r."

1168 **purple flower** i.e., the anemone   1175 **breach** break (in the
stalk)   1177 **guise** custom

Thus weary of the world, away she hies,
And yokes her silver doves, by whose swift aid
Their mistress, mounted, through the empty skies
In her light chariot quickly is conveyed,
    Holding their course to Paphos, where their queen
    Means to immure herself and not be seen.

1190

FINIS

1193 **Paphos** (where Venus dwells in Cyprus)

LVCRECE.

LONDON.

Printed by Richard Field, for Iohn Harrison; and are
to be fold at the figne of the white Greyhound
in Paules Churh-yard. 1594.

The Rape of Lucrece title page (1594).

THE RAPE OF LUCRECE

To the Right Honorable
Henry Wriothesley
Earl of Southampton, and Baron of Titchfield

The love I dedicate to your Lordship is without end;
whereof this pamphlet without beginning is but a   *5*
superfluous moiety. The warrant I have of your honor-
able disposition, not the worth of my untutored lines,
makes it assured of acceptance. What I have done is
yours; what I have to do is yours; being part in all I
have, devoted yours. Were my worth greater, my duty   *10*
would show greater; meantime, as it is, it is bound to
your Lordship, to whom I wish long life still length-
ened with all happiness.

Your Lordship's in all duty,

William Shakespeare   *15*

THE ARGUMENT

Lucius Tarquinius (for his excessive pride surnamed
Superbus), after he had caused his own father-in-law
Servius Tullius to be cruelly murdered, and, contrary
to the Roman laws and customs, not requiring or stay-
ing for the people's suffrages, had possessed himself   *5*
of the kingdom, went, accompanied with his sons and
other noblemen of Rome, to besiege Ardea; during

Ded.   5 **without beginning** i.e., the narrative begins *in medias res*
6 **moiety** small part

which siege the principal men of the army meeting
one evening at the tent of Sextus Tarquinius, the
King's son, in their discourses after supper every one
commended the virtues of his own wife; among whom
Collatinus extolled the incomparable chastity of his
wife Lucretia. In that pleasant humor they all posted
to Rome; and intending by their secret and sudden
arrival to make trial of that which every one had be-
fore avouched, only Collatinus finds his wife (though
it were late in the night) spinning amongst her maids;
the other ladies were all found dancing and reveling,
or in several disports. Whereupon the noblemen
yielded Collatinus the victory, and his wife the fame.
At that time Sextus Tarquinius being inflamed with
Lucrece' beauty, yet smothering his passions for the
present, departed with the rest back to the camp; from
whence he shortly after privily withdrew himself, and
was (according to his estate) royally entertained and
lodged by Lucrece at Collatium. The same night he
treacherously stealeth into her chamber, violently
ravished her, and early in the morning speedeth away.
Lucrece, in this lamentable plight, hastily dispatcheth
messengers, one to Rome for her father, another to
the camp for Collatine. They came, the one accom-
panied with Junius Brutus, the other with Publius
Valerius; and finding Lucrece attired in mourning
habit, demanded the cause of her sorrow. She, first
taking an oath of them for her revenge, revealed the
actor and whole manner of his dealing, and withal
suddenly stabbed herself. Which done, with one con-
sent they all vowed to root out the whole hated family
of the Tarquins; and bearing the dead body to Rome,
Brutus acquainted the people with the doer and man-
ner of the vile deed, with a bitter invective against
the tyranny of the King; wherewith the people were
so moved that with one consent and a general ac-
clamation the Tarquins were all exiled, and the state
government changed from kings to consuls.

The Rape of Lucrece

From the besiegèd Ardea all in post,
Borne by the trustless wings of false desire,
Lust-breathèd Tarquin leaves the Roman host
And to Collatium bears the lightless fire
Which, in pale embers hid, lurks to aspire   5
    And girdle with embracing flames the waist
    Of Collatine's fair love, Lucrece the chaste.

Haply that name of "chaste" unhap'ly set
This bateless edge on his keen appetite;
When Collatine unwisely did not let   10
To praise the clear unmatchèd red and white
Which triumphed in that sky of his delight,
    Where mortal stars, as bright as heaven's beauties,
    With pure aspects did him peculiar duties.

For he the night before, in Tarquin's tent,   15
Unlocked the treasure of his happy state:
What priceless wealth the heavens had him lent
In the possession of his beauteous mate;
Reck'ning his fortune at such high proud rate
    That kings might be espousèd to more fame,   20
    But king nor peer to such a peerless dame.

---

1 **all in post** in great haste   2 **trustless** treacherous   3 **Lust-
breathèd** inspired by lust   4 **lightless** smoldering   5 **aspire** as-
cend   8 **Haply** perhaps   9 **bateless** unbated   9 **appetite** lust
10 **let** forbear   12 **that sky of his delight** i.e., Lucrece's face
13 **mortal stars** i.e., Lucrece's eyes   14 **aspects** (1) looks (2) as-
trological influences   14 **peculiar** private

281

O happiness enjoyed but of a few,
And if possessed, as soon decayed and done
As is the morning's silver-melting dew
25 Against the golden splendor of the sun!
An expired date, canceled ere well begun.
    Honor and beauty, in the owner's arms,
    Are weakly fortressed from a world of harms.

Beauty itself doth of itself persuade
30 The eyes of men without an orator.
What needeth then apologies be made,
To set forth that which is so singular?
Or why is Collatine the publisher
    Of that rich jewel he should keep unknown
35 From thievish ears, because it is his own?

Perchance his boast of Lucrece' sov'reignty
Suggested this proud issue of a king;
For by our ears our hearts oft tainted be.
Perchance that envy of so rich a thing,
40 Braving compare, disdainfully did sting
    His high-pitched thoughts, that meaner men should
        vaunt
    That golden hap which their superiors want.

But some untimely thought did instigate
His all too timeless speed, if none of those.
45 His honor, his affairs, his friends, his state,
Neglected all, with swift intent he goes
To quench the coal which in his liver glows.
    O rash false heat, wrapped in repentant cold,
    Thy hasty spring still blasts and ne'er grows old!

22 **of** by   23 **done** consumed   26 **date** lease   31 **apologies** i.e.,
vindications   33 **publisher** proclaimer   37 **Suggested** prompted
37 **issue** i.e., son   40 **Braving compare** challenging comparison
42 **hap** luck   42 **want** lack   44 **timeless** untimely   45 **state** sta-
tus, estate   47 **liver** (thought to have been the seat of sexual desire)
49 **still blasts** always is blasted

When at Collatium this false lord arrivèd, 50
Well was he welcomed by the Roman dame,
Within whose face Beauty and Virtue strivèd
Which of them both should underprop her fame.
When Virtue bragged, Beauty would blush for shame;
    When Beauty boasted blushes, in despite 55
    Virtue would stain that o'er with silver white.

But Beauty in that white entitulèd
From Venus' doves, doth challenge that fair field;
Then Virtue claims from Beauty Beauty's red,
Which Virtue gave the Golden Age to gild 60
Their silver cheeks, and called it then their shield,
    Teaching them thus to use it in the fight,
    When shame assailed, the red should fence the
      white.

This heraldry in Lucrece' face was seen,
Argued by Beauty's red and Virtue's white; 65
Of either's color was the other queen,
Proving from world's minority their right.
Yet their ambition makes them still to fight,
    The sovereignty of either being so great
    That oft they interchange each other's seat. 70

This silent war of lilies and of roses,
Which Tarquin viewed in her fair face's field,
In their pure ranks his traitor eye encloses;
Where, lest between them both it should be killed,
The coward captive vanquishèd doth yield 75
    To those two armies that would let him go
    Rather than triumph in so false a foe.

---

57 **entitulèd** having a claim   58 **field** (1) field of battle (2) ground
of a shield   60 **gild** color (with a blush)   63 **fence** defend
65 **Argued** expressed   67 **minority** youth (i.e., the Golden Age of
line 60)

Now thinks he that her husband's shallow tongue,
The niggard prodigal that praised her so,
80   In that high task hath done her beauty wrong,
Which far exceeds his barren skill to show.
Therefore that praise which Collatine doth owe
    Enchanted Tarquin answers with surmise,
    In silent wonder of still-gazing eyes.

85   This earthly saint, adorèd by this devil,
Little suspecteth the false worshipper;
For unstained thoughts do seldom dream on evil;
Birds never limed no secret bushes fear.
So guiltless she securely gives good cheer
90   And reverend welcome to her princely guest,
    Whose inward ill no outward harm expressed;

For that he colored with his high estate,
Hiding base sin in pleats of majesty;
That nothing in him seemed inordinate,
95   Save sometime too much wonder of his eye,
Which, having all, all could not satisfy;
    But poorly rich, so wanteth in his store
    That, cloyed with much, he pineth still for more.

But she, that never coped with stranger eyes,
100 Could pick no meaning from their parling looks,
Nor read the subtle shining secrecies
Writ in the glassy margents of such books.
She touched no unknown baits, nor feared no hooks;
    Nor could she moralize his wanton sight,
105   More than his eyes were opened to the light.

83 **answers** pays   83 **surmise** amazement   88 **limed** caught by
bird-lime (a sticky substance smeared upon branches)   89 **securely**
unsuspectingly   90 **reverend**   reverent   92 **colored**   cloaked
94 **That** so that   97 **store** wealth   99 **coped with** encountered
99 **stranger** i.e., strangers'   100 **parling** speaking   102 **glassy**
margents margins (of his eyes)   104 **moralize** interpret   104 **sight**
glance

He stories to her ears her husband's fame,
Won in the fields of fruitful Italy;
And decks with praises Collatine's high name,
Made glorious by his manly chivalry,
With bruisèd arms and wreaths of victory.   *110*
　　Her joy with heaved-up hand she doth express,
　　And wordless so greets heaven for his success.

Far from the purpose of his coming thither
He makes excuses for his being there.
No cloudy show of stormy blust'ring weather   *115*
Doth yet in his fair welkin once appear,
Till sable Night, mother of dread and fear,
　　Upon the world dim darkness doth display
　　And in her vaulty prison stows the day.

For then is Tarquin brought unto his bed,   *120*
Intending weariness with heavy sprite;
For, after supper, long he questionèd
With modest Lucrece, and wore out the night.
Now leaden slumber with life's strength doth fight,
　　And everyone to rest himself betakes,   *125*
　　Save thieves, and cares, and troubled minds that
　　　　wakes.

As one of which doth Tarquin lie revolving
The sundry dangers of his will's obtaining;
Yet ever to obtain his will resolving,
Though weak-built hopes persuade him to abstaining.   *130*
Despair to gain doth traffic oft for gaining;
　　And when great treasure is the meed proposèd,
　　Though death be adjunct, there's no death supposèd.

110 **bruisèd arms** battered armor   111 **heaved-up** uplifted
116 **welkin** sky   121 **Intending** pretending   121 **sprite** spirit
122 **questionèd** talked   131 **traffic** trade   132 **meed** reward
133 **adjunct** i.e., the consequence   134 **fond** infatuated

Those that much covet are with gain so fond
135 That what they have not, that which they possess
They scatter and unloose it from their bond,
And so by hoping more they have but less;
Or, gaining more, the profit of excess
    Is but to surfeit, and such griefs sustain
140   That they prove bankrout in this poor rich gain.

The aim of all is but to nurse the life
With honor, wealth, and ease in waning age;
And in this aim there is such thwarting strife
That one for all, or all for one we gage:
145 As life for honor in fell battle's rage;
    Honor for wealth; and oft that wealth doth cost
    The death of all, and all together lost;

So that in vent'ring ill we leave to be
The things we are for that which we expect;
150 And this ambitious foul infirmity,
In having much, torments us with defect
Of that we have: so then we do neglect
    The thing we have, and all for want of wit,
    Make something nothing by augmenting it.

155 Such hazard now must doting Tarquin make,
Pawning his honor to obtain his lust;
And for himself himself he must forsake.
Then where is truth, if there be no self-trust?
When shall he think to find a stranger just,
160   When he himself himself confounds, betrays
    To sland'rous tongues and wretched hateful days?

---

140 **bankrout** bankrupt   144 **gage** pledge   145 **As** for example
145 **fell** fierce   148 **vent'ring** risking   148 **leave** cease   151 **de-
fect** the insufficiency   160 **confounds** destroys

Now stole upon the time the dead of night,
When heavy sleep had closed up mortal eyes.
No comfortable star did lend his light,
No noise but owls, and wolves' death-boding cries;   *165*
Now serves the season that they may surprise
   The silly lambs: pure thoughts are dead and still,
   While lust and murder wakes to stain and kill.

And now this lustful lord leapt from his bed,
Throwing his mantle rudely o'er his arm;   *170*
Is madly tossed between desire and dread:
Th' one sweetly flatters, th' other feareth harm;
But honest fear, bewitched with lust's foul charm,
   Doth too too oft betake him to retire,
   Beaten away by brainsick rude desire.   *175*

His falchion on a flint he softly smiteth,
That from the cold stone sparks of fire do fly;
Whereat a waxen torch forthwith he lighteth,
Which must be lodestar to his lustful eye;
And to the flame thus speaks advisedly: *180*
   "As from this cold flint I enforced this fire,
   So Lucrece must I force to my desire."

Here pale with fear he doth premeditate
The dangers of his loathsome enterprise,
And in his inward mind he doth debate   *185*
What following sorrow may on this arise;
Then looking scornfully, he doth despise
   His naked armor of still-slaught'red lust
   And justly thus controls his thoughts unjust:

---

164 **comfortable** comforting   167 **silly** innocent   175 **brainsick**
mad   176 **falchion** curved sword   176 **softly** silently   179 **lode-
star** guiding star   180 **advisedly** deliberately   188 **His naked ...
lust** i.e., his armor, lust, is no armor, for when lust is fulfilled it is
killed

190   "Fair torch, burn out thy light, and lend it not
     To darken her whose light excelleth thine;
     And die, unhallowed thoughts, before you blot
     With your uncleanness that which is divine.
     Offer pure incense to so pure a shrine.
195   Let fair humanity abhor the deed
         That spots and stains love's modest snow-white
            weed.

    "O shame to knighthood and to shining arms!
     O foul dishonor to my household's grave!
     O impious act including all foul harms!
200   A martial man to be soft fancy's slave!
     True valor still a true respect should have;
       Then my digression is so vile, so base,
         That it will live engraven in my face.

    "Yea, though I die, the scandal will survive
205   And be an eyesore in my golden coat.
     Some loathsome dash the herald will contrive
     To cipher me how fondly I did dote;
     That my posterity, shamed with the note,
       Shall curse my bones, and hold it for no sin
210   To wish that I their father had not been.

    "What win I if I gain the thing I seek?
     A dream, a breath, a froth of fleeting joy.
     Who buys a minute's mirth to wail a week?
     Or sells eternity to get a toy?
215   For one sweet grape who will the vine destroy?
       Or what fond beggar, but to touch the crown,
         Would with the scepter straight be stroken down?

196 **weed** garment, i.e., chastity   198 **my houshold's grave** the tomb of my ancestors   200 **soft fancy's** i.e., love's   201 **still** always   201 **respect** regard   205 **coat** coat of arms   206 **loathsome dash** i.e., a mark of disgrace   207 **cipher** show   207 **fondly** foolishly

"If Collatinus dream of my intent,
Will he not wake, and in a desp'rate rage
Post hither this vile purpose to prevent?   220
This siege that hath engirt his marriage,
This blur to youth, this sorrow to the sage,
    This dying virtue, this surviving shame,
    Whose crime will bear an ever-during blame?

"O, what excuse can my invention make   225
When thou shalt charge me with so black a deed?
Will not my tongue be mute, my frail joints shake,
Mine eyes forgo their light, my false heart bleed?
The guilt being great, the fear doth still exceed;
    And extreme fear can neither fight nor fly,   230
    But cowardlike with trembling terror die.

"Had Collatinus killed my son or sire,
Or lain in ambush to betray my life,
Or were he not my dear friend, this desire
Might have excuse to work upon his wife,   235
As in revenge or quittal of such strife;
    But as he is my kinsman, my dear friend,
    The shame and fault finds no excuse nor end.

"Shameful it is—ay, if the fact be known.
Hateful it is—there is no hate in loving.   240
I'll beg her love—but she is not her own.
The worst is but denial and reproving.
My will is strong, past reason's weak removing.
    Who fears a sentence or an old man's saw
    Shall by a painted cloth be kept in awe."   245

221 **engirt** surrounded to attack   224 **ever-during** ever-enduring
236 **quittal** requital   243 **will** desire   243 **removing** dissuasion
244 **sentence** moral judgment   244 **saw** moral saying   245 **painted
cloth** wall hanging on which were painted moral texts and illustrative
Biblical and classical subjects

Thus graceless holds he disputation
'Tween frozen conscience and hot-burning will,
And with good thoughts makes dispensation,
Urging the worser sense for vantage still;
250   Which in a moment doth confound and kill
    All pure effects, and doth so far proceed
    That what is vile shows like a virtuous deed.

Quoth he, "She took me kindly by the hand
And gazed for tidings in my eager eyes,
255   Fearing some hard news from the warlike band
Where her belovèd Collatinus lies.
O, how her fear did make her color rise!
    First red as roses that on lawn we lay,
    Then white as lawn, the roses took away.

260   "And how her hand, in my hand being locked,
Forced it to tremble with her loyal fear!
Which strook her sad, and then it faster rocked
Until her husband's welfare she did hear;
Whereat she smilèd with so sweet a cheer
265   That, had Narcissus seen her as she stood,
    Self-love had never drowned him in the flood.

"Why hunt I then for color or excuses?
All orators are dumb when beauty pleadeth;
Poor wretches have remorse in poor abuses;
270   Love thrives not in the heart that shadows dreadeth.
Affection is my captain, and he leadeth;
    And when his gaudy banner is displayed,
    The coward fights and will not be dismayed.

248 **makes dispensation** dispenses   249 **vantage** advantage
251 **effects** emotions   258 **lawn** (fine) linen   262 **Which** i.e., the
fact that his hand trembled   262 **it** i.e., her heart   265 **Narcissus** a
beautiful youth who fell in love with his own reflection   267 **color**
pretext   269 **Poor wretches ... abuses** remorse is felt only by lesser
men in their petty transgressions   270 **shadows dreadeth** i.e., has
scruples   271 **Affection** desire   273 **The coward** i.e., even the
coward

"Then childish fear avaunt, debating die!
Respect and reason wait on wrinkled age!   275
My heart shall never countermand mine eye.
Sad pause and deep regard beseems the sage;
My part is youth, and beats these from the stage.
    Desire my pilot is, beauty my prize;
    Then who fears sinking where such treasure lies?"   280

As corn o'ergrown by weeds, so heedful fear
Is almost choked by unresisted lust.
Away he steals with open list'ning ear,
Full of foul hope and full of fond mistrust;
Both which, as servitors to the unjust,   285
    So cross him with their opposite persuasion
    That now he vows a league, and now invasion.

Within his thought her heavenly image sits,
And in the selfsame seat sits Collatine.
That eye which looks on her confounds his wits;   290
That eye which him beholds, as more divine,
Unto a view so false will not incline;
    But with a pure appeal seeks to the heart,
    Which once corrupted takes the worser part;

And therein heartens up his servile powers,   295
Who, flatt'red by their leader's jocund show,
Stuff up his lust, as minutes fill up hours;
And as their captain, so their pride doth grow,
Paying more slavish tribute than they owe.
    By reprobate desire thus madly led,   300
    The Roman lord marcheth to Lucrece' bed.

---

275 **Respect** prudence 275 **wait on** attend 277 **Sad** serious
281 **corn** grain 286 **cross** thwart 287 **league** peace 293 **seeks
to** applies to 295 **his servile powers** i.e., the senses

The locks between her chamber and his will,
Each one by him enforced, retires his ward;
But as they open, they all rate his ill,
305 Which drives the creeping thief to some regard.
The threshold grates the door to have him heard;
    Night-wand'ring weasels shriek to see him there;
    They fright him, yet he still pursues his fear.

As each unwilling portal yields him way,
310 Through little vents and crannies of the place
The wind wars with his torch to make him stay,
And blows the smoke of it into his face,
Extinguishing his conduct in this case;
    But his hot heart, which fond desire doth scorch,
315 Puffs forth another wind that fires the torch;

And being lighted, by the light he spies
Lucretia's glove, wherein her needle sticks;
He takes it from the rushes where it lies,
And griping it, the needle his finger pricks,
320 As who should say, "This glove to wanton tricks
    Is not inured; return again in haste;
    Thou seest our mistress' ornaments are chaste."

But all these poor forbiddings could not stay him;
He in the worst sense consters their denial:
325 The doors, the wind, the glove, that did delay him,
He takes for accidental things of trial;
Or as those bars which stop the hourly dial,
    Who with a ling'ring stay his course doth let,
    Till every minute pays the hour his debt.

303 **retires his ward** draws back its bolt ("ward")   304 **rate his ill**
condemn his evil intentions (by creaking)   305 **regard** caution
307 **weasels** (kept in Roman houses in place of cats to catch rats)
313 **conduct** conductor (i.e., the torch)   318 **rushes** (used as floor
coverings)   321 **inured** accustomed   324 **consters** construes
326 **accidental things of trial** chance happenings   327 **bars** lines
on the face of a clock   328 **Who** which   328 **let** delay

"So, so," quoth he, "these lets attend the time, 330
Like little frosts that sometime threat the spring
To add a more rejoicing to the prime
And give the sneapèd birds more cause to sing.
Pain pays the income of each precious thing:
    Huge rocks, high winds, strong pirates, shelves and
        sands, 335
    The merchant fears ere rich at home he lands."

Now is he come unto the chamber door
That shuts him from the heaven of his thought,
Which with a yielding latch, and with no more,
Hath barred him from the blessèd thing he sought. 340
So from himself impiety hath wrought
    That for his prey to pray he doth begin,
    As if the heavens should countenance his sin.

But in the midst of his unfruitful prayer,
Having solicited th' eternal power 345
That his foul thoughts might compass his fair fair,
And they would stand auspicious to the hour,
Even there he starts; quoth he, "I must deflow'r.
    The powers to whom I pray abhor this fact;
    How can they then assist me in the act? 350

"Then Love and Fortune be my gods, my guide:
My will is backed with resolution.
Thoughts are but dreams till their effects be tried;
The blackest sin is cleared with absolution;
Against love's fire fear's frost hath dissolution. 355
    The eye of heaven is out, and misty night
    Covers the shame that follows sweet delight."

330 **lets** hindrances 332 **prime** spring 333 **sneapèd** chilled
334 **income** harvest, gain 341 **wrought** i.e., wrought him 346
compass his fair fair possess his virtuous beauty

This said, his guilty hand plucked up the latch,
And with his knee the door he opens wide.
360 The dove sleeps fast that this night owl will catch.
Thus treason works ere traitors be espied.
Who sees the lurking serpent steps aside;
　　But she, sound sleeping, fearing no such thing,
　　Lies at the mercy of his mortal sting.

365 Into the chamber wickedly he stalks
And gazeth on her yet unstainèd bed.
The curtains being close, about he walks,
Rolling his greedy eyeballs in his head.
By their high treason is his heart misled,
370 　　Which gives the watchword to his hand full soon
　　To draw the cloud that hides the silver moon.

Look as the fair and fiery-pointed sun,
Rushing from forth a cloud, bereaves our sight,
Even so, the curtain drawn, his eyes begun
375 To wink, being blinded with a greater light.
Whether it is that she reflects so bright
　　That dazzleth them, or else some shame supposèd;
　　But blind they are, and keep themselves enclosèd.

O, had they in that darksome prison died,
380 Then had they seen the period of their ill!
Then Collatine again by Lucrece' side
In his clear bed might have reposèd still.
But they must ope, this blessèd league to kill,
　　And holy-thoughted Lucrece to their sight
385 　　Must sell her joy, her life, her world's delight.

364 **sting** (1) lust (2) penis   372 **Look as** as   373 **bereaves** takes
away   375 **wink** close   377 **supposèd** imagined   380 **period**
end   380 **ill** evil   382 **clear** unstained

Her lily hand her rosy cheek lies under,
Coz'ning the pillow of a lawful kiss;
Who, therefore angry, seems to part in sunder,
Swelling on either side to want his bliss;
Between whose hills her head entombèd is;   390
    Where like a virtuous monument she lies,
    To be admired of lewd unhallowed eyes.

Without the bed her other fair hand was,
On the green coverlet; whose perfect white
Showed like an April daisy on the grass,   395
With pearly sweat resembling dew of night.
Her eyes like marigolds had sheathed their light,
    And canopied in darkness sweetly lay
    Till they might open to adorn the day.

Her hair like golden threads played with her breath—   400
O modest wantons, wanton modesty—
Showing life's triumph in the map of death,
And death's dim look in life's mortality.
Each in her sleep themselves so beautify
    As if between them twain there were no strife,   405
    But that life lived in death, and death in life.

Her breasts like ivory globes circled with blue,
A pair of maiden worlds unconquerèd,
Save of their lord no bearing yoke they knew,
And him by oath they truly honorèd.   410
These worlds in Tarquin new ambition bred,
    Who like a foul usurper went about
    From this fair throne to heave the owner out.

What could he see but mightily he noted?
What did he note but strongly he desirèd?   415
What he beheld, on that he firmly doted,
And in his will his willful eye he tirèd.
With more than admiration he admirèd
    Her azure veins, her alabaster skin,
    Her coral lips, her snow-white dimpled chin.   420

387 **Coz'ning** cheating   402 **map** image   417 **will** lust

As the grim lion fawneth o'er his prey,
Sharp hunger by the conquest satisfied,
So o'er this sleeping soul doth Tarquin stay,
His rage of lust by gazing qualified;
425   Slacked, not suppressed; for, standing by her side,
    His eye, which late this mutiny restrains,
    Unto a greater uproar tempts his veins.

And they, like straggling slaves for pillage fighting,
Obdurate vassals fell exploits effecting,
430   In bloody death and ravishment delighting,
Nor children's tears nor mothers' groans respecting,
Swell in their pride, the onset still expecting.
    Anon his beating heart, alarum striking,
    Gives the hot charge and bids them do their liking.

435   His drumming heart cheers up his burning eye,
His eye commends the leading to his hand;
His hand, as proud of such a dignity,
Smoking with pride, marched on to make his stand
On her bare breast, the heart of all her land;
440   Whose ranks of blue veins, as his hand did scale,
    Left their round turrets destitute and pale.

They, must'ring to the quiet cabinet
Where their dear governess and lady lies,
Do tell her she is dreadfully beset
445   And fright her with confusion of their cries.
She, much amazed, breaks ope her locked-up eyes,
    Who, peeping forth this tumult to behold,
    Are by his flaming torch dimmed and controlled.

---

421 **fawneth** rejoices   431 **Nor...nor** neither...nor   432 **pride**
lust   433 **alarum** call to attack in battle   435 **cheers up** encourages   436 **commends** entrusts   442 **must'ring** rallying   442 **the
quiet cabinet** i.e., the heart   448 **controlled** overpowered

Imagine her as one in dead of night,
From forth dull sleep by dreadful fancy waking,   450
That thinks she hath beheld some ghastly sprite,
Whose grim aspect sets every joint a-shaking.
What terror 'tis! but she, in worser taking,
    From sleep disturbèd, heedfully doth view
    The sight which makes supposèd terror true.   455

Wrapped and confounded in a thousand fears,
Like to a new-killed bird she trembling lies.
She dares not look; yet winking there appears
Quick-shifting antics, ugly in her eyes.
Such shadows are the weak brain's forgeries,   460
    Who, angry that the eyes fly from their lights,
    In darkness daunts them with more dreadful sights.

His hand, that yet remains upon her breast
(Rude ram, to batter such an ivory wall),
May feel her heart (poor citizen) distressed,   465
Wounding itself to death, rise up and fall,
Beating her bulk, that his hand shakes withal.
    This moves in him more rage and lesser pity,
    To make the breach and enter this sweet city.

First like a trumpet doth his tongue begin   470
To sound a parley to his heartless foe;
Who o'er the white sheet peers her whiter chin,
The reason of this rash alarm to know,
Which he by dumb demeanor seeks to show;
    But she with vehement prayers urgeth still   475
    Under what color he commits this ill.

453 **taking** fear 459 **antics** grotesque figures 460 **shadows** shapes 464 **ram** battering-ram 467 **bulk** body 471 **heartless** frightened 474 **dumb demeanor** dumb show 476 **color** (1) pretext (2) flag (3) anger (choler)

Thus he replies: "The color in thy face,
That even for anger makes the lily pale
And the red rose blush at her own disgrace,
480 Shall plead for me and tell my loving tale.
Under that color am I come to scale
     Thy never-conquered fort; the fault is thine,
     For those thine eyes betray thee unto mine.

"Thus I forestall thee, if thou mean to chide:
485 Thy beauty hath ensnared thee to this night,
Where thou with patience must my will abide,
My will that marks thee for my earth's delight,
Which I to conquer sought with all my might;
     But as reproof and reason beat it dead,
490   By thy bright beauty was it newly bred.

"I see what crosses my attempt will bring,
I know what thorns the growing rose defends,
I think the honey guarded with a sting:
All this beforehand counsel comprehends.
495 But Will is deaf, and hears no heedful friends;
     Only he hath an eye to gaze on Beauty,
     And dotes on what he looks, 'gainst law or duty.

"I have debated even in my soul,
What wrong, what shame, what sorrow I shall breed;
500 But nothing can affection's course control
Or stop the headlong fury of his speed.
I know repentant tears ensue the deed,
     Reproach, disdain, and deadly enmity;
     Yet strive I to embrace mine infamy."

This said, he shakes aloft his Roman blade,   505
Which, like a falcon tow'ring in the skies,
Coucheth the fowl below with his wings' shade,
Whose crooked beak threats if he mount he dies.
So under his insulting falchion lies
    Harmless Lucretia, marking what he tells   510
    With trembling fear, as fowl hear falcons' bells.

"Lucrece," quoth he, "this night I must enjoy thee.
If thou deny, then force must work my way;
For in thy bed I purpose to destroy thee.
That done, some worthless slave of thine I'll slay,   515
To kill thine honor with thy life's decay;
    And in thy dead arms do I mean to place him,
    Swearing I slew him, seeing thee embrace him.

"So thy surviving husband shall remain
The scornful mark of every open eye;   520
Thy kinsmen hang their heads at this disdain,
Thy issue blurred with nameless bastardy;
And thou, the author of their obloquy,
    Shalt have thy trespass cited up in rhymes
    And sung by children in succeeding times.   525

"But if thou yield, I rest thy secret friend;
The fault unknown is as a thought unacted.
A little harm done to a great good end
For lawful policy remains enacted.
The poisonous simple sometimes is compacted   530
    In a pure compound; being so applied,
    His venom in effect is purified.

507 **Coucheth** makes cower   509 **falchion** curved sword (with
play on "falcon")   521 **disdain** disgrace   529 **enacted** recorded
530 **simple** medicine   530 **compacted** compounded

"Then, for thy husband and thy children's sake,
Tender my suit; bequeath not to their lot
535 The shame that from them no device can take,
The blemish that will never be forgot;
Worse than a slavish wipe or birth-hour's blot;
    For marks descried in men's nativity
    Are nature's faults, not their own infamy."

540 Here with a cockatrice' dead-killing eye
He rouseth up himself and makes a pause;
While she, the picture of pure piety,
Like a white hind under the gripe's sharp claws,
Pleads, in a wilderness where are no laws,
545   To the rough beast that knows no gentle right
    Nor aught obeys but his foul appetite.

But when a black-faced cloud the world doth threat,
In his dim mist th' aspiring mountains hiding,
From earth's dark womb some gentle gust doth get,
550 Which blows these pitchy vapors from their biding,
Hind'ring their present fall by this dividing,
    So his unhallowed haste her words delays,
    And moody Pluto winks while Orpheus plays.

Yet, foul night-waking cat, he doth but dally,
555 While in his hold-fast foot the weak mouse panteth.
Her sad behavior feeds his vulture folly,
A swallowing gulf that even in plenty wanteth.
His ear her prayers admits, but his heart granteth
    No penetrable entrance to her plaining.
560   Tears harden lust, though marble wear with raining.

534 **Tender** regard   537 **slavish wipe** i.e., brand mark on a slave
537 **birth-hour's blot** birth mark   540 **cockatrice'** basilisk's
(mythical serpent which killed with a glance)   543 **hind** doe   543
gripe's griffin's (?) eagle's (?)   549 **doth get** makes its way   551
present immediate   553 **Pluto ... Orpheus** Pluto, the ruler of the
underworld, charmed by Orpheus' music, shut his eyes and allowed
Orpheus to lead his wife, Eurydice, back toward the world   556 **vul-
ture folly** ravenous madness   557 **wanteth** hungers   559 **plain-
ing** lament

Her pity-pleading eyes are sadly fixèd
In the remorseless wrinkles of his face.
Her modest eloquence with sighs is mixèd,
Which to her oratory adds more grace.
She puts the period often from his place,   565
    And midst the sentence so her accent breaks
    That twice she doth begin ere once she speaks.

She conjures him by high almighty Jove,
By knighthood, gentry, and sweet friendship's oath,
By her untimely tears, her husband's love,   570
By holy human law and common troth,
By heaven and earth, and all the power of both,
    That to his borrowed bed he make retire
    And stoop to honor, not to foul desire.

Quoth she, "Reward not hospitality   575
With such black payment as thou hast pretended;
Mud not the fountain that gave drink to thee;
Mar not the thing that cannot be amended.
End thy ill aim before thy shoot be ended.
    He is no woodman that doth bend his bow   580
    To strike a poor unseasonable doe.

"My husband is thy friend; for his sake spare me.
Thyself art mighty; for thine own sake leave me.
Myself a weakling; do not then ensnare me.
Thou look'st not like deceit; do not deceive me.   585
My sighs like whirlwinds labor hence to heave thee.
    If ever man were moved with woman's moans,
    Be movèd with my tears, my sighs, my groans;

562 **remorseless wrinkles** pitiless frowns   565 **She puts ... place**
she often makes a pause in the middle of a sentence   566 **accent**
speech   574 **stoop to** submit to   576 **pretended** proposed   579
shoot act of shooting (with pun on "suit"?)   580 **woodman** hunter
586 **heave** move

"All which together, like a troubled ocean,
590   Beat at thy rocky and wrack-threat'ning heart,
To soften it with their continual motion;
For stones dissolved to water do convert.
O, if no harder than a stone thou art,
      Melt at my tears and be compassionate!
595   Soft pity enters at an iron gate.

"In Tarquin's likeness I did entertain thee;
Hast thou put on his shape to do him shame?
To all the host of heaven I complain me.
Thou wrong'st his honor, wound'st his princely name.
600   Thou art not what thou seem'st; and if the same,
      Thou seem'st not what thou art, a god, a king;
      For kings like gods should govern everything.

"How will thy shame be seeded in thine age
When thus thy vices bud before thy spring?
605   If in thy hope thou dar'st do such outrage,
What dar'st thou not when once thou art a king?
O, be rememb'red, no outrageous thing
      From vassal actors can be wiped away;
      Then kings' misdeeds cannot be hid in clay.

610   "This deed will make thee only loved for fear;
But happy monarchs still are feared for love.
With foul offenders thou perforce must bear
When they in thee the like offenses prove.
If but for fear of this, thy will remove;
615   For princes are the glass, the school, the book,
      Where subjects' eyes do learn, do read, do look.

592 **convert** change   603 **seeded** matured   608 **vassal actors**
i.e., subjects, acting on orders   609 **in clay** i.e., in death   614 **If but
for** if only for   614 **thy will remove** dissuade your lust   615 **glass**
looking glass

"And wilt thou be the school where Lust shall learn?
Must he in thee read lectures of such shame?
Wilt thou be glass wherein it shall discern
Authority for sin, warrant for blame,   620
To privilege dishonor in thy name?
    Thou back'st reproach against long-living laud
    And mak'st fair reputation but a bawd.

"Hast thou command? By him that gave it thee,
From a pure heart command thy rebel will!   625
Draw not thy sword to guard iniquity,
For it was lent thee all that brood to kill.
Thy princely office how canst thou fulfill
    When, patterned by thy fault, foul Sin may say,
    He learned to sin, and thou didst teach the way?   630

"Think but how vile a spectacle it were
To view thy present trespass in another.
Men's faults do seldom to themselves appear;
Their own transgressions partially they smother.
This guilt would seem death-worthy in thy brother.   635
    O, how are they wrapped in with infamies
    That from their own misdeeds askaunce their eyes!

"To thee, to thee, my heaved-up hands appeal,
Not to seducing lust, thy rash relier.
I sue for exiled majesty's repeal;   640
Let him return, and flatt'ring thoughts retire.
His true respect will prison false desire
    And wipe the dim mist from thy doting eyne,
    That thou shalt see thy state, and pity mine."

---

622 **Thou back'st** you support   622 **laud** praise   624 **him** i.e.,
God   637 **askaunce** turn aside   639 **lust, thy rash relier** i.e., lust
which you rashly rely on   640 **repeal** return from exile   642 **re-
spect** respectfulness   642 **prison** imprison   643 **eyne** eyes

645 "Have done," quoth he. "My uncontrollèd tide
    Turns not, but swells the higher by this let.
    Small lights are soon blown out; huge fires abide
    And with the wind in greater fury fret.
    The petty streams that pay a daily debt
650   To their salt sovereign with their fresh falls' haste,
      Add to his flow, but alter not his taste."

    "Thou art," quoth she, "a sea, a sovereign king;
    And, lo, there falls into thy boundless flood
    Black lust, dishonor, shame, misgoverning,
655 Who seek to stain the ocean of thy blood.
    If all these petty ills shall change thy good,
      Thy sea within a puddle's womb is hearsèd,
      And not the puddle in thy sea dispersèd.

    "So shall these slaves be king, and thou their slave;
660 Thou nobly base, they basely dignified;
    Thou their fair life, and they thy fouler grave;
    Thou loathèd in their shame, they in thy pride.
    The lesser thing should not the greater hide.
      The cedar stoops not to the base shrub's foot,
665   But low shrubs wither at the cedar's root.

    "So let thy thoughts, low vassals to thy state"—
    "No more," quoth he. "By heaven, I will not hear
      thee!
    Yield to my love; if not, enforcèd hate,
    Instead of love's coy touch, shall rudely tear thee.
670 That done, despitefully I mean to bear thee
      Unto the base bed of some rascal groom,
      To be thy partner in this shameful doom."

---

646 **let** hindrance   650 **salt sovereign** i.e., the ocean   650 **falls'** flows'   657 **hearsèd** entombed   669 **coy** gentle   670 **despitefully** cruelly

This said, he sets his foot upon the light,
For light and lust are deadly enemies;
Shame folded up in blind concealing night,   675
When most unseen, then most doth tyrannize.
The wolf hath seized his prey; the poor lamb cries,
     Till with her own white fleece her voice controled
     Entombs her outcry in her lips' sweet fold;

For with the nightly linen that she wears   680
He pens her piteous clamors in her head,
Cooling his hot face in the chastest tears
That ever modest eyes with sorrow shed.
O, that prone lust should stain so pure a bed,
     The spots whereof, could weeping purify,   685
     Her tears should drop on them perpetually!

But she hath lost a dearer thing than life,
And he hath won what he would lose again.
This forcèd league doth force a further strife;
This momentary joy breeds months of pain;   690
This hot desire converts to cold disdain;
     Pure Chastity is rifled of her store,
     And Lust, the thief, far poorer than before.

Look as the full-fed hound or gorgèd hawk,
Unapt for tender smell or speedy flight,   695
Make slow pursuit, or altogether balk
The prey wherein by nature they delight,
So surfeit-taking Tarquin fares this night:
     His taste delicious, in digestion souring,
     Devours his will, that lived by foul devouring.   700

678 **white fleece** i.e., bedclothes   678 **controled** overwhelmed
680 **nightly linen** turban (?)   684 **prone** (1) impulsive (2) prostrate
695 **tender smell** weak scent   696 **balk** neglect to pursue

O, deeper sin than bottomless conceit
Can comprehend in still imagination!
Drunken Desire must vomit his receipt
Ere he can see his own abomination.
705   While Lust is in his pride, no exclamation
      Can curb his heat or rein his rash desire
      Till, like a jade, Self-will himself doth tire.

And then with lank and lean discolored cheek,
With heavy eye, knit brow, and strengthless pace,
710   Feeble Desire, all recreant, poor, and meek,
      Like to a bankrout beggar wails his case.
      The flesh being proud, Desire doth fight with Grace,
        For there it revels; and when that decays,
        The guilty rebel for remission prays.

715   So fares it with this fault-full lord of Rome,
Who this accomplishment so hotly chasèd;
For now against himself he sounds this doom,
That through the length of times he stands disgracèd.
Besides, his soul's fair temple is defacèd;
720   To whose weak ruins muster troops of cares,
      To ask the spotted princess how she fares.

She says her subjects with foul insurrection
Have battered down her consecrated wall,
And by their mortal fault brought in subjection
725   Her immortality and made her thrall
To living death and pain perpetual;
      Which in her prescience she controllèd still,
      But her foresight could not forestall their will.

701 **bottomless conceit** infinite imagination   703 **his receipt** what
it has received 705 **exclamation** exhortation 710 **recreant**
cowed 713 **that** i.e., lust 721 **the spotted princess** i.e., Tar-
quin's defiled soul 722 **subjects** i.e., the senses 724 **mortal**
deadly 727 **Which** i.e., her subjects 727 **prescience** foreknowl-
edge (i.e., in theory)

Ev'n in this thought through the dark night he stealeth,
A captive victor that hath lost in gain;   730
Bearing away the wound that nothing healeth,
The scar that will despite of cure remain;
Leaving his spoil perplexed in greater pain.
    She bears the load of lust he left behind,
    And he the burden of a guilty mind.   735

He like a thievish dog creeps sadly thence;
She like a wearied lamb lies panting there.
He scowls, and hates himself for his offense;
She desperate with her nails her flesh doth tear.
He faintly flies, sweating with guilty fear;   740
    She stays, exclaiming on the direful night;
    He runs, and chides his vanished loathed delight.

He thence departs a heavy convertite;
She there remains a hopeless castaway.
He in his speed looks for the morning light;   745
She prays she never may behold the day,
"For day," quoth she, "night's scapes doth open lay,
    And my true eyes have never practiced how
    To cloak offenses with a cunning brow.

"They think not but that every eye can see   750
The same disgrace which they themselves behold;
And therefore would they still in darkness be,
To have their unseen sin remain untold;
For they their guilt with weeping will unfold
    And grave, like water that doth eat in steel,   755
    Upon my cheeks what helpless shame I feel."

Here she exclaims against repose and rest,
And bids her eyes hereafter still be blind.
She wakes her heart by beating on her breast,
And bids it leap from thence, where it may find   760
Some purer chest to close so pure a mind.
    Frantic with grief thus breathes she forth her spite
    Against the unseen secrecy of night:

733 **spoil** victim 743 **heavy convertite** sad penitent 744 **castaway** lost soul 747 **scapes** transgressions 755 **grave** engrave 755 **water** i.e., acid 761 **close** enclose

"O comfort-killing Night, image of hell,
765 Dim register and notary of shame,
Black stage for tragedies and murders fell,
Vast sin-concealing chaos, nurse of blame,
Blind muffled bawd, dark harbor for defame!
      Grim cave of death, whisp'ring conspirator
770   With close-tongued treason and the ravisher!

"O hateful, vaporous, and foggy Night,
Since thou art guilty of my cureless crime,
Muster thy mists to meet the eastern light,
Make war against proportioned course of time;
775 Or if thou wilt permit the sun to climb
      His wonted height, yet ere he go to bed,
      Knit poisonous clouds about his golden head.

"With rotten damps ravish the morning air;
Let their exhaled unwholesome breaths make sick
780 The life of purity, the supreme fair,
Ere he arrive his weary noontide prick;
And let thy musty vapors march so thick
      That in their smoky ranks his smoth'red light
      May set at noon and make perpetual night.

785 "Were Tarquin Night, as he is but Night's child,
The silver-shining queen he would distain;
Her twinkling handmaids too, by him defiled,
Through Night's black bosom should not peep again.
So should I have co-partners in my pain;
790   And fellowship in woe doth woe assuage,
      As palmers' chat makes short their pilgrimage;

---

765 **notary** recorder   768 **defame** disgrace   770 **close-tongued**
secretive   774 **proportioned** orderly   780 **the supreme fair** i.e.,
the sun   781 **Ere he arrive ... prick** before he reaches wearied at
the point of noon (on a sun dial)   785 **Night's child** i.e., wicked
786 **distain** defile   791 **palmers'** pilgrims' (those who had been to
the Holy Land wore a palm leaf)

"Where now I have no one to blush with me,
To cross their arms and hang their heads with mine,
To mask their brows and hide their infamy;
But I alone, alone must sit and pine,   795
Seasoning the earth with show'rs of silver brine,
    Mingling my talk with tears, my grief with groans,
    Poor wasting monuments of lasting moans.

"O Night, thou furnace of foul reeking smoke,
Let not the jealous Day behold that face   800
Which underneath thy black all-hiding cloak
Immodestly lies martyred with disgrace!
Keep still possession of thy gloomy place,
    That all the faults which in thy reign are made
    May likewise be sepulchered in thy shade!   805

"Make me not object to the telltale Day.
The light will show, charactered in my brow,
The story of sweet chastity's decay,
The impious breach of holy wedlock vow.
Yea, the illiterate, that know not how   810
    To cipher what is writ in learnèd books,
    Will quote my loathsome trespass in my looks.

"The nurse to still her child will tell my story
And fright her crying babe with Tarquin's name.
The orator to deck his oratory   815
Will couple my reproach to Tarquin's shame.
Feast-finding minstrels, tuning my defame,
    Will tie the hearers to attend each line,
    How Tarquin wrongèd me, I Collatine.

792 **Where now** whereas   793 **To cross their arms** (folded arms
were a sign of melancholy)   794 **To mask their brows** (a hat pulled
down over one's face was a sign of melancholy)   800 **jealous**
watchful   807 **charactered** lettered (accent on second syllable)
811 **cipher** decipher   812 **quote** mark   818 **tie** hold

820 "Let my good name, that senseless reputation,
    For Collatine's dear love be kept unspotted.
    If that be made a theme for disputation,
    The branches of another root are rotted,
    And undeserved reproach to him allotted
825   That is as clear from this attaint of mine
        As I ere this was pure to Collatine.

    "O unseen shame, invisible disgrace!
    O unfelt sore, crest-wounding private scar!
    Reproach is stamped in Collatinus' face,
830 And Tarquin's eye may read the mot afar,
    How he in peace is wounded, not in war.
        Alas, how many bear such shameful blows
        Which not themselves, but he that gives them
            knows!

    "If, Collatine, thine honor lay in me,
835 From me by strong assault it is bereft;
    My honey lost, and I, a dronelike bee,
    Have no perfection of my summer left,
    But robbed and ransacked by injurious theft.
        In thy weak hive a wand'ring wasp hath crept
840   And sucked the honey which thy chaste bee kept.

    "Yet am I guilty of thy honor's wrack;
    Yet for thy honor did I entertain him:
    Coming from thee, I could not put him back,
    For it had been dishonor to disdain him.
845 Besides, of weariness he did complain him
        And talked of virtue: O unlooked-for evil,
        When virtue is profaned in such a devil!

820 **senseless** (1) impalpable (2) free from sensuality   825 **attaint**
disgrace   828 **crest-wounding** i.e., disgraceful to the family crest
830 **mot** motto (with allusion to the parable of the mote and the beam,
Matthew 7:3)

"Why should the worm intrude the maiden bud?
Or hateful cuckoos hatch in sparrows' nests?
Or toads infect fair founts with venom mud?   850
Or tyrant folly lurk in gentle breasts?
Or kings be breakers of their own behests?
    But no perfection is so absolute
    That some impurity doth not pollute.

"The agèd man that coffers up his gold   855
Is plagued with cramps and gouts and painful fits,
And scarce hath eyes his treasure to behold,
But like still-pining Tantalus he sits
And useless barns the harvest of his wits,
    Having no other pleasure of his gain   860
    But torment that it cannot cure his pain.

"So then he hath it when he cannot use it,
And leaves it to be mast'red by his young,
Who in their pride do presently abuse it;
Their father was too weak, and they too strong,   865
To hold their cursèd-blessèd fortune long.
    The sweets we wish for turn to loathèd sours
    Even in the moment that we call them ours.

"Unruly blasts wait on the tender spring;
Unwholesome weeds take root with precious flow'rs;   870
The adder hisses where the sweet birds sing;
What virtue breeds iniquity devours.
We have no good that we can say is ours,
    But ill-annexèd opportunity
    Or kills his life or else his quality.   875

852 **behests** commands   858 **Tantalus** (in Hades, Tantalus was
surrounded by food and drink that he could never touch)   859 **barns**
stores   864 **presently** immediately   874 **ill-annexèd opportunity**
disastrously connected chance   875 **Or . . . quality** either kills its
(good's) life or its nature

"O Opportunity, thy guilt is great!
'Tis thou that execut'st the traitor's treason;
Thou sets the wolf where he the lamb may get;
Whoever plots the sin, thou point'st the season.
880   'Tis thou that spurn'st at right, at law, at reason;
    And in thy shady cell, where none may spy him,
    Sits Sin, to seize the souls that wander by him.

"Thou mak'st the vestal violate her oath;
Thou blow'st the fire when temperance is thawed;
885   Thou smother'st honesty, thou murd'rest troth.
Thou foul abettor, thou notorious bawd,
Thou plantest scandal and displacest laud.
    Thou ravisher, thou traitor, thou false thief,
    Thy honey turns to gall, thy joy to grief.

890   "Thy secret pleasure turns to open shame,
Thy private feasting to a public fast,
Thy smoothing titles to a ragged name,
Thy sug'red tongue to bitter wormwood taste:
Thy violent vanities can never last.
895   How comes it then, vile Opportunity,
    Being so bad, such numbers seek for thee?

"When wilt thou be the humble suppliant's friend,
And bring him where his suit may be obtainèd?
When wilt thou sort an hour great strifes to end?
900   Or free that soul which wretchedness hath chainèd?
Give physic to the sick, ease to the painèd?
    The poor, lame, blind, halt, creep, cry out for thee;
    But they ne'er meet with Opportunity.

"The patient dies while the physician sleeps;
905   The orphan pines while the oppressor feeds;
Justice is feasting while the widow weeps;
Advice is sporting while infection breeds.
Thou grant'st no time for charitable deeds:
    Wrath, envy, treason, rape, and murder's rages,
910   Thy heinous hours wait on them as their pages.

887 **laud** praise 892 **smoothing** flattering 899 **sort** choose
907 **Advice** (medical) knowledge

"When Truth and Virtue have to do with thee,
A thousand crosses keep them from thy aid.
They buy thy help; but Sin ne'er gives a fee,
He gratis comes; and thou art well apaid
As well to hear as grant what he hath said.   915
    My Collatine would else have come to me
    When Tarquin did, but he was stayed by thee.

"Guilty thou art of murder and of theft,
Guilty of perjury and subornation,
Guilty of treason, forgery, and shift,   920
Guilty of incest, that abomination:
An accessary by thine inclination
    To all sins past and all that are to come,
    From the creation to the general doom.

"Misshapen Time, copesmate of ugly Night,   925
Swift subtle post, carrier of grisly care,
Eater of youth, false slave to false delight,
Base watch of woes, sin's packhorse, virtue's snare!
Thou nursest all, and murd'rest all that are.
    O, hear me then, injurious shifting Time;   930
    Be guilty of my death, since of my crime.

"Why hath thy servant Opportunity
Betrayed the hours thou gav'st me to repose?
Canceled my fortunes, and enchainèd me
To endless date of never-ending woes?   935
Time's office is to fine the hate of foes,
    To eat up errors by opinion bred,
    Not spend the dowry of a lawful bed.

912 **crosses** hindrances   919 **subornation** bribing someone to
commit a crime   920 **shift** cheating   925 **copesmate** companion,
paramour   926 **subtle post** sly post-rider   928 **watch** watchman
936 **fine** end

"Time's glory is to calm contending kings,
940 To unmask falsehood and bring truth to light,
To stamp the seal of time in agèd things,
To wake the morn and sentinel the night,
To wrong the wronger till he render right,
       To ruinate proud buildings with thy hours,
945   And smear with dust their glitt'ring golden tow'rs;

"To fill with wormholes stately monuments,
To feed oblivion with decay of things,
To blot old books and alter their contents,
To pluck the quills from ancient ravens' wings,
950 To dry the old oak's sap and cherish springs,
       To spoil antiquities of hammered steel
       And turn the giddy round of Fortune's wheel;

"To show the beldame daughters of her daughter,
To make the child a man, the man a child,
955 To slay the tiger that doth live by slaughter,
To tame the unicorn and lion wild,
To mock the subtle in themselves beguiled,
       To cheer the ploughman with increaseful crops
       And waste huge stones with little water-drops.

960 "Why work'st thou mischief in thy pilgrimage,
Unless thou couldst return to make amends?
One poor retiring minute in an age
Would purchase thee a thousand thousand friends,
Lending him wit that to bad debtors lends.
965   O this dread night, wouldst thou one hour come
         back,
       I could prevent this storm and shun thy wrack!

942 **sentinel** guard   944 **ruinate** reduce to ruin   950 **cherish
springs** renew (1) the water of springs, or (2) young saplings (i.e.,
new growth of any kind)   953 **beldame** old woman   959 **waste**
wear away   962 **retiring** returning

"Thou ceaseless lackey to Eternity,
With some mischance cross Tarquin in his flight.
Devise extremes beyond extremity
To make him curse this cursèd crimeful night.   970
Let ghastly shadows his lewd eyes affright,
    And the dire thought of his committed evil
    Shape every bush a hideous shapeless devil.

"Disturb his hours of rest with restless trances;
Afflict him in his bed with bedrid groans;   975
Let there bechance him pitiful mischances
To make him moan, but pity not his moans.
Stone him with hard'nèd hearts harder than stones,
    And let mild women to him lose their mildness,
    Wilder to him than tigers in their wildness.   980

"Let him have time to tear his curlèd hair,
Let him have time against himself to rave,
Let him have time of Time's help to despair,
Let him have time to live a loathèd slave,
Let him have time a beggar's orts to crave,   985
    And time to see one that by alms doth live
    Disdain to him disdainèd scraps to give.

"Let him have time to see his friends his foes
And merry fools to mock at him resort;
Let him have time to mark how slow time goes   990
In time of sorrow, and how swift and short
His time of folly and his time of sport;
    And ever let his unrecalling crime
    Have time to wail th' abusing of his time.

967 **ceaseless lackey** ever-present servant   985 **orts** scraps   993
unrecalling irrevocable

995 "O Time, thou tutor both to good and bad,
    Teach me to curse him that thou taught'st this ill.
    At his own shadow let the thief run mad,
    Himself himself seek every hour to kill.
    Such wretched hands such wretched blood should
        spill,
1000   For who so base would such an office have
        As sland'rous deathsman to so base a slave?

    "The baser is he, coming from a king,
    To shame his hope with deeds degenerate.
    The mightier man, the mightier is the thing
1005 That makes him honored or begets him hate;
    For greatest scandal waits on greatest state.
        The moon being clouded presently is missed,
        But little stars may hide them when they list.

    "The crow may bathe his coal-black wings in mire
1010 And unperceived fly with the filth away;
    But if the like the snow-white swan desire,
    The stain upon his silver down will stay.
    Poor grooms are sightless night, kings glorious day;
        Gnats are unnoted wheresoe'er they fly,
1015   But eagles gazed upon with every eye.

    "Out, idle words, servants to shallow fools,
    Unprofitable sounds, weak arbitrators!
    Busy yourselves in skill-contending schools;
    Debate where leisure serves with dull debaters;
1020 To trembling clients be you mediators:
        For me, I force not argument a straw,
        Since that my case is past the help of law.

1001 **sland'rous deathsman** disgraced executioner   1003 **hope**
expectations (as heir)   1013 **grooms** servants   1013 **sightless** in-
visible   1017 **arbitrators** arbiters (or compromisers)   1018 **in
skill-contending schools** i.e., in mere debates   1020 **clients** suitors
at law   1021 **force not argument a straw** care not a straw for argu-
ment

"In vain I rail at Opportunity,
At Time, at Tarquin, and uncheerful Night;
In vain I cavil with mine infamy;   *1025*
In vain I spurn at my confirmed despite:
This helpless smoke of words doth me no right.
    The remedy indeed to do me good
    Is to let forth my foul defilèd blood.

"Poor hand, why quiver'st thou at this decree?   *1030*
Honor thyself to rid me of this shame;
For if I die, my honor lives in thee;
But if I live, thou liv'st in my defame.
Since thou couldst not defend thy loyal dame
    And wast afeared to scratch her wicked foe,   *1035*
    Kill both thyself and her for yielding so."

This said, from her betumbled couch she starteth,
To find some desp'rate instrument of death;
But this no slaughterhouse no tool imparteth
To make more vent for passage of her breath,   *1040*
Which, thronging through her lips, so vanisheth
    As smoke from Aetna that in air consumes
    Or that which from dischargèd cannon fumes.

"In vain," quoth she, "I live, and seek in vain
Some happy mean to end a hapless life.   *1045*
I feared by Tarquin's falchion to be slain,
Yet for the selfsame purpose seek a knife;
But when I feared I was a loyal wife.
    So am I now—O no, that cannot be:
    Of that true type hath Tarquin rifled me.   *1050*

1026 **spurn** kick 1026 **despite** wrong 1027 **smoke of words**
mere talk 1039 **imparteth** provides 1050 **true type** stamp

"O, that is gone for which I sought to live,
And therefore now I need not fear to die.
To clear this spot by death, at least I give
A badge of fame to slander's livery,
1055 A dying life to living infamy.
  Poor helpless help, the treasure stol'n away,
  To burn the guiltless casket where it lay!

"Well, well, dear Collatine, thou shalt not know
The stainèd taste of violated troth.
1060 I will not wrong thy true affection so,
To flatter thee with an infringèd oath.
This bastard graff shall never come to growth:
  He shall not boast who did thy stock pollute
  That thou art doting father of his fruit.

1065 "Nor shall he smile at thee in secret thought,
Nor laugh with his companions at thy state;
But thou shalt know thy int'rest was not bought
Basely with gold, but stol'n from forth thy gate.
For me, I am the mistress of my fate,
1070   And with my trespass never will dispense
  Till life to death acquit my forced offense.

"I will not poison thee with my attaint
Nor fold my fault in cleanly coined excuses;
My sable ground of sin I will not paint
1075 To hide the truth of this false night's abuses.
My tongue shall utter all; mine eyes, like sluices,
  As from a mountain spring that feeds a dale,
  Shall gush pure streams to purge my impure tale."

1054 **badge** mark (crest, coat of arms) worn on a servant's sleeve
1054 **livery** garment   1062 **graff** graft, shoot   1067 **int'rest**
property   1070 **dispense** pardon   1074 **sable** black

By this lamenting Philomēl had ended
The well-tuned warble of her nightly sorrow,   1080
And solemn night with slow sad gait descended
To ugly hell; when, lo, the blushing morrow
Lends light to all fair eyes that light will borrow;
　　But cloudy Lucrece shames herself to see
　　And therefore still in night would cloist'red be.   1085

Revealing day through every cranny spies
And seems to point her out where she sits weeping;
To whom she sobbing speaks, "O eye of eyes
Why pry'st thou through my window? Leave thy
　　peeping.
Mock with thy tickling beams eyes that are sleeping.   1090
　　Brand not my forehead with thy piercing light.
　　For day hath naught to do what's done by night."

Thus cavils she with everything she sees.
True grief is fond and testy as a child,
Who wayward once, his mood with naught agrees.   1095
Old woes, not infant sorrows, bear them mild:
Continuance tames the one; the other wild,
　　Like an unpracticed swimmer plunging still,
　　With too much labor drowns for want of skill.

So she, deep drenchèd in a sea of care,   1100
Holds disputation with each thing she views,
And to herself all sorrow doth compare;
No object but her passion's strength renews;
And as one shifts, another straight ensues.
　　Sometime her grief is dumb and hath no words;   1105
　　Sometime 'tis mad and too much talk affords.

1079 **Philomel** the nightingale (who, according to legend, had origi-
nally been a woman, ravished by Tereus—see lines 1128-34)   1090
tickling lightly touching   1094 **fond and testy** foolish and irritable
1095 **wayward once** once becoming angry   1096 **them** themselves
1104 **straight ensues** straightway follows

The little birds that tune their morning's joy
Make her moans mad with their sweet melody:
For mirth doth search the bottom of annoy;
1110 Sad souls are slain in merry company;
Grief best is pleased with grief's society:
    True sorrow then is feelingly suffised
    When with like semblance it is sympathized.

'Tis double death to drown in ken of shore;
1115 He ten times pines that pines beholding food;
To see the salve doth make the wound ache more;
Great grief grieves most at that would do it good;
Deep woes roll forward like a gentle flood,
    Who, being stopped, the bounding banks o'erflows;
1120   Grief dallied with, nor law nor limit knows.

"You mocking birds," quoth she, "your tunes entomb
Within your hollow swelling feath'red breasts,
And in my hearing be you mute and dumb;
My restless discord loves no stops nor rests.
1125 A woeful hostess brooks not merry guests.
    Relish your nimble notes to pleasing ears;
    Distress likes dumps when time is kept with tears.

"Come, Philomel, that sing'st of ravishment,
Make thy sad grove in my disheveled hair.
1130 As the dank earth weeps at thy languishment,
So I at each sad strain will strain a tear
And with deep groans the diapason bear;
    For burden-wise I'll hum on Tarquin still,
    While thou on Tereus descants better skill.

1107 **tune** sing   1109 **search the bottom of annoy** pierce to the depths of grief   1112 **suffised** contented   1114 **ken** sight   1120 **dallied with** trifled with   1124 **stops, rests** (1) cessation of discord (2) musical pauses   1126 **Relish** make pleasant (sauce)   1127 **dumps** slow mournful tunes   1132 **diapason** bass accompaniment   1133 **burden-wise** a burden was (1) a bass accompaniment (2) the refrain of a song   1134 **descants better skill** (1) sings better (2) sings more intricately

"And whiles against a thorn thou bear'st thy part   *1135*
To keep thy sharp woes waking, wretched I,
To imitate thee well, against my heart
Will fix a sharp knife to affright mine eye,
Who if it wink shall thereon fall and die.
    These means, as frets upon an instrument,   *1140*
    Shall tune our heartstrings to true languishment.

"And for, poor bird, thou sing'st not in the day,
As shaming any eye should thee behold,
Some dark deep desert, seated from the way,
That knows not parching heat nor freezing cold,   *1145*
Will we find out; and there we will unfold
    To creatures stern sad tunes, to change their kinds.
    Since men prove beasts, let beasts bear gentle
        minds."

As the poor frighted deer that stands at gaze,
Wildly determining which way to fly,   *1150*
Or one encompassed with a winding maze,
That cannot tread the way out readily;
So with herself is she in mutiny,
    To live or die which of the twain were better,
    When life is shamed and death reproach's debtor.   *1155*

"To kill myself," quoth she, "alack, what were it
But with my body my poor soul's pollution?
They that lose half with greater patience bear it
Than they whose whole is swallowed in confusion.
That mother tries a merciless conclusion   *1160*
    Who, having two sweet babes, when death takes
      one,
    Will slay the other and be nurse to none.

1139 **Who** which (i.e., her heart)   1139 **it wink** i.e., her eye closes
1140 **frets** ridges fastened across the fingerboard of a stringed instrument to regulate fingering   1142 **And for** and because   1143 **shaming** being ashamed   1144 **desert, seated from the way** deserted place situated away from a path   1147 **kinds** natures   1149 **at gaze** i.e., bewildered   1155 **death reproach's debtor** i.e., her death (suicide) would be the occasion of reproach   1159 **confusion** destruction   1160 **conclusion** experiment

"My body or my soul, which was the dearer
When the one pure, the other made divine?
1165 Whose love of either to myself was nearer
When both were kept for heaven and Collatine?
Ay me, the bark pilled from the lofty pine,
    His leaves will wither and his sap decay:
    So must my soul, her bark being pilled away.

"Her house is sacked, her quiet interrupted,
Her mansion battered by the enemy;
Her sacred temple spotted, spoiled, corrupted,
Grossly engirt with daring infamy.
Then let it not be called impiety
1175   If in this blemished fort I make some hole
    Through which I may convey this troubled soul.

"Yet die I will not till my Collatine
Have heard the cause of my untimely death,
That he may vow, in that sad hour of mine,
1180 Revenge on him that made me stop my breath.
My stainèd blood to Tarquin I'll bequeath,
    Which, by him tainted, shall for him be spent
    And as his due writ in my testament.

"My honor I'll bequeath unto the knife
1185 That wounds my body so dishonorèd.
'Tis honor to deprive dishonored life:
The one will live, the other being dead.
So of shame's ashes shall my fame be bred,
    For in my death I murder shameful scorn;
1190   My shame so dead, mine honor is new born.

"Dear lord of that dear jewel I have lost,
What legacy shall I bequeath to thee?
My resolution, love, shall be thy boast,
By whose example thou revenged mayst be.
1195 How Tarquin must be used, read it in me:
    Myself thy friend will kill myself thy foe,
    And for my sake serve thou false Tarquin so.

1167 **pilled** peeled 1173 **engirt** besieged 1175 **fort** i.e., her
body 1186 **deprive** take away

"This brief abridgment of my will I make:
My soul and body to the skies and ground;
My resolution, husband, do thou take;   1200
Mine honor be the knife's that makes my wound;
My shame be his that did my fame confound;
    And all my fame that lives disbursèd be
    To those that live and think no shame of me.

"Thou, Collatine, shalt oversee this will.   1205
How was I overseen that thou shalt see it!
My blood shall wash the slander of mine ill;
My life's foul deed my life's fair end shall free it.
Faint not, faint heart, but stoutly say, 'So be it.'
    Yield to my hand, my hand shall conquer thee: 1210
    Thou dead, both die, and both shall victors be."

This plot of death when sadly she had laid
And wiped the brinish pearl from her bright eyes,
With untuned tongue she hoarsely calls her maid,
Whose swift obedience to her mistress hies;   1215
For fleet-winged duty with thought's feathers flies.
    Poor Lucrece' cheeks unto her maid seem so
    As winter meads when sun doth melt their snow.

Her mistress she doth give demure good-morrow
With soft-slow tongue, true mark of modesty,   1220
And sorts a sad look to her lady's sorrow,
For why her face wore sorrow's livery;
But durst not ask of her audaciously
    Why her two suns were cloud-eclipsèd so,
    Nor why her fair cheeks overwashed with woe.   1225

1205 **oversee** execute   1206 **overseen** deceived   1207 **wash**
wash away   1207 **ill** sin   1214 **untuned** discordant   1219 **de-
mure** modest   1221 **sorts** fits   1222 **For why** because

But as the earth doth weep, the sun being set,
Each flower moist'ned like a melting eye,
Even so the maid with swelling drops 'gan wet
Her circled eyne, enforced by sympathy
1230 Of those fair suns set in her mistress' sky,
    Who in a salt-waved ocean quench their light,
    Which makes the maid weep like the dewy night.

A pretty while these pretty creatures stand,
Like ivory conduits coral cisterns filling.
1235 One justly weeps, the other takes in hand
No cause, but company, of her drops spilling.
Their gentle sex to weep are often willing,
    Grieving themselves to guess at others' smarts,
    And then they drown their eyes or break their
        hearts.

1240 For men have marble, women waxen minds,
And therefore are they formed as marble will;
The weak oppressed, th' impression of strange kinds
Is formed in them by force, by fraud, or skill.
Then call them not the authors of their ill,
1245   No more than wax shall be accounted evil
    Wherein is stamped the semblance of a devil.

Their smoothness, like a goodly champain plain,
Lays open all the little worms that creep;
In men, as in a rough-grown grove, remain
1250 Cave-keeping evils that obscurely sleep.
Through crystal walls each little mote will peep.
    Though men can cover crimes with bold stern looks,
    Poor women's faces are their own faults' books.

1229 **circled eyne** rounded eyes (?) eyes encircled with dark rings (?)
1234 **coral cisterns** i.e., their reddened eyes (?) 1235 **takes in hand** acknowledges 1241 **will** i.e., as marble will have them formed
1247 **champain** level 1248 **Lays open** reveals 1250 **Cave-keeping** dwelling in caves 1251 **mote** speck

No man inveigh against the with'red flow'r,
But chide rough winter that the flow'r hath killed. *1255*
Nor that devoured, but that which doth devour,
Is worthy blame; O, let it not be hild
Poor women's faults that they are so fulfilled
    With men's abuses! those proud lords to blame
    Make weak-made women tenants to their shame. *1260*

The precedent whereof in Lucrece view,
Assailed by night with circumstances strong
Of present death, and shame that might ensue
By that her death, to do her husband wrong.
Such danger to resistance did belong *1265*
    That dying fear through all her body spread;
    And who cannot abuse a body dead?

By this, mild patience bid fair Lucrece speak
To the poor counterfeit of her complaining.
"My girl," quoth she, "on what occasion break *1270*
Those tears from thee that down thy cheeks are
    raining?
If thou dost weep for grief of my sustaining,
    Know, gentle wench, it small avails my mood;
    If tears could help, mine own would do me good.

"But tell me, girl, when went" (and there she stayed *1275*
Till after a deep groan) "Tarquin from hence?"
"Madam, ere I was up," replied the maid,
"The more to blame my sluggard negligence.
Yet with the fault I thus far can dispense:
    Myself was stirring ere the break of day, *1280*
    And ere I rose was Tarquin gone away.

1254 **No man** let no man   1257 **hild** held   1258 **fulfilled** filled
1261 **precedent** example 1266 **dying** i.e., unnerving 1269 **coun-
terfeit** image 1272 **of my sustaining** that I sustain 1273 **mood**
grief

"But, lady, if your maid may be so bold,
She would request to know your heaviness."
"O, peace," quoth Lucrece. "If it should be told,
1285 The repetition cannot make it less;
For more it is than I can well express,
    And that deep torture may be called a hell
    When more is felt than one hath power to tell.

"Go get me hither paper, ink, and pen;
1290 Yet save that labor, for I have them here.
What should I say? One of my husband's men
Bid thou be ready by and by to bear
A letter to my lord, my love, my dear.
    Bid him with speed prepare to carry it;
1295   The cause craves haste, and it will soon be writ."

Her maid is gone, and she prepares to write,
First hovering o'er the paper with her quill.
Conceit and grief an eager combat fight;
What wit sets down is blotted straight with will.
1300 This is too curious good, this blunt and ill.
    Much like a press of people at a door,
    Throng her inventions, which shall go before.

At last she thus begins: "Thou worthy lord
Of that unworthy wife that greeteth thee,
1305 Health to thy person! next vouchsafe t' afford
(If ever, love, thy Lucrece thou wilt see)
Some present speed to come and visit me.
    So, I commend me, from our house in grief.
    My woes are tedious, though my words are brief."

1283 **heaviness** cause of grief   1292 **by and by** immediately
1298 **Conceit** thought   1300 **curious** cleverly   1302 **which shall
go before** which one shall enter first

Here folds she up the tenure of her woe,   1310
Her certain sorrow writ uncertainly.
By this short schedule Collatine may know
Her grief, but not her grief's true quality;
She dares not thereof make discovery,
    Lest he should hold it her own gross abuse   1315
    Ere she with blood had stained her stained excuse.

Besides, the life and feeling of her passion
She hoards, to spend when he is by to hear her,
When sighs and groans and tears may grace the
        fashion
Of her disgrace, the better so to clear her   1320
From that suspicion which the world might bear her.
    To shun this blot, she would not blot the letter
    With words till action might become them better.

To see sad sights moves more than hear them told,
For then the eye interprets to the ear   1325
The heavy motion that it doth behold
When every part a part of woe doth bear.
'Tis but a part of sorrow that we hear.
    Deep sounds make lesser noise than shallow fords,
    And sorrow ebbs, being blown with wind of words.   1330

Her letter now is sealed, and on it writ,
"At Ardea to my lord with more than haste."
The post attends, and she delivers it,
Charging the sour-faced groom to hie as fast
As lagging fowls before the Northern blast;   1335
    Speed more than speed but dull and slow she
        deems:
    Extremity still urgeth such extremes.

1310 **tenure** statement 1312 **schedule** summary 1316 **her
stained excuse** her account of her stain 1317 **passion** suffering
1326 **heavy motion** melancholy action 1329 **sounds** soundings
(naval term) 1334 **sour-faced** sad-faced (?) long-faced (out of re-
spect)

The homely villain cursies to her low;
And, blushing on her, with a steadfast eye,
1340 Receives the scroll without or yea or no
And forth with bashful innocence doth hie.
But they whose guilt within their bosoms lie
    Imagine every eye beholds their blame,
    For Lucrece thought he blushed to see her shame,

1345 When, seely groom (God wot), it was defect
Of spirit, life, and bold audacity;
Such harmless creatures have a true respect
To talk in deeds, while others saucily
Promise more speed, but do it leisurely.
1350   Even so this pattern of the worn-out age
    Pawned honest looks, but laid no words to gage.

His kindled duty kindled her mistrust,
That two red fires in both their faces blazèd.
She thought he blushed as knowing Tarquin's lust,
1355 And, blushing with him, wistly on him gazèd;
Her earnest eye did make him more amazèd.
    The more she saw the blood his cheeks replenish,
    The more she thought he spied in her some blemish.

But long she thinks till he return again,
1360 And yet the duteous vassal scarce is gone;
The weary time she cannot entertain,
For now 'tis stale to sigh, to weep and groan:
So woe hath wearied woe, moan tirèd moan,
    That she her plaints a little while doth stay,
1365   Pausing for means to mourn some newer way.

1338 **homely villain cursies** simple servant bows   1339 **blushing on her** i.e., blushing toward her   1345 **seely** simple   1345 **wot** knows   1346 **life** liveliness   1347 **respect** aspect   1348 **To talk in deeds** to act and not to talk   1350 **worn-out** past   1351 **Pawned** pledged   1351 **gage** i.e., to bind him (as by an oath)   1355 **wistly** earnestly   1359 **long she thinks** i.e., she thinks time passes slowly   1361 **entertain** occupy   1364 **stay** stop

At last she calls to mind where hangs a piece
Of skillful painting, made for Priam's Troy,
Before the which is drawn the power of Greece,
For Helen's rape the city to destroy,
Threat'ning cloud-kissing Ilion with annoy;   1370
  Which the conceited painter drew so proud
  As heaven, it seemed, to kiss the turrets bowed.

A thousand lamentable objects there,
In scorn of nature, art gave lifeless life;
Many a dry drop seemed a weeping tear   1375
Shed for the slaught'red husband by the wife.
The red blood reeked, to show the painter's strife,
  And dying eyes gleamed forth their ashy lights,
  Like dying coals burnt out in tedious nights.

There might you see the laboring pioner   1380
Begrimed with sweat, and smearèd all with dust;
And from the tow'rs of Troy there would appear
The very eyes of men through loopholes thrust,
Gazing upon the Greeks with little lust:
  Such sweet observance in this work was had   1385
  That one might see those far-off eyes look sad.

In great commanders grace and majesty
You might behold triumphing in their faces;
In youth, quick bearing and dexterity;
And here and there the painter interlaces   1390
Pale cowards marching on with trembling paces,
  Which heartless peasants did so well resemble
  That one would swear he saw them quake and
    tremble.

1367 **made for** depicting 1367 **Priam's Troy** Priam was the king
of Troy during the Trojan War 1368 **is drawn the power of Greece**
the Greek army is assembled 1369 **Helen's rape** the abduction of
Helen 1370 **Ilion** Troy 1370 **annoy** destruction 1371 **con-
ceited** ingenious 1372 **As** that 1374 **In scorn of** to rival
1377 **strife** effort 1380 **pioner** engineer 1384 **lust** pleasure
1385 **sweet observance** loving accuracy 1389 **quick** lively
1392 **heartless** cowardly

In Ajax and Ulysses, O, what art
1395   Of physiognomy might one behold!
The face of either ciphered either's heart;
Their face their manners most expressly told:
In Ajax' eyes blunt rage and rigor rolled;
    But the mild glance that sly Ulysses lent
1400   Showed deep regard and smiling government.

There pleading might you see grave Nestor stand,
As 'twere encouraging the Greeks to fight,
Making such sober action with his hand
That it beguiled attention, charmed the sight.
1405   In speech it seemed his beard, all silver white,
    Wagged up and down, and from his lips did fly
    Thin winding breath which purled up to the sky.

About him were a press of gaping faces,
Which seemed to swallow up his sound advice,
1410   All jointly list'ning, but with several graces,
As if some mermaid did their ears entice,
Some high, some low—the painter was so nice.
    The scalps of many, almost hid behind,
    To jump up higher seemed, to mock the mind.

1415   Here one man's hand leaned on another's head,
His nose being shadowed by his neighbor's ear;
Here one, being thronged, bears back, all boll'n and
      red;
Another, smothered, seems to pelt and swear;
And in their rage such signs of rage they bear
1420   As, but for loss of Nestor's golden words,
    It seemed they would debate with angry swords.

1394 **Ajax and Ulysses** Greek leaders 1396 **ciphered** depicted
1400 **deep regard . . . government** profound wisdom and successful
rule 1401 **Nestor** an aged Greek leader 1407 **purled** curled
1410 **several** distinct 1412 **nice** precise 1417 **thronged** crushed
in the crowd 1417 **boll'n** swollen 1418 **pelt** scold

For much imaginary work was there;
Conceit deceitful, so compact, so kind,
That for Achilles' image stood his spear,
Griped in an armèd hand; himself behind   1425
Was left unseen, save to the eye of mind:
    A hand, a foot, a face, a leg, a head
    Stood for the whole to be imaginèd.

And from the walls of strong-besiegèd Troy
When their brave hope, bold Hector, marched to field,   1430
Stood many Troyan mothers, sharing joy
To see their youthful sons bright weapons wield;
And to their hope they such odd action yield
    That through their light joy seemèd to appear
    (Like bright things stained) a kind of heavy fear.   1435

And from the strond of Dardan, where they fought,
To Simois' reedy banks the red blood ran,
Whose waves to imitate the battle sought
With swelling ridges, and their ranks began
To break upon the gallèd shore, and than   1440
    Retire again, till, meeting greater ranks,
    They join, and shoot their foam at Simois' banks.

To this well-painted piece is Lucrece come,
To find a face where all distress is stelled.
Many she sees where cares have carvèd some,   1445
But none where all distress and dolor dwelled
Till she despairing Hecuba beheld,
    Staring on Priam's wounds with her old eyes,
    Which bleeding under Pyrrhus' proud foot lies.

1423 **Conceit** conception   1423 **kind** natural   1424 **Achilles**
chief warrior of the Greeks   1430 **Hector** son of Priam and chief
warrior of the Trojans   1433 **odd action yield** contrary gestures ex-
press   1436 **strond of Dardan** shore of Troas (the country of which
Troy was the chief city)   1437 **Simois** river near Troy   1440 **gal-
lèd** eroded   1440 **than** then   1444 **stelled** portrayed   1447
Hecuba wife of Priam   1449 **Pyrrhus** Greek warrior, slayer of
Priam

1450 In her the painter had anatomized
     Time's ruin, beauty's wrack, and grim care's reign;
     Her cheeks with chops and wrinkles were disguised;
     Of what she was no semblance did remain.
     Her blue blood, changed to black in every vein,
1455   Wanting the spring that those shrunk pipes had fed,
         Showed life imprisoned in a body dead.

     On this sad shadow Lucrece spends her eyes
     And shapes her sorrow to the beldame's woes,
     Who nothing wants to answer her but cries
1460 And bitter words to ban her cruel foes.
         The painter was no god to lend her those;
         And therefore Lucrece swears he did her wrong
         To give her so much grief and not a tongue.

     "Poor instrument," quoth she, "without a sound:
1465 I'll tune thy woes with my lamenting tongue,
     And drop sweet balm in Priam's painted wound,
     And rail on Pyrrhus that hath done him wrong,
     And with my tears quench Troy that burns so long,
         And with my knife scratch out the angry eyes
1470   Of all the Greeks that are thine enemies.

     "Show me the strumpet that began this stir,
     That with my nails her beauty I may tear.
     Thy heat of lust, fond Paris, did incur
     This load of wrath that burning Troy doth bear.
1475 Thy eye kindled the fire that burneth here,
         And here in Troy, for trespass of thine eye,
         The sire, the son, the dame and daughter die.

1450 **anatomized** dissected   1452 **chops** cracks   1452 **disguised**
disfigured   1460 **ban** curse   1465 **tune** sing   1471 **stir** action
(i.e., war)

"Why should the private pleasure of some one
Become the public plague of many moe?
Let sin, alone committed, light alone   1480
Upon his head that hath transgressèd so;
Let guiltless souls be freed from guilty woe:
    For one's offense why should so many fall,
    To plague a private sin in general?

"Lo, here weeps Hecuba, here Priam dies,   1485
Here manly Hector faints, here Troilus sounds,
Here friend by friend in bloody channel lies,
And friend to friend gives unadvisèd wounds,
And one man's lust these many lives confounds.
    Had doting Priam checked his son's desire,   1490
    Troy had been bright with fame, and not with fire."

Here feelingly she weeps Troy's painted woes,
For sorrow, like a heavy hanging bell,
Once set on ringing, with his own weight goes;
Then little strength rings out the doleful knell.   1495
So Lucrece, set awork, sad tales doth tell
    To penciled pensiveness and colored sorrow:
    She lends them words, and she their looks doth
      borrow.

She throws her eyes about the painting round,
And who she finds forlorn, she doth lament.   1500
At last she sees a wretched image bound
That piteous looks to Phrygian shepherds lent.
His face, though full of cares, yet showed content;
    Onward to Troy with the blunt swains he goes,
    So mild that patience seemed to scorn his woes.   1505

1479 **moe** more 1484 **in general** on the general public
1486 **Troilus** a son of Priam 1486 **sounds** swoons 1488 **unad-
visèd** unintentional 1489 **confounds** destroys 1497 **penciled,
colored** painted 1499 **round** all around 1501 **wretched image**
i.e., Sinon, the Trojan traitor 1502 **piteous . . . lent** i.e., aroused
compassionate looks from the Phrygian shepherds 1504 **blunt**
simple 1505 **patience** i.e., his patience

In him the painter labored with his skill
To hide deceit, and give the harmless show
An humble gait, calm looks, eyes wailing still,
A brow unbent that seemed to welcome woe,
1510 Cheeks neither red nor pale, but mingled so
　　That blushing red no guilty instance gave
　　Nor ashy pale the fear that false hearts have;

But, like a constant and confirmèd devil,
He entertained a show so seeming just,
1515 And therein so ensconced his secret evil,
That jealousy itself could not mistrust
False creeping craft and perjury should thrust
　　Into so bright a day such black-faced storms
　　Or blot with hell-born sin such saintlike forms.

1520 The well-skilled workman this mild image drew
For perjured Sinon, whose enchanting story
The credulous old Priam after slew;
Whose words like wildfire burnt the shining glory
Of rich-built Ilion, that the skies were sorry,
1525 　　And little stars shot from their fixèd places
　　When their glass fell, wherein they viewed their
　　　　faces.

This picture she advisedly perused
And chid the painter for his wondrous skill,
Saying, some shape in Sinon's was abused;
1530 So fair a form lodged not a mind so ill.
And still on him she gazed, and gazing still,
　　Such signs of truth in his plain face she spied,
　　That she concludes the picture was belied.

1507 **show** appearance　1509 **unbent** unfurrowed　1514 **entertained a show** kept up an appearance　1516 **jealousy** suspicion
1521 **enchanting story** i.e., bewitching lie　1526 **glass** mirror (i.e., shining Troy)　1527 **advisedly** thoughtfully　1529 **some shape...abused** some other person's form had been falsely represented as Sinon's　1533 **belied** proved false

"It cannot be," quoth she, "that so much guile"—
She would have said "can lurk in such a look"; 1535
But Tarquin's shape came in her mind the while,
And from her tongue "can lurk" from "cannot" took.
"It cannot be" she in that sense forsook
    And turned it thus: "It cannot be, I find,
    But such a face should bear a wicked mind; 1540

"For even as subtile Sinon here is painted,
So sober-sad, so weary, and so mild
(As if with grief or travail he had fainted),
To me came Tarquin armèd, to beguiled
With outward honesty, but yet defiled 1545
    With inward vice. As Priam him did cherish,
    So did I Tarquin; so my Troy did perish.

"Look, look, how list'ning Priam wets his eyes,
To see those borrowed tears that Sinon sheeds!
Priam, why art thou old, and yet not wise? 1550
For every tear he falls a Troyan bleeds.
His eye drops fire, no water thence proceeds:
    Those round clear pearls of his that move thy pity
    Are balls of quenchless fire to burn thy city.

"Such devils steal effects from lightless hell, 1555
For Sinon in his fire doth quake with cold,
And in that cold hot burning fire doth dwell.
These contraries such unity do hold
Only to flatter fools and make them bold.
    So Priam's trust false Sinon's tears doth flatter 1560
    That he finds means to burn his Troy with water."

1544 **beguiled** beguile   1549 **borrowed** i.e., false   1549 **sheeds**
sheds   1551 **falls** lets fall   1559 **flatter** deceive   1559 **make
them bold** give them confidence

Here, all enraged, such passion her assails
That patience is quite beaten from her breast.
She tears the senseless Sinon with her nails,
1565 Comparing him to that unhappy guest
Whose deed hath made herself herself detest.
 At last she smilingly with this gives o'er:
 "Fool, fool!" quoth she, "his wounds will not be
  sore."

Thus ebbs and flows the current of her sorrow,
1570 And time doth weary time with her complaining.
She looks for night, and then she longs for morrow,
And both she thinks too long with her remaining.
Short time seems long in sorrow's sharp sustaining;
 Though woe be heavy, yet it seldom sleeps,
1575 And they that watch see time how slow it creeps;

Which all this time hath overslipped her thought
That she with painted images hath spent,
Being from the feeling of her own grief brought
By deep surmise of others' detriment,
1580 Losing her woes in shows of discontent.
 It easeth some, though none it ever curèd,
 To think their dolor others have endurèd.

But now the mindful messenger, come back,
Brings home his lord and other company;
1585 Who finds his Lucrece clad in mourning black,
And round about her tear-distainèd eye
Blue circles streamed, like rainbows in the sky.
 These water-galls in her dim element
 Foretell new storms to those already spent.

1565 **unhappy** unfortunate 1567 **gives o'er** ceases 1574 **heavy**
(1) distressing (2) sleepy 1576 **overslipped her thought** i.e., gone
unnoticed 1579 **surmise** contemplation 1580 **shows** representa-
tions 1586 **tear-distainèd** tear-stained 1588 **water-galls** atmo-
spheric conditions attendant upon rainbows 1588 **element** sky

Which when her sad-beholding husband saw,   *1590*
Amazedly in her sad face he stares.
Her eyes, though sod in tears, looked red and raw,
Her lively color killed with deadly cares.
He hath no power to ask her how she fares;
    Both stood like old acquaintance in a trance,   *1595*
    Met far from home, wond'ring each other's chance.

At last he takes her by the bloodless hand,
And thus begins: "What uncouth ill event
Hath thee befall'n, that thou dost trembling stand?
Sweet love, what spite hath thy fair color spent?   *1600*
Why art thou thus attired in discontent?
    Unmask, dear dear, this moody heaviness,
    And tell thy grief, that we may give redress."

Three times with sighs she gives her sorrow fire,
Ere once she can discharge one word of woe.   *1605*
At length addressed to answer his desire,
She modestly prepares to let them know
Her honor is ta'en prisoner by the foe,
    While Collatine and his consorted lords
    With sad attention long to hear her words.   *1610*

And now this pale swan in her wat'ry nest
Begins the sad dirge of her certain ending:
"Few words," quoth she, "shall fit the trespass best,
Where no excuse can give the fault amending.
In me moe woes than words are now depending,   *1615*
    And my laments would be drawn out too long
    To tell them all with one poor tirèd tongue.

1592 **sod** sodden   1596 **chance** fortune   1598 **uncouth** unknown
1600 **spite** feeling of annoyance   1602 **Unmask** disclose
1604 **fire** i.e., fire to ignite a discharge (from a cannon)   1606 **ad-
dressed** prepared   1609 **consorted** associated   1612 **ending**
death   1615 **moe** more   1615 **depending** impending

"Then be this all the task it hath to say:
Dear husband, in the interest of thy bed
1620 A stranger came and on that pillow lay
Where thou wast wont to rest thy weary head;
And what wrong else may be imaginèd
    By foul enforcement might be done to me,
    From that, alas, thy Lucrece is not free.

1625 "For in the dreadful dead of dark midnight,
With shining falchion in my chamber came
A creeping creature with a flaming light
And softly cried, 'Awake, thou Roman dame,
And entertain my love; else lasting shame
1630   On thee and thine this night I will inflict,
    If thou my love's desire do contradict.

" 'For some hard-favored groom of thine,' quoth he,
'Unless thou yoke thy liking to my will,
I'll murder straight, and then I'll slaughter thee
1635 And swear I found you where you did fulfill
The loathsome act of lust, and so did kill
    The lechers in their deed: this act will be
    My fame and thy perpetual infamy.'

"With this I did begin to start and cry;
1640 And then against my heart he set his sword,
Swearing, unless I took all patiently,
I should not live to speak another word.
So should my shame still rest upon record,
    And never be forgot in mighty Rome
1645   Th' adulterate death of Lucrece and her groom.

1619 **interest** possession   1629 **entertain** receive   1633 **yoke** submit

"Mine enemy was strong, my poor self weak
And far the weaker with so strong a fear.
My bloody judge forbod my tongue to speak;
No rightful plea might plead for justice there.
His scarlet lust came evidence to swear   *1650*
    That my poor beauty had purloined his eyes;
    And when the judge is robbed, the prisoner dies.

"O, teach me how to make mine own excuse,
Or (at the least) this refuge let me find:
Though my gross blood be stained with this abuse,   *1655*
Immaculate and spotless is my mind;
That was not forced, that never was inclined
    To accessary yieldings, but still pure
    Doth in her poisoned closet yet endure."

Lo, here, the hopeless merchant of this loss,   *1660*
With head declined and voice dammed up with woe,
With sad-set eyes and wreathèd arms across,
From lips new-waxen pale begins to blow
The grief away that stops his answer so.
    But, wretched as he is, he strives in vain;   *1665*
    What he breathes out his breath drinks up again.

As through an arch the violent roaring tide
Outruns the eye that doth behold his haste,
Yet in the eddy boundeth in his pride
Back to the strait that forced him on so fast;   *1670*
In rage sent out, recalled in rage being past:
    Even so his sighs, his sorrows, make a saw,
    To push grief on, and back the same grief draw.

1648 **forbod** forbade 1660 **merchant** i.e., Collatine 1662 **wreathèd arms** (arms folded were a sign of melancholy) 1672 **saw** i.e., sawlike motion

Which speechless woe of his poor she attendeth
1675 And his untimely frenzy thus awaketh:
"Dear lord, thy sorrow to my sorrow lendeth
Another power; no flood by raining slaketh;
My woe too sensible thy passion maketh
    More feeling-painful. Let it then suffice
1680   To drown one woe, one pair of weeping eyes.

"And for my sake when I might charm thee so,
For she that was thy Lucrece (now attend me)
Be suddenly revengèd on my foe—
Thine, mine, his own. Suppose thou dost defend me
1685 From what is past; the help that thou shalt lend me
    Comes all too late, yet let the traitor die;
    For sparing justice feeds iniquity.

"But ere I name him, you fair lords," quoth she,
Speaking to those that came with Collatine,
1690 "Shall plight your honorable faiths to me
With swift pursuit to 'venge this wrong of mine;
For 'tis a meritorious fair design
    To chase injustice with revengeful arms:
    Knights by their oaths should right poor ladies'
        harms."

1695 At this request, with noble disposition
Each present lord began to promise aid,
As bound in knighthood to her imposition,
Longing to hear the hateful foe bewrayed.
But she, that yet her sad task hath not said,
1700   The protestation stops. "O, speak!" quoth she,
    "How may this forcèd stain be wiped from me?

1675 **frenzy** trance   1678 **sensible** sensitive   1681 **so** in such
things   1698 **bewrayed** revealed

"What is the quality of my offense,
Being constrained with dreadful circumstance?
May my pure mind with the foul act dispense,
My low-declinèd honor to advance?   1705
May any terms acquit me from this chance?
    The poisoned fountain clears itself again;
    And why not I from this compellèd stain?"

With this they all at once began to say,
Her body's stain her mind untainted clears;   1710
While with a joyless smile she turns away
The face, that map which deep impression bears
Of hard misfortune, carved in it with tears.
    "No, no!" quoth she, "no dame hereafter living
    By my excuse shall claim excuse's giving."   1715

Here with a sigh as if her heart would break
She throws forth Tarquin's name: "He, he!" she says,
But more than "he" her poor tongue could not speak,
Till after many accents and delays,
Untimely breathings, sick and short assays,   1720
    She utters this: "He, he! fair lords, 'tis he
    That guides this hand to give this wound to me."

Even here she sheathèd in her harmless breast
A harmful knife, that thence her soul unsheathèd.
That blow did bail it from the deep unrest   1725
Of that polluted prison where it breathèd.
Her contrite sighs unto the clouds bequeathèd
    Her wingèd sprite, and through her wounds doth fly
    Life's lasting date from canceled destiny.

1702 **quality** nature   1704 **dispense** be reconciled   1705 **ad-
vance** raise   1719 **accents** emphasized sounds   1720 **assays**
attempts   1723 **harmless** innocent   1725 **bail** release   1729
Life's ... canceled destiny i.e., eternal life is freed (canceled) by fly-
ing from life on earth (destiny)

1730 Stone-still, astonished with this deadly deed,
     Stood Collatine and all his lordly crew,
     Till Lucrece' father, that beholds her bleed,
     Himself on her self-slaught'red body threw,
     And from the purple fountain Brutus drew
1735   The murd'rous knife, and as it left the place,
         Her blood, in poor revenge, held it in chase;

     And bubbling from her breast, it doth divide
     In two slow rivers, that the crimson blood
     Circles her body in on every side,
1740 Who like a late-sacked island vastly stood
     Bare and unpeopled in this fearful flood.
         Some of her blood still pure and red remained,
         And some looked black, and that false Tarquin
             stained.

     About the mourning and congealèd face
1745 Of that black blood a wat'ry rigoll goes,
     Which seems to weep upon the tainted place;
     And ever since, as pitying Lucrece' woes,
     Corrupted blood some watery token shows,
         And blood untainted still doth red abide,
1750   Blushing at that which is so putrefied.

     "Daughter, dear daughter!" old Lucretius cries,
     "That life was mine which thou hast here deprivèd;
     If in the child the father's image lies,
     Where shall I live now Lucrece is unlivèd?
1755 Thou wast not to this end from me derivèd.
         If children predecease progenitors,
         We are their offspring, and they none of ours.

1740 **vastly** like a waste   1745 **wat'ry rigoll** (when blood coagu-
lates it separates into a congealed blot and a serum, "wat'ry rigoll")

"Poor broken glass, I often did behold
In thy sweet semblance my old age new born;
But now that fair fresh mirror, dim and old,   1760
Shows me a bare-boned death by time outworn.
O, from thy cheeks my image thou hast torn
    And shivered all the beauty of my glass,
    That I no more can see what once I was.

"O time, cease thou thy course, and last no longer,   1765
If they surcease to be that should survive.
Shall rotten death make conquest of the stronger
And leave the falt'ring feeble souls alive?
The old bees die, the young possess their hive;
    Then live, sweet Lucrece, live again and see   1770
    Thy father die, and not thy father thee."

By this, starts Collatine as from a dream
And bids Lucretius give his sorrow place;
And then in key-cold Lucrece' bleeding stream
He falls, and bathes the pale fear in his face,   1775
And counterfeits to die with her a space;
    Till manly shame bids him possess his breath,
    And live to be revengèd on her death.

The deep vexation of his inward soul
Hath served a dumb arrest upon his tongue;   1780
Who, mad that sorrow should his use control,
Or keep him from heart-easing words so long,
Begins to talk; but through his lips do throng
    Weak words, so thick come in his poor heart's aid
    That no man could distinguish what he said.   1785

1758 **glass** mirror   1761 **death** skull   1763 **shivered** shattered
1766 **surcease** cease   1774 **key-cold** i.e., cold as metal   1776 **coun-
terfeits to die** swoons (and seems transported as by an orgasm)
1780 **served a dumb arrest** enforced a silence (as if by a warrant)
1784 **thick** quickly

Yet sometime "Tarquin" was pronouncèd plain,
But through his teeth, as if the name he tore.
This windy tempest, till it blow up rain,
Held back his sorrow's tide, to make it more.
1790 At last it rains, and busy winds give o'er;
    Then son and father weep with equal strife
    Who should weep most, for daughter or for wife.

The one doth call her his, the other his;
Yet neither may possess the claim they lay.
1795 The father says, "She's mine." "O, mine, she is!"
Replies her husband, "do not take away
My sorrow's interest; let no mourner say
    He weeps for her, for she was only mine,
    And only must be wailed by Collatine."

1800 "O," quoth Lucretius, "I did give that life
Which she too early and too late hath spilled."
"Woe, woe!" quoth Collatine, "she was my wife,
I owed her, and 'tis mine that she hath killed."
"My daughter" and "my wife" with clamors filled
1805   The dispersed air, who, holding Lucrece' life,
    Answered their cries, "my daughter" and "my
        wife."

Brutus, who plucked the knife from Lucrece' side,
Seeing such emulation in their woe,
Began to clothe his wit in state and pride,
1810 Burying in Lucrece' wound his folly's show.
He with the Romans was esteemèd so
    As seely jeering idiots are with kings,
    For sportive words and utt'ring foolish things;

1797 **sorrow's interest** right to sorrow   1801 **late** recently
1803 **owed** owned   1805 **The dispersed air** i.e., the boundless
air (which has received Lucrece's "life" or spirit upon her death)
1810 **folly's show** appearance of folly   1812 **seely** simple
1813 **sportive** merry

But now he throws that shallow habit by
Wherein deep policy did him disguise,   *1815*
And armed his long-hid wits advisedly
To check the tears in Collatinus' eyes.
"Thou wrongèd lord of Rome," quoth he, "arise!
  Let my unsounded self, supposed a fool,
  Now set thy long-experienced wit to school.   *1820*

"Why, Collatine, is woe the cure for woe?
Do wounds help wounds, or grief help grievous deeds?
Is it revenge to give thyself a blow
For his foul act by whom thy fair wife bleeds?
Such childish humor from weak minds proceeds;   *1825*
  Thy wretched wife mistook the matter so,
  To slay herself that should have slain her foe.

"Courageous Roman, do not steep thy heart
In such relenting dew of lamentations;
But kneel with me, and help to bear thy part   *1830*
To rouse our Roman gods with invocations
That they will suffer these abominations
  (Since Rome herself in them doth stand disgracèd)
  By our strong arms from forth her fair streets
    chasèd.

"Now, by the Capitol that we adore,   *1835*
And by this chaste blood so unjustly stainèd,
By heaven's fair sun that breeds the fat earth's store,
By all our country rights in Rome maintainèd,
And by chaste Lucrece' soul that late complainèd
  Her wrongs to us, and by this bloody knife,   *1840*
  We will revenge the death of this true wife."

1814 **habit** cloak (here, of a king's jester)   1815 **policy** calculation
1819 **unsounded** unplumbed   1821 **Why** (exclamation of impa-
tience)   1829 **relenting** melting   1832 **suffer** allow   1834 **chasèd**
i.e., to be chased   1837 **fat earth's store** fertile earth's abundance

This said, he strook his hand upon his breast
And kissed the fatal knife to end his vow;
And to his protestation urged the rest,
1845 Who, wond'ring at him, did his words allow.
    Then jointly to the ground their knees they bow,
        And that deep vow which Brutus made before,
        He doth again repeat, and that they swore.

When they had sworn to this advisèd doom,
1850 They did conclude to bear dead Lucrece thence,
To show her bleeding body thorough Rome,
And so to publish Tarquin's foul offense;
    Which being done with speedy diligence,
        The Romans plausibly did give consent
1855   To Tarquin's everlasting banishment.

FINIS

1842 **strook** struck 1844 **protestation** vow 1845 **allow** approve 1849 **advisèd doom** considered judgment 1854 **plausibly** with applause (i.e., with a "general acclamation"; see Argument, page 280, lines 43–44)

The Phoenix and the Turtle

Let the bird of loudest lay
On the sole Arabian tree
Herald sad and trumpet be,
To whose sound chaste wings obey.

But thou shrieking harbinger,   5
Foul precurrer of the fiend,
Augur of the fever's end,
To this troop come thou not near.

From this session interdict
Every fowl of tyrant wing,   10
Save the eagle, feath'red king:
Keep the obsequy so strict.

The Phoenix and the Turtle the phoenix, a unique legendary bird,
was said to fly periodically to Arabia, where, after building a nest of
spices, it was consumed in flame, and from its ashes a new phoenix
arose; it is a symbol of immortality. The turtle, i.e., the turtle dove, is
a symbol of true love. **1 lay** song **2 sole** unique **3 sad** serious
3 trumpet trumpeter **4 chaste wings** i.e., other good birds **5
shrieking harbinger** screech owl (?) **6 precurrer** precursor (ap-
parently Shakespeare's coinage) **7 Augur of the fever's end**
prophet of death **9 session** formal gathering, as of a parliament or a
court **9 interdict** ban **10 fowl of tyrant wing** bird of prey, unso-
cial bird (in contrast to those of "chaste wings," line 4) **12 obsequy**
funeral rite

Let the priest in surplice white,
That defunctive music can,
15   Be the death-divining swan,
Lest the requiem lack his right.

And thou treble-dated crow,
That thy sable gender mak'st
With the breath thou giv'st and tak'st,
20   'Mongst our mourners shalt thou go.

Here the anthem doth commence:
Love and constancy is dead,
Phoenix and the turtle fled
In a mutual flame from hence.

25   So they loved, as love in twain
Had the essence but in one;
Two distincts, division none:
Number there in love was slain.

Hearts remote, yet not asunder;
30   Distance and no space was seen
'Twixt this turtle and his queen;
But in them it were a wonder.

So between them love did shine
That the turtle saw his right
35   Flaming in the phoenix' sight:
Either was the other's mine.

14 **defunctive music can** is skilled in funeral music   15 **death-divining** foretelling death (the swan allegedly sang only once, just before it died)   16 **his right** its due (?) his (i.e., the swan's) rite of requiem (?)   17 **treble-dated** long-lived   18–19 **That thy . . . tak'st** that breeds your black offspring with the breath you exhale and inhale (alluding to a belief that some birds conceived and laid eggs at the bill)   25 **as** that   26 **essence** nature   27 **distincts** distinct or separate things   28 **Number . . . slain** i.e., because the two were one, and Elizabethan proverbial lore held that "one is no number"   29 **remote** apart   32 **But . . . wonder** i.e., in any others except them it would have been a marvel   34 **his right** what was due to him   36 **mine** (1) my own property (2) source of hidden treasure

Property was thus appallèd,
That the self was not the same;
Single nature's double name
Neither two nor one was callèd.   *40*

Reason, in itself confounded,
Saw division grow together,
To themselves yet either neither,
Simple were so well compounded;

That it cried, "How true a twain   *45*
Seemeth this concordant one!
Love hath reason, reason none,
If what parts can so remain."

Whereupon it made this threne
To the phoenix and the dove,   *50*
Co-supremes and stars of love,
As chorus to their tragic scene.

THRENOS

Beauty, truth, and rarity,
Grace in all simplicity,
Here enclosed, in cinders lie.   *55*

Death is now the phoenix' nest,
And the turtle's loyal breast
To eternity doth rest,

Leaving no posterity:
'Twas not their infirmity,   *60*
It was married chastity.

37 **Property** essential nature, peculiar quality   41 **confounded**
perplexed   44 **Simple** i.e., simples, elementary elements (?) indi-
vidual ingredients (?)   44 **compounded** made into a new unity
45 **it** i.e., Reason   48 **If . . . remain** i.e., if what divides into two
can remain one   49 **threne** funeral song (Greek: *threnos*)   51 **Co-
supremes** joint rulers   53 **rarity** excellence   55 **cinders** ashes
61 **married chastity** faithful married love (?) abstinence (?)

Truth may seem, but cannot be;
Beauty brag, but 'tis not she:
Truth and Beauty buried be.

65   To this urn let those repair
That are either true or fair;
For these dead birds sigh a prayer.

FINIS

63 **she** i.e., true Beauty

A Lover's Complaint

From off a hill whose concave womb reworded
A plaintful story from a sist'ring vale,
My spirits t' attend this double voice accorded,
And down I laid to list the sad-tuned tale;
Ere long espied a fickle maid full pale,   5
Tearing of papers, breaking rings atwain,
Storming her world with sorrow's wind and rain.

Upon her head a platted hive of straw,
Which fortified her visage from the sun,
Whereon the thought might think sometime it saw   10
The carcass of a beauty spent and done.
Time had not scythèd all that youth begun,
Nor youth all quit; but, spite of heaven's fell rage,
Some beauty peeped through lattice of seared age.

Oft did she heave her napkin to her eyne,   15
Which on it had conceited characters,
Laund'ring the silken figures in the brine
That seasoned woe had pelleted in tears,
And often reading what contents it bears;
As often shrieking undistinguished woe,   20
In clamors of all size, both high and low.

1 **womb reworded** i.e., valley echoed 2 **sist'ring** nearby (?) similar (?) 3 **accorded** agreed (?) inclined (?) 5 **fickle** unstable
6 **papers** love letters 8 **platted hive** woven hat 10 **thought** mind 12 **scythèd** cut down 13 **all quit** entirely gone 13 **fell** deadly 14 **lattice** i.e., wrinkles 15 **heave . . . eyne** lift her handkerchief to her eyes 16 **conceited** ingenious, fanciful 18 **seasoned** (1) matured (2) salted (playing on "brine" in previous line)
18 **pelleted** made round (i.e., like hailstones or like pellets of meat or dough) 20 **undistinguished woe** incoherent cries

Sometimes her leveled eyes their carriage ride,
As they did batt'ry to the spheres intend;
Sometime diverted their poor balls are tied
To th' orbèd earth; sometimes they do extend
Their view right on; anon their gazes lend
To every place at once, and, nowhere fixed,
The mind and sight distractedly commixed.

Her hair, nor loose nor tied in formal plat,
Proclaimed in her a careless hand of pride;
For some, untucked, descended her sheaved hat,
Hanging her pale and pinèd cheek beside;
Some in her threaden fillet still did bide
And, true to bondage, would not break from thence,
Though slackly braided in loose negligence.

A thousand favors from a maund she drew,
Of amber, crystal, and of bedded jet,
Which one by one she in a river threw,
Upon whose weeping margent she was set,
Like usury, applying wet to wet,
Or monarch's hands that lets not bounty fall
Where want cries some but where excess begs all.

Of folded schedules had she many a one
Which she perused, sighed, tore, and gave the flood;
Cracked many a ring of posied gold and bone,
Bidding them find their sepulchers in mud;
Found yet moe letters sadly penned in blood,
With sleided silk feat and affectedly
Enswathed, and sealed to curious secrecy.

25

30

35

40

45

22 **leveled** aimed (the image is of a firearm on a gun-carriage)
23 **As . . . intend** as if they intended to direct their fire against the
stars 29 **nor . . . nor** neither . . . nor 29 **plat** knot 30 **a careless
hand of pride** a hand indifferent to show 31 **sheaved** straw
33 **threaden fillet** headband 36 **maund** basket 37 **bedded** in-
laid (emendation to "beaded" is plausible) 39 **weeping margent**
wet bank 40 **Like usury** i.e., adding to the original amount
42 **cries some** cries out for some 43 **schedules** papers with
writing 45 **posied** inscribed with mottoes 47 **moe** more
48 **sleided** raveled 48–49 **feat and affectedly/Enswathed** tied
neatly and elaborately (or neatly and lovingly) 49 **curious**
painstaking

These often bathed she in her fluxive eyes,   50
And often kissed, and often gave to tear;
Cried, "O false blood, thou register of lies,
What unapprovèd witness dost thou bear!
Ink would have seemed more black and damnèd here!"
This said, in top of rage the lines she rents,   55
Big discontent so breaking their contents.

A reverend man that grazed his cattle nigh,
Sometime a blusterer that the ruffle knew
Of court, of city, and had let go by
The swiftest hours, observèd as they flew,   60
Towards this afflicted fancy fastly drew,
And, privileged by age, desires to know
In brief the grounds and motives of her woe.

So slides he down upon his grainèd bat,
And comely-distant sits he by her side;   65
When he again desires her, being sat,
Her grievance with his hearing to divide:
If that from him there may be aught applied
Which may her suffering ecstasy assuage,
'Tis promised in the charity of age.   70

"Father," she says, "though in me you behold
The injury of many a blasting hour,
Let it not tell your judgment I am old;
Not age, but sorrow, over me hath power.
I might as yet have been a spreading flower,   75
Fresh to myself, if I had self-applied
Love to myself, and to no love beside.

50 **fluxive** flowing   53 **unapprovèd** unconfirmed, not proved by
deeds   57 **reverend** aged   58 **ruffle** bustle   59–60 **had ... flew**
i.e., had learned about the world through observation during the busy
days of youth   61 **fancy** lovesick lady   61 **fastly** near (?) quickly
(?)   64 **grainèd bat** shepherd's staff on which the grain was show-
ing   65 **comely-distant** at an appropriate distance   69 **ecstasy** fit,
passion

"But, woe is me, too early I attended
A youthful suit—it was to gain my grace—
80 Of one by nature's outwards so commended,
That maidens' eyes stuck over all his face:
Love lacked a dwelling, and made him her place;
And when in his fair parts she did abide,
She was new lodged and newly deified.

85 "His browny locks did hang in crooked curls,
And every light occasion of the wind
Upon his lips their silken parcels hurls.
What's sweet to do, to do will aptly find;
Each eye that saw him did enchant the mind,
90 For on his visage was in little drawn
What largeness thinks in Paradise was sawn.

"Small show of man was yet upon his chin;
His phoenix down began but to appear,
Like unshorn velvet, on that termless skin
95 Whose bare out-bragged the web it seemed to wear.
Yet showed his visage by that cost more dear;
And nice affections wavering stood in doubt
If best were as it was, or best without.

"His qualities were beauteous as his form,
100 For maiden-tongued he was, and thereof free;
Yet, if men moved him, was he such a storm
As oft 'twixt May and April is to see,
When winds breathe sweet, unruly though they be.
His rudeness so with his authorized youth
105 Did livery falseness in a pride of truth.

78 **attended** heeded 86 **occasion** chance movement 91 **What...
sawn** what was seen (or possibly "sown") in large in paradise
93 **phoenix down** i.e., newborn fuzz 94 **termless** young (?) inde-
scribable (?) 95 **Whose...wear** i.e., the skin excelled the covering
(?) 96 **cost** display, ornament 97 **nice affections** delicate tastes
100 **maiden-tongued** modestly spoken 100 **thereof free** not shy
in speaking 104–05 **His rudeness...truth** his agitated behavior,
with his privilege of youth, covered falseness with the appearance of
honesty

"Well could he ride, and often men would say,
'That horse his mettle from his rider takes.
Proud of subjection, noble by the sway,
What rounds, what bounds, what course, what stop he
    makes!'
And controversy hence a question takes,   110
Whether the horse by him became his deed,
Or he his manage by th' well-doing steed.

"But quickly on this side the verdict went:
His real habitude gave life and grace
To appertainings and to ornament,   115
Accomplished in himself, not in his case.
All aids, themselves made fairer by their place,
Came for additions; yet their purposed trim
Pieced not his grace but were all graced by him.

"So on the tip of his subduing tongue   120
All kind of arguments and question deep,
All replication prompt and reason strong,
For his advantage still did wake and sleep.
To make the weeper laugh, the laugher weep,
He had the dialect and different skill,   125
Catching all passions in his craft of will,

"That he did in the general bosom reign
Of young, of old, and sexes both enchanted
To dwell with him in thoughts, or to remain
In personal duty, following where he haunted.   130
Consents bewitched, ere he desire, have granted,
And dialogued for him what he would say,
Asked their own wills and made their wills obey.

109 **rounds, bounds, stop** (terms of horsemanship, or "manage")
111–12 **Whether...steed** whether the horse showed his good quali-
ties because of the man, or whether the man showed his skill at horse-
manship ("manage") because of the horse's skill   113 **this** i.e.,
the following   114 **real habitude** true character   116 **case**
outside, belongings   118 **for** as   119 **Pieced not** did not add to
122 **replication** reply, repartee   126 **craft of will** skill to persuade
127 **That** so that   130 **In personal duty** i.e., as servants to him
130 **haunted** frequented

"Many there were that did his picture get,
135 To serve their eyes, and in it put their mind,
Like fools that in th' imagination set
The goodly objects which abroad they find
Of lands and mansions, theirs in thought assigned,
And laboring in moe pleasures to bestow them
140 Than the true gouty landlord which doth owe them.

"So many have, that never touched his hand,
Sweetly supposed them mistress of his heart.
My woeful self, that did in freedom stand
And was my own fee-simple, not in part,
145 What with his art in youth and youth in art,
Threw my affections in his charmèd power,
Reserved the stalk and gave him all my flower.

"Yet did I not, as some my equals did,
Demand of him, nor being desirèd yielded;
150 Finding myself in honor so forbid,
With safest distance I mine honor shielded.
Experience for me many bulwarks builded
Of proofs new-bleeding, which remained the foil
Of this false jewel, and his amorous spoil.

155 "But, ah, who ever shunned by precedent
The destined ill she must herself assay?
Or forced examples, 'gainst her own content,
To put the by-past perils in her way?
Counsel may stop awhile what will not stay;
160 For when we rage, advice is often seen
By blunting us to make our wits more keen.

---

140 **gouty** rheumatic, i.e., old 140 **owe** own 144 **fee-simple,
not in part** absolute possession, without restriction 146 **charmèd**
enchanting 148 **my equals** i.e., girls of my age 152 **Experience**
knowledge 153 **proofs new-bleeding** examples of others newly ru-
ined 153 **foil** dark background (to display a jewel) 156 **assay** ex-
perience 157 **forced examples** comparisons with her own case
which seem to her far-fetched, though she is made to consider them
160 **rage** are impassioned

"Nor gives it satisfaction to our blood,
That we must curb it upon others' proof,
To be forbod the sweets that seems so good
For fear of harms that preach in our behoof.   165
O appetite, from judgment stand aloof!
The one a palate hath that needs will taste,
Though Reason weep and cry, 'It is thy last.'

"For further I could say this man's untrue,
And knew the patterns of his foul beguiling;   170
Heard where his plants in others' orchards grew;
Saw how deceits were gilded in his smiling;
Knew vows were ever brokers to defiling;
Thought characters and words merely but art,
And bastards of his foul adulterate heart.   175

"And long upon these terms I held my city,
Till thus he 'gan besiege me: 'Gentle maid,
Have of my suffering youth some feeling pity
And be not of my holy vows afraid.
That's to ye sworn to none was ever said;   180
For feasts of love I have been called unto,
Till now did ne'er invite nor never woo.

" 'All my offenses that abroad you see
Are errors of the blood, none of the mind.
Love made them not. With acture they may be,   185
Where neither party is nor true nor kind.
They sought their shame that so their shame did find,
And so much less of shame in me remains
By how much of me their reproach contains.

---

162 **blood** passion   163 **others' proof** the experience of others
164 **forbod** forbidden   169 **say this man's untrue** tell of this
man's untruth   173 **brokers** panders   174 **characters and words**
written and spoken words   180 **That's** what's   184 **blood** lust
185 **acture** action (as opposed to volition)

190 " 'Among the many that mine eyes have seen,
Not one whose flame my heart so much as warmèd,
Or my affection put to th' smallest teen,
Or any of my leisures ever charmèd.
Harm have I done to them, but ne'er was harmèd;
195 Kept hearts in liveries, but mine own was free
And reigned commanding in his monarchy.

" 'Look here what tributes wounded fancies sent me
Of pallid pearls and rubies red as blood,
Figuring that they their passions likewise lent me
200 Of grief and blushes, aptly understood
In bloodless white and the encrimsoned mood;
Effects of terror and dear modesty,
Encamped in hearts, but fighting outwardly.

" 'And, lo, behold these talents of their hair,
205 With twisted metal amorously empleached,
I have received from many a several fair,
Their kind acceptance weepingly beseeched,
With th' annexions of fair gems enriched,
And deep-brained sonnets that did amplify
210 Each stone's dear nature, worth, and quality.

" 'The diamond, why, 'twast beautiful and hard,
Whereto his invised properties did tend;
The deep-green em'rald, in whose fresh regard
Weak sights their sickly radiance do amend;
215 The heaven-hued sapphire, and the opal blend
With objects manifold: each several stone,
With wit well blazoned, smiled or made some moan.

192 **teen** distress   195 **in liveries** as servants   201 **mood** mode
204 **talents** treasures   205 **empleached** intertwined   206 **several
fair** different lady   208 **annexions** additions   210 **dear** valuable
212 **invised** inward-looking, self-regarding (?) (Latin *invisus* = se-
cret)   214 **radiance** power of vision   215–16 **opal ... manifold**
blended opal, with many other objects (?)   216 **several** separate
217 **blazoned** proclaimed

" 'Lo, all these trophies of affections hot,
Of pensived and subdued desires the tender,
Nature hath charged me that I hoard them not,   220
But yield them up where I myself must render,
That is, to you, my origin and ender.
For these of force must your oblations be,
Since I their altar, you enpatron me.

" 'O, then, advance of yours that phraseless hand,   225
Whose white weighs down the airy scale of praise!
Take all these similes to your own command,
Hollowed with sighs that burning lungs did raise.
What me, your minister, for you obeys,
Works under you; and to your audit comes   230
Their distract parcels in combinèd sums.

" 'Lo, this device was sent me from a nun,
Or sister sanctified, of holiest note,
Which late her noble suit in court did shun,
Whose rarest havings made the blossoms dote;   235
For she was sought by spirits of richest coat,
But kept cold distance, and did thence remove
To spend her living in eternal love.

" 'But, O my sweet, what labor is 't to leave
The thing we have not, mast'ring what not strives,   240
Paling the place which did no form receive,
Playing patient sports in unconstrainèd gyves?
She that her fame so to herself contrives,
The scars of battle 'scapeth by the flight
And makes her absence valiant, not her might.   245

219 **tender** offering   223 **oblations** offerings   224 **Since . . . en-
patron me** i.e., I am the altar at which they are offered to you, my pa-
tron saint   225 **phraseless** indescribable   227 **similes** love-tokens
(jewels and sonnets)   228 **Hollowed** (1) blown up, shaped (2) hal-
lowed   229 **What . . . obeys** whatever obeys me, your servant ("min-
ister")   230 **audit** accounting   231 **distract parcels** separate items
234 **suit** wooing   235 **havings** personal qualities   235 **blossoms**
i.e., flower of the nobility   236 **coat** coats of arms   238 **eternal love**
love of things heavenly   241 **Paling** fencing (but "Paling" is an emen-
dation for "Playing"; "Leaving" and "Flying" have also been sug-
gested)   241 **the place** i.e., the nun's heart, which had never received
the impression of love   242 **unconstrainèd gyves** fetters that do not
constrain (because willingly put on)   243 **her . . . contrives** creates
for herself a reputation (for renouncing love)   245 **might** power

" 'O, pardon me, in that my boast is true:
The accident which brought me to her eye
Upon the moment did her force subdue,
And now she would the cagèd cloister fly.
250 Religious love put out religion's eye.
Not to be tempted, would she be inured,
And now, to tempt all, liberty procured.

" 'How mighty then you are, O hear me tell:
The broken bosoms that to me belong
255 Have emptied all their fountains in my well,
And mine I pour your ocean all among.
I strong o'er them, and you o'er me being strong,
Must for your victory us all congest,
As compound love to physic your cold breast.

260 " 'My parts had pow'r to charm a sacred nun,
Who, disciplined, ay, dieted in grace,
Believed her eyes when they t'assail begun,
All vows and consecrations giving place.
O most potential love! vow, bond, nor space
265 In thee hath neither sting, knot, nor confine,
For thou art all, and all things else are thine.

" 'When thou impressest, what are precepts worth
Of stale example? When thou wilt inflame,
How coldly those impediments stand forth
270 Of wealth, of filial fear, law, kindred, fame!
Love's arms are peace, 'gainst rule, 'gainst sense,
        'gainst shame;
And sweetens, in the suff'ring pangs it bears,
The aloes of all forces, shocks, and fears.

250 **Religious** devoted   251 **inured** hardened   252 **And . . . pro-
cured** and now she has procured liberty to try ("tempt") all things (?)
254 **bosoms** hearts   258 **congest** gather together   259 **physic**
cure   262 **Believed . . . begun** trusted her eyes when, filled with
his image, they assailed her chastity   264 **potential** powerful
267 **impressest** conscripts   271 **arms are** warfare produces
273 **aloes** bitterness

" 'Now all these hearts that do on mine depend,
Feeling it break, with bleeding groans they pine;   *275*
And supplicant their sighs to you extend,
To leave the batt'ry that you make 'gainst mine,
Lending soft audience to my sweet design,
And credent soul to that strong-bonded oath
That shall prefer and undertake my troth.'   *280*

"This said, his wat'ry eyes he did dismount,
Whose sights till then were leveled on my face;
Each cheek a river running from a fount
With brinish current downward flowed apace.
O, how the channel to the stream gave grace!   *285*
Who glazed with crystal gate the glowing roses
That flame through water which their hue encloses.

"O father, what a hell of witchcraft lies
In the small orb of one particular tear!
But with the inundation of the eyes   *290*
What rocky heart to water will not wear?
What breast so cold that is not warmèd here?
O cleft effect! Cold modesty, hot wrath,
Both fire from hence and chill extincture hath.

"For, lo, his passion, but an art of craft,   *295*
Even there resolved my reason into tears;
There my white stole of chastity I daffed,
Shook off my sober guards and civil fears;
Appear to him as he to me appears,
All melting, though our drops this diff'rence bore: *300*
His poisoned me, and mine did him restore.

275 **bleeding groans** (every sigh was thought to lessen life by drawing blood from the heart) 279 **credent** believing 280 **prefer** advance, promote 280 **undertake my troth** support my love 281 **dismount** lower 286 **Who** which 286 **gate** barrier (the idea is that his cheeks beneath his ears are like roses beneath glass) 293 **cleft** double 296 **resolved** dissolved 297 **daffed** doffed, put off 298 **civil** moral 299 **Appear** I appear 300 **drops** medicinal drops

"In him a plenitude of subtle matter,
Applied to cautels, all strange forms receives,
Of burning blushes, or of weeping water,
305 Or sounding paleness; and he takes and leaves,
In either's aptness, as it best deceives,
To blush at speeches rank, to weep at woes,
Or to turn white and sound at tragic shows;

"That not a heart which in his level came
310 Could 'scape the hail of his all-hurting aim,
Showing fair nature as both kind and tame;
And, veiled in them, did win whom he would maim.
Against the thing he sought he would exclaim:
When he most burned in heart-wished luxury,
315 He preached pure maid and praised cold chastity.

"Thus merely with the garment of a Grace,
The naked and concealèd fiend he covered,
That th' unexperient gave the tempter place,
Which, like a cherubin, above them hovered.
320 Who, young and simple, would not be so lovered?
Ay me! I fell, and yet do question make
What I should do again for such a sake.

"O, that infected moisture of his eye,
O, that false fire which in his cheek so glowed,
325 O, that forced thunder from his heart did fly,
O, that sad breath his spongy lungs bestowed,
O, all that borrowed motion, seeming owed,
Would yet again betray the fore-betrayed
And new-pervert a reconcilèd maid!"

FINIS

303 **cautels** tricks   305 **sounding** swooning   305 **takes and leaves**
alternately uses   306 **In either's aptness** i.e., according as it serves
his purpose   307 **rank** lustful   308 **sound** swoon   309 **level** range
of eye (literally: aim, line of fire)   310 **hail** bullets   311 **Showing . . .
tame** appearing to be harmless and friendly   312 **them** i.e., kind-
ness and tameness (or possibly the "strange forms" of line 303)
314 **luxury** lechery   318 **unexperient** inexperienced   319 **Which**
who   323 **infected** unnatural   327 **borrowed . . . owed** assumed
behavior that seemed his own   329 **reconcilèd** penitent

The Passionate Pilgrim

IV

Sweet Cytherea, sitting by a brook
With young Adonis, lovely, fresh, and green,
Did court the lad with many a lovely look,
Such looks as none could look but beauty's queen.
She told him stories, to delight his ear;   5
She showed him favors, to allure his eye;
To win his heart she touched him here and there—
Touches so soft still conquer chastity.
But whether unripe years did want conceit,
Or he refused to take her figured proffer,   10
The tender nibbler would not touch the bait,
But smile and jest at every gentle offer.
    Then fell she on her back, fair queen, and toward.
    He rose and ran away. Ah, fool too froward!

IV 1 **Cytherea** Venus 2 **green** young 3 **lovely** loving 9
conceit understanding 13 **toward** willing 14 **froward** refrac-
tory

VI

Scarce had the sun dried up the dewy morn,
And scarce the herd gone to the hedge for shade,
When Cytherea (all in love forlorn),
A longing tarriance for Adonis made
5   Under an osier growing by a brook,
A brook where Adon used to cool his spleen.
Hot was the day; she hotter that did look
For his approach that often there had been.
Anon he comes, and throws his mantle by,
10   And stood stark naked on the brook's green brim.
The sun looked on the world with glorious eye,
Yet not so wistly as this queen on him.
    He, spying her, bounced in whereas he stood.
    "O Jove," quoth she, "why was not I a flood!"

VII

Fair is my love, but not so fair as fickle;
Mild as a dove, but neither true nor trusty;
Brighter than glass, and yet as glass is, brittle;
Softer than wax, and yet as iron rusty:
5   A lily pale, with damask dye to grace her;
    None fairer, nor none falser to deface her.

Her lips to mine how often hath she joinèd,
Between each kiss her oaths of true love swearing!
How many tales to please me hath she coinèd,
10   Dreading my love, the loss whereof still fearing!
    Yet, in the midst of all her pure protestings,
    Her faith, her oaths, her tears, and all were jestings.

VI   3 **Cytherea** Venus   4 **tarriance** awaiting   5 **osier** willow
6 **spleen** hot temper   12 **wistly** eagerly   13 **whereas** where

VII   5 **damask** pale red   6 **to deface her** to her discredit   9
coinèd counterfeited

She burnt with love, as straw with fire flameth;
She burnt out love, as soon as straw outburneth;
She framed the love, and yet she foiled the framing;   15
She bade love last, and yet she fell a-turning.
　　Was this a lover, or a lecher, whether?
　　Bad in the best, though excellent in neither.

IX

Fair was the morn when the fair queen of love,
·　·　·　·　·　·　·　·　·　·　·　·　·　·
Paler for sorrow than her milk-white dove,
For Adon's sake, a youngster proud and wild,
Her stand she takes upon a steep-up hill.   5
Anon Adonis comes with horn and hounds.
She, silly queen, with more than love's good will,
Forbade the boy he should not pass those grounds.
"Once," quoth she, "did I see a fair sweet youth
Here in these brakes deep-wounded with a boar,   10
Deep in the thigh, a spectacle of ruth!
See, in my thigh," quoth she, "here was the sore."
　　She showèd hers; he saw more wounds than one,
　　And blushing fled and left her all alone.

X

Sweet rose, fair flower, untimely plucked, soon vaded,
Plucked in the bud, and vaded in the spring!
Bright orient pearl, alack, too timely shaded!
Fair creature, killed too soon by death's sharp sting!
　　Like a green plum that hangs upon a tree,   5
　　And falls, through wind, before the fall should be.

13 **fire** (two syllables)　15 **framed** formed　15 **foiled** thwarted
16 **fell a-turning** i.e., turned to others (for sex)　17 **whether** which
of the two　18 **neither** (also, the sexual organs are "nether" parts)
IX　2 (a line rhyming with "wild" is lost)　11 **ruth** pity　X 1, 2
vaded (1) departed (2) faded　3 **timely** soon

I weep for thee, and yet no cause I have;
For why, thou left'st me nothing in thy will.
And yet thou left'st me more than I did crave,
10　For why, I cravèd nothing of thee still.
　　　O yes, dear friend, I pardon crave of thee:
　　　Thy discontent thou didst bequeath to me.

XII·

Crabbèd age and youth cannot live together:
Youth is full of pleasance, age is full of care;
Youth like summer morn, age like winter weather;
Youth like summer brave, age like winter bare.
5　Youth is full of sport, age's breath is short;
Youth is nimble, age is lame;
Youth is hot and bold, age is weak and cold;
Youth is wild, and age is tame.
Age, I do abhor thee; youth, I do adore thee:
10　O, my love, my love is young!
Age, I do defy thee. O sweet shepherd hie thee,
For methinks thou stays too long.

XIII

Beauty is but a vain and doubtful good;
A shining gloss that vadeth suddenly;
A flower that dies when first it 'gins to bud;
A brittle glass that's broken presently;
5　　A doubtful good, a gloss, a glass, a flower,
　　Lost, vaded, broken, dead within an hour.

8, 10 **For why** because　XII　2 **pleasance** gaiety　4 **brave** splendid　11 **defy** reject　11 **hie thee** hurry　XIII　2 **vadeth** (1) departs (2) fades　4 **presently** soon

And as goods lost are seld or never found,
As vaded gloss no rubbing will refresh,
As flowers dead lie witherèd on the ground,
As broken glass no cement can redress: 10
   So beauty blemished once, for ever lost,
   In spite of physic, painting, pain, and cost.

XIV

Good night, good rest; ah, neither be my share!
She bade good night that kept my rest away,
And daffed me to a cabin hanged with care
To descant on the doubts of my decay.
   "Farewell," quoth she, "and come again tomor-
     row."   5
Fare well I could not, for I supped with sorrow.

Yet at my parting sweetly did she smile,
In scorn or friendship, nill I conster whether.
'T may be she joyed to jest at my exile;
'T may be, again to make me wander thither: 10
   "Wander"—a word for shadows like myself
   As take the pain but cannot pluck the pelf.

Lord, how mine eyes throw gazes to the east!
My heart doth charge the watch; the morning rise
Doth cite each moving sense from idle rest,   15
Not daring trust the office of mine eyes,
   While Philomela sits and sings, I sit and mark,
   And wish her lays were tunèd like the lark;

7 **seld** seldom   10 **cement** (stress on first syllable)   12 **physic** medicine   12 **cost** expenditure   XIV   3 **daffed me** sent me off   4 **descant** lament (literally, compose musical variations)   8 **nill I conster whether** I do not know which   12 **As** who   12 **pelf** reward   14 **charge the watch** order the watchman to proclaim day (?)   15 **cite** summon   17 **Philomela** the nightingale   18 **lays** songs

For she doth welcome daylight with her ditty
20 And drives away dark dreaming night.
The night so packed, I post unto my pretty;
Heart hath his hope, and eyes their wishèd sight;
    Sorrow changed to solace and solace mixed with sorrow;
For why, she sighed and bade me come tomorrow.

25 Were I with her, the night would post too soon,
But now are minutes added to the hours;
To spite me now, each minute seems a moon;
Yet not for me, shine sun to succor flowers!
    Pack night, peep day! Good day, of night now borrow:
30 Short, night, tonight, and length thyself tomorrow.

XV

It was a lording's daughter, the fairest one of three,
That likèd of her master as well as well might be,
Till looking on an Englishman, the fair'st that eye could see,
    Her fancy fell a-turning.
Long was the combat doubtful that love with love did
5   fight,
To leave the master loveless, or kill the gallant knight:
To put in practice either, alas, it was a spite
    Unto the silly damsel!
But one must be refusèd; more mickle was the pain
10 That nothing could be usèd to turn them both to gain,
For of the two the trusty knight was wounded with
        disdain:
    Alas, she could not help it!
Thus art with arms contending was victor of the day,
Which by a gift of learning did bear the maid away:
15 Then, lullaby, the learned man hath got the lady gay;
    For now my song is ended.

21 **packed** disposed of 21 **post** hurry 24 **For why** because 26
added to i.e., like 27 **moon** month 30 **Short . . . length** shorten
. . . lengthen XV 1 **lording's** lord's 2 **master** teacher 8 **silly**
inexperienced 9 **more mickle** greater 13 **art** learning

XVII

My flocks feed not, my ewes breed not,
My rams speed not, all is amiss:
Love is dying, faith's defying,
Heart's denying, causer of this.
All my merry jigs are quite forgot, 5
All my lady's love is lost, God wot.
Where her faith was firmly fixed in love,
There a nay is placed without remove.
One silly cross wrought all my loss.
    O frowning Fortune, cursèd fickle dame! 10
For now I see inconstancy
    More in women than in men remain.

In black mourn I, all fears scorn I,
Love hath forlorn me, living in thrall.
Heart is bleeding, all help needing— 15
O cruel speeding, fraughted with gall!
My shepherd's pipe can sound no deal;
My wether's bell rings doleful knell;
My curtail dog, that wont to have played,
Plays not at all, but seems afraid; 20
With sighs so deep procures to weep,
    In howling wise, to see my doleful plight.
How sighs resound through heartless ground,
    Like a thousand vanquished men in bloody fight!

XVII 3 **defying** rejection 4 **denying** (perhaps it should be
emended to *renying* = disowning) 5 **jigs** songs or dance tunes 6
wot knows 8 **nay** denial 9 **cross** misfortune 16 **speeding** lot
16 **fraughted** laden 17 **no deal** not at all 19 **curtail dog** dog
with docked tail 23 **heartless** (1) pitiless (2) cowardly

25 Clear wells spring not, sweet birds sing not,
    Green plants bring not forth their dye.
    Herds stands weeping, flocks all sleeping,
    Nymphs back peeping fearfully.
    All our pleasure known to us poor swains,
30 All our merry meetings on the plains,
    All our evening sport from us is fled,
    All our love is lost, for Love is dead.
    Farewell, sweet lass! Thy like ne'er was
        For a sweet content, the cause of all my moan.
35 Poor Corydon must live alone.
        Other help for him I see that there is none.

XVIII

    When as thine eye hath chose the dame
    And stalled the deer that thou shouldst strike,
    Let reason rule things worthy blame,
    As well as fancy's partial might;
5   Take counsel of some wiser head,
        Neither too young, nor yet unwed.

    And when thou com'st thy tale to tell,
    Smooth not thy tongue with filèd talk,
    Lest she some subtile practice smell—
10 A cripple soon can find a halt;
        But plainly say thou lov'st her well,
        And set thy person forth to sell.

    And to her will frame all thy ways.
    Spare not to spend, and chiefly there
15 Where thy desert may merit praise
    By ringing in thy lady's ear.
        The strongest castle, tower, and town,
        The golden bullet beats it down.

XVIII   2 **stalled the deer** got the deer within range (with pun on
"dear")   4 **fancy's partial might** (a desperate emendation for the
text's "fancy (partyall might)" which seems meaningless. The emenda-
tion, and its context, means that sexual behavior ["things worthy blame"]
should be governed by impartial reason and by the partial power of love
["fancy"])   8 **filèd** polished   9 **practice** deception   10 **A cripple . . .
halt** a cripple knows a limp (and so a woman can recognize a deceiver)

Serve always with assurèd trust
And in thy suit be humble-true.   *20*
Unless thy lady prove unjust,
Press never thou to choose a new.
    When time shall serve, be thou not slack
    To proffer, though she put thee back.

What though her frowning brows be bent,   *25*
Her cloudy looks will calm ere night;
And then too late she will repent
That thus dissembled her delight,
    And twice desire, ere it be day,
    That which with scorn she put away.   *30*

What though she strive to try her strength,
And ban and brawl and say thee nay,
Her feeble force will yield at length,
When craft hath taught her thus to say:
    "Had women been so strong as men,   *35*
    In faith, you had not had it then."

The wiles and guiles that women work,
Dissembled with an outward show,
The tricks and toys that in them lurk,
The cock that treads them shall not know.   *40*
    Have you not heard it said full oft,
    A woman's nay doth stand for naught?

Think women still to strive with men
To sin and never for to saint.
There is no heaven: be holy then   *45*
When time with age shall them attaint.
    Were kisses all the joys in bed,
    One woman would another wed.

---

32 ban **curse** 45 **There is no heaven** i.e., there is no heavenly bliss
in serving women (?)

But soft, enough! too much, I fear,
50   Lest that my mistress hear my song.
She will not stick to round me on th' ear,
To teach my tongue to be so long.
    Yet will she blush, here be it said,
    To hear her secrets so bewrayed.

FINIS

49 **soft** stop   51 **stick to round me on th' ear** hesitate to scold me
54 **bewrayed** revealed

Commentaries

HALLETT SMITH

From Elizabethan Poetry

The most famous of the Ovidian poems to appear is of course Shakespeare's *Venus and Adonis,* which came from the press of Richard Field in 1593. Shakespeare uses the same six-line stanza which Lodge had used for *Scillaes Metamorphosis,* not the couplets of Marlowe. His material comes mainly from the tenth book of Ovid's *Metamorphoses,* but as in other Elizabethan Ovidian poems, the legend has been modified by the Salmacis-Hermaphroditus story in Book IV and the Narcissus story in Book III.

The comparison between Marlowe's *Hero and Leander* and Shakespeare's *Venus and Adonis* is a critic's set piece. The two poems, close together in time and belonging to the same tradition, offer a chance to compare the genius of these two poets as their plays can never do. On the whole, the judgment in the competition has been in favor of Marlowe. It is well expressed in a recent illuminating essay by W. B. C. Watkins.* In commenting on the "natural imagery drawn from first-hand observation of the fields and woods," for which Shakespeare's poem is usually praised, Watkins remarks, "In attempting to combine a conservatory atmosphere and the out-of-doors, an ornate style and simplicity of observation, Shakespeare may have had in mind something more than merely another Ovidian poem, or something different, but he failed."

Shakespeare chose one of the most familiar of Ovid's stories

From *Elizabethan Poetry* by Hallett Smith (Cambridge, Mass.: Harvard University Press, 1952. Copyright, 1952, by the President and Fellows of Harvard College). Reprinted by permission of the publisher.
*"Shakespeare's Banquet of Sense," *Southern Review* 7 (1942): 710.

for artistic treatment. It was common enough in paintings and
tapestries, and it had been done in the poetical description of a
painting by Lydgate and by Spenser.* Spenser's description is
that of an appropriate decoration for his Castle Ioyeous. The
room in which it hangs gives an impression of royalty and rich
purveyance, as Spenser emphasizes, so luxurious that it con-
veys to visitors

> The image of superfluous riotize,
> Exceeding much the state of meane degree.†

As Mr. Hard points out, the tapestry is apparently in four panels,
portraying the enamorment of Venus, her enticements, Adonis
sleeping, and the metamorphosis of the slain Adonis into a
flower. It is described by Spenser as

> A worke of rare deuice, and wondrous wit.

The lascivious aspects of the picture presumably derive from an
identification with part of the Salmacis story,

> And whilest he bath'd, with her two crafty spyes,
> She secretly would search each daintie lim.‡

Although Venus does all the wooing, the reluctance of Adonis is
not stressed, and Spenser gives the impression that the goddess
won him.** That the whole purpose of this tapestry was aphro-
disiac is made explicit in the activities of the occupants of the
room.†† The attitude of Britomart and the Red Cross Knight
toward these festivities, if not toward the arras, was one of
proper disapproval.‡‡ Even the serious and moral poets, in the
1590s, drew their Ovidian pictures with some warmth. Such
survivors of the allegorical tradition as Abraham Fraunce, writing

---

*For a discussion of the vogue of tapestries and their subjects, see Fred-
erick Hard, "Spenser's 'Clothes of Arras and of Toure,' " *SP* 27 (1930):
162–85.
  †*Faerie Queene,* III, I, xxxiii.
  ‡III, I, xxxvi. Spenser's source, according to H. G. Lotspeich, is Natalis
Comes for everything except the transformation to a flower (Variorum
Faerie Queene, Book III, p. 208).
  **III, I, xxxvii.
  ††III, I, xxxix.
  ‡‡III, I, xl.

for the Countess of Pembroke a series of tales from the *Metamorphoses* under the title *The Third Part of the Countesse of Pembrokes Yuychurch. Entituled Amintas Dale* (1592), gave a fairly lascivious version of the love-making of Venus.* Furthermore, Fraunce associates Venus and Adonis with Hero and Leander:

> Sometimes, louely records for Adonis sake, she reciteth;
> How Laeander dyde, as he swamme to the bewtiful Hero.†

Venus and Adonis is a crude production in comparison with *Hero and Leander.* A much larger part of it is contained in the dialogue of the two characters, and the action is almost confined to the event of the horse and the breeding jennet. There is nothing like the variety of color, of surface finish, that Marlowe's poem exhibits. And curiously, Shakespeare's queen of love herself seems considerably less divine than the semi-human figures of Hero and Leander.

Marlowe had sensed that Ovid got some of his most telling erotic effects by utilizing reluctance, innocence, and naïveté; he therefore did not scruple to make Leander a novice, for all of his sophistic arguments against virginity. But Shakespeare, in trying to imitate this, betrayed something of his own provincial background. Instead of an erotic innocent, Adonis is something of an adolescent lout. He is from the country and very conscious that he hasn't been around. This makes the attempts to emphasize his beauty ridiculous, and the final impression Adonis leaves is not that of a creature of a world of myth but of a young fellow from Stratford ill at ease in the presence of a court lady.

> Faire Queene (quoth he) if anie loue you owe me,
> Measure my strangenesse with my vnripe yeares,

---

*Sig. M₂r. The relevant lines are quoted by Bush, *Mythology and the Renaissance Tradition,* p. 145, n. 15. The best critical account of Fraunce is to be found in Kathrine Koller, "Abraham Fraunce and Edmund Spenser," *ELH* 7 (1940): 108–20.

†Sig. M₂r. This association is unusual, though the Venus and Adonis story is a common ornament for other Ovidian tales. It is represented on the sleeves of Hero's dress in Marlowe's poem (I, 11–14) and on the dress of Venus in Lodge's *Scillaes Metamorphosis.* But the "louely records" are not, for Fraunce, simply ornaments; they are part of Venus' repertoire of erotic persuasion.

> Before I know myselfe, seeke not to know me,
> No fisher but the vngrowne frie forbeares,
>   The mellow plum doth fall, the green sticks fast,
>   Or being early pluckt, is sower to tast.*

Venus herself represents no ideal picture of physical love. She is dominated by the imagery, which most often and most significantly revolves around the hard and violent appetite of the hawk.†

The critics have often remarked that Shakespeare tempers the erotic atmosphere of the poem with references to the fields and open air. The description of the horse and the account given by Venus of the coursing of the hare, the images of the dive-dapper and the snail, of the lark mounting from his moist cabinet on high, are frequently admired for their own sake. The question of their appropriateness to an Ovidian poem is a more difficult one. Watkins suggests that in one respect Shakespeare is closer to Ovid than Marlowe is: that he "does not exclude any possible suggestion of the physically unpleasant from the portrayal of sensual beauty, though he fails to maintain Ovid's sense of proportion."‡ But it is a question of the particular nature of the physically unpleasant which is admitted into the myth. The "vultur thought" and the comparison with the ravenous appetite of animals are a criticism of the feelings of Venus, and that new world of joy evoked by the struggle of Marlowe's lovers is a very different thing. The associations in Shakespeare's mind become clearer from *Lucrece,* where Tarquin's thoughts as he proceeds to the rape are compared to the vulture, and this leads naturally to the sense of repletion and disgust when such feelings are satisfied, again in terms of the hawk:

> Looke as the full-fed Hound, or gorged Hawke,
> Vnapt for tender smell, or speedie flight,
> Make slow pursuite, or altogether bauk,
> The praie wherein by nature they delight;**

Venus and Adonis, lines 523–28, in *The Poems,* ed. H. E. Rollins (Philadelphia, 1938), vol. 22 of *A New Variorum Edition of Shakespeare.*
†Lines 55–60, 547–58.
‡"Shakespeare's Banquet of Sense," p. 728.
**The Rape of Lucrece,* lines 694–97.

and we are reminded of the sonnet which begins "Th' expense of spirit in a waste of shame." Marlowe can indicate this fierceness of sexual appetite without his imagination being dominated by it. The lines

> Love is not full of pity, as men say,
> But deaf and cruel, where he means to prey,

are followed immediately by

> She trembling strove; this strife of hers (like that
> Which made the world) another world begat
> Of unknown joy.*

In the style of *Venus and Adonis* Shakespeare was no doubt influenced by two opposing models: the painting or tapestry, which would give him such visual details as Venus' lightness on the primroses (151–52), Adonis' "bonnet" (339), and the horse,† and a rhetorical or dramatic tradition which would persuade him to put so much of his narrative into direct speech. There is not such an abrupt break between *Venus and Adonis* and *Lucrece* as the critics have usually made out.

If, as it is reasonable to suppose, Shakespeare had in mind the taste of the young Earl of Southampton when he chose a subject and style for his maiden effort, he was probably right in attempting something in the Ovidian-erotic tradition. It was courtiers like Southampton who fancied the genre most, and, as the references to Shakespeare's poem show, it was the young who were especially attracted to it. But considering how much of the rustic Englishman Shakespeare still had about him, it was a bold experiment. The rusticity shows through. The poet cannot escape from the barnyard, the hawking field, and the rabbit hunt. His senses are still coarsened, and the Ovidian theme is not quite strong enough to refine them for him. The catalogue of the senses, which Chapman was later to make into a structure for his Ovidian poem, is crudely handled here (433–50). When Shakespeare decorates his discourse, it is either with description from nature or rhetorical involutions, and

---

Hero and Leander, II, 287–88; 291–93.
†See A. H. R. Fairchild, *Shakespeare and the Arts of Design* (Columbia, Missouri, 1937), pp. 137–39, for a discussion of the horse passage.

they are both to be used sparingly in this type of poem. The decoration which is suitable and functional is that of the fragment of myth. Marlowe's poem is rich in these decorations and Shakespeare's is poor in them.

Modern criticism of the poem has not been as successful as its auspicious beginning, with Coleridge, would suggest. Coleridge used the poem for illustrative material on two general subjects: the evidence of genius in a young writer and the celebrated distinction between fancy and imagination. These are of course relevant to the poem, and turned back upon it with closer analysis they might have produced very fruitful results. But the critics have followed other courses, with the result that judgment on the poem is without an appropriate frame of reference; it varies from E. W. Sievers' "*Venus and Adonis . . .* is really the foundation of the entire structure of Shakespeare's philosophy of life" to John Bailey's "Much of it is rather empty and verbose, more is crude in taste, at once sensuous and sentimental, without reserve or reticence, dignity or manliness or morals."* Professor H. T. Price interprets very elaborately the imagery of *Venus and Adonis,* after the manner of G. Wilson Knight, finds the poem to be the expression of the most savage irony known to him in literature, and says in conclusion, "I am the only man of our days to say in print that he has really received from *Venus and Adonis* the joy that Shakespeare intended to communicate."†

Viewed from within the convention to which it belongs, Shakespeare's poem shows the difficulty of acclimatizing the new Ovidian poem in English. Marlowe had done it, but his success hung precariously on a skill and taste which even his greatest contemporary did not have in 1593. Considering the nature of Shakespeare's artistic development, it might be said that the failure of *Venus and Adonis* predicts the success of *A Midsummer Night's Dream.* Shakespeare was unwilling or unable to shed a basic English earthiness; had he done so he might have matched *Hero and Leander* but he might never have produced Bottom or Falstaff or Juliet's nurse. Tucker Brooke used to say that just as Keats wrote *Endymion* to decockneyize himself, Shakespeare wrote *Venus and Adonis* as the quickest way out of the mental climate of Stratford. It is

---

*Variorum *Poems,* ed. Rollins, pp. 486, 513–14.
†"The Function of Imagery in *Venus and Adonis,*" *Papers of the Michigan Academy of Science, Arts, and Letters* 31 (1945): 275–97.

fortunate for his later work that he did not succeed in getting completely out.

Whatever modern criticism may say about *Venus and Adonis,* in its own time "the younger sort," as Gabriel Harvey said, found in the poem a triumph of fancy and delight. There were at least ten editions in Shakespeare's lifetime, and the poem was, as Professor Bentley says, "probably Shakespeare's best-known composition between 1590 and 1616."* Some of its popularity was due to its erotic subject matter, and there are many allusions to prove that in the eyes of some contemporaries "Shakespeare's poems were the favorite reading of loose and degenerate people, and that, as a consequence, they led to looseness and degeneracy."† But of course the critics who objected to the salacious qualities of *Venus and Adonis* would also object to Ovid, even in the *Metamorphoses,* unless they happened to consider him an allegorical poet. It is amusing to hear a character in the Cambridge play of 1601, *The Return from Parnassus, or The Scourge of Simony,* praise *Venus and Adonis* and *The Rape of Lucrece* but suggest wistfully that Shakespeare would be a better writer

> Could but a grauer subiect him content,
> Without loues foolish lazy languishment.‡

The greatest testimony to the vogue of *Venus and Adonis* comes not from allusions but from the many Ovidian poems of the next decade which borrowed from it and *Hero and Leander.* Even poets who considered Spenser the greatest English bard, as many of them did, turned to Marlowe and Shakespeare for models of the mythological poem.

---

*G. E. Bentley, *Shakespeare and Jonson,* 2 vols. (Chicago, 1945), I, 41. *Venus and Adonis* did not maintain this position through the seventeenth century. See Bentley's list, I, 109, and his comment on I, 117, that "the poem's vogue was largely a sixteenth-century one."
†Variorum *Poems,* ed. Rollins, p. 456.
‡Ed. by W. D. Macray (Oxford, 1886), p. 87.

C. S. LEWIS

From English Literature in the Sixteenth Century

Venus and Adonis, if it were his only work, might not now be highly praised; but his next poem might stand higher if it stood alone and were compared solely with other Elizabethan products, not with his own masterpieces. *The Rape of Lucrece* (1594) presumably discharges the promise made in the Epistle to *Venus and Adonis* of "some graver labour." It is heroic poetry as the heroic was understood before Virgil had been sufficiently distinguished from Lucan and Ovid; and it differs from its predecessor in merit as much as in kind. The theme would at that time have tempted almost any other poet to one more "tragedy" modeled on the *Mirror for Magistrates,* and only those who have read many such "tragedies" can adequately thank Shakespeare for rejecting that form. It is, however, very much a work of its own age. It contains prettinesses and puerilities which the later Shakespeare would have seen to be unsuitable to his heartrending subject. The conceit which makes Lucrece's pillow "angrie" at 388 would have been tolerable in *Hero and Leander* but is here repellent; and so is the aetiological myth at 1747, or the competitive laments of the husband and the father at Lucrece's death. There is some of Kyd's fustian in the apostrophe to Night (764–77). It is hard not to smile when Lucrece invites the nightingale to use her hair as a grove (1129), but Edward Lear may be partly to blame. The passage in which she becomes preoccupied, like Troilus or a lover in the *Arcadia,* about the style of her letter to her husband is more difficult to judge: perhaps it is not impossible that a woman of the nineties, brought up by a humanist tutor, might, even at such a moment,

From *English Literature in the Sixteenth Century* by C. S. Lewis (Oxford: The Clarendon Press, 1954). Reprinted by permission of the publisher.

have remembered the claims of *eloquentia.* These are merely
local imperfections. But there is also, whether we reckon it an
imperfection or not, something in the structure of the whole
poem which is not quite congenial to our taste. It starts indeed
with twenty-one lines of purposeful narration, not rivaled in
that age outside the *Faerie Queene*: then our sails flap in three
stanzas of digression. And we must be prepared for this
throughout. Shakespeare's version of the story is about twelve
times as long as Ovid's in the *Fasti* and, even so, omits the
earlier stages. Much of this length is accounted for by digres-
sion (131–54 or 1237–53), *exclamatio* (701–14), *sententiae*
(131–54), and *descriptio* (1366–1526). The technique is in fact
that of the medieval rhetoricians. Even in those passages which,
taken as a whole, are narrative, a great deal of gnomic amplifi-
cation is brought in. We have "theme and variations." Thus at
211 ("What win I if I gain the thing I seek?") Tarquin states the
theme of the game not being worth the candle in two lines: it is
then varied for five. At 1002 Lucrece states her theme (*noblesse
oblige*) in two lines and then varies it for twelve. At 1107 we
have theme in two lines and again twelve lines of variation. Mi-
nor instances occur throughout. We must not put this down too
exclusively to the Age, for Shakespeare was in fact fonder of
amplification than many other Elizabethans and used it, some-
times rather grossly, in his earlier plays. There is nothing in *Lu-
crece* quite so crude as Gaunt's successive variations on the
theme "His rash fierce blaze of riot cannot last" in *Richard II*
(2.1.33 et seq.). There is a free use of simple one-for-one paral-
lelism, as in the Psalms;

> The shame that from them no device can take,
> The blemish that will never be forgot,

or

> Bearing away the wound that nothing healeth,
> The scarre that will despite of cure remaine.

Whether the method shall prove tedious or delightful depends
on style, in the narrowest sense of the word: that is, on the volu-
bility of phrase which makes the variant seem effortless, and on
phonetic qualities. Thus in *shame, device,* and *blemish* we have
long monosyllable, disyllable in rising rhythm, disyllable in

falling rhythm. In the second example we have the alliteration of *away* and *wound* and the very subtle consonantal pattern of *scarre, despite,* and *cure.* The first consonant group (*sk*) is not repeated, but one of its elements recurs in *-spite* and the other in *cure.*

Another example is:

> To stamp the seal of time in aged things   (941)

No one reads such a line without pleasure. Yet its emotional content is weak and its intellectual weaker still: to say that time stamps the seal of time on things that have existed a long time is near tautology. The charm depends partly, as before, on the distribution of a consonant group between the simple consonants of two later words (*st, s, t*), and partly on the fact that all the stressed syllables are long and all have different vowels.

But *Lucrece* has more than formal beauties to offer us. If not continuously, yet again and again, our sympathies are fully engaged. The rape itself, from the moment at which Tarquin strikes his falchion on the flint to the moment when he "creeps sadly thence" is presented with a terror and horror unequaled in Elizabethan narrative verse. And here, certainly, the digression on "drunken desire" before and after its "vomit" is fully justified. "The spotted princess" (Tarquin's soul) is admirable: still a princess, unable to abdicate, and there's the tragedy. Lucrece, too rhetorical in her agonies, is not quite so good as Tarquin, but she has her great moments: "I sue for exil'd majestie's repeal," pleading "in a wilderness where are no laws." And of all the good things that Shakespeare said about Time he puts perhaps the best into her mouth:

> Why work'st thou mischief in thy pilgrimage
> Unless thou couldst return to make amendes?

She should not have gone on (good though the line is) to add "Thou ceaslesse lackeye to eternitie." It matters nothing that the historical Lucretia would have known neither Plato nor Boethius: the Elizabethan Lucrece ought not to have displayed her learning at that moment. For of course the characters are to be judged as Elizabethans throughout: even Christianity creeps in at 624 and 1156–58.

KENNETH MUIR AND SEAN O'LOUGHLIN

From The Voyage to Illyria

The broad and superficial outline of *The Phoenix and the Turtle* is not difficult to trace. We have various birds summoned to join in the obsequies of two loyal and faithful birds, the phoenix and the turtle. The birds summoned are birds of good omen, or, more curiously, chaste but of ill omen. The fidelity of the dead birds had been a source of wonder and admiration, so close were the links that joined them. Reason, marveling, but not comprehending, made the lament over their ashes. It is in the closer interpretation of the poem that critics, as we have already seen, confess themselves baffled. "Ranjee" rightly disagrees with the late Professor Herford, who called it "a pleasant jest," and with Grosart, who indulged in a farrago about Elizabeth and Essex, but his own interpretation on the basis of the work of emblematists like Gabriello Simeoni and Arnold Freitag seems to us totally mistaken. Only Mr. Murry, in the essay on poetry in *Discoveries,* appears to have come within striking distance of the problem. Our own attempt, made independently, resembles his in some respects, though it has important differences.

It is clear, we have said, that Shakespeare had glanced at *Love's Martyr,* but there was another book, *The Phoenix Nest,* published in 1593, the contents of which were certainly in his mind. In Matthew Roydon's elegy on Sir Philip Sidney there is a passage of some importance. The author describes the mourners at the funeral thus:

> The skie bred Egle roiall bird,
> Percht there vpon an oke aboue,
> The Turtle by him neuer stird,

From *The Voyage to Illyria* by Kenneth Muir and Sean O'Loughlin (London: Methuen & Co. Ltd., 1937). Reprinted by permission of the authors.

> Example of immortall loue.
>> The swan that sings about to dy,
>> Leauing Meander stood thereby.
>
> And that which was of woonder most,
> The Phoenix left sweete Arabie.

This coincidence is not fortuitous, since the line in Shakespeare's poem, "Death is now the *Phoenix* nest," suggests another link. Furthermore, the idea of chastity is the subject of a subsequent poem in the same book, and, in "An excellent Dialogue between Constancie and Inconstancie" which comes immediately after it, we have a reference to "loue, which is for the most part, reason beyond reason." It seems natural to suppose that this is the "source" of "Loue hath Reason, Reason none."

We have now to discover the idea in Shakespeare's mind which attracted to itself all these fragments, which are related, in their original setting, only by their proximity. In view of what we propose to establish later on, we can say that *The Phoenix and the Turtle* came not long after the final break with Southampton. It must be emphasized that this break is not to be confused with the estrangement mentioned in the *Sonnets* themselves, but was a deeper and more disturbing one, which came after the last sonnet had been written. Despite this, the poem is not one of despair, but of quiet assurance. "Hope creates From its own wreck the thing it contemplates." Therein lies its significance. Southampton had destroyed the love for which the poet had been willing to sacrifice everything. "Take all my loues, my loue, yea take them all," and Shakespeare now proclaims that though their mutual love is ended in the actual world, it exists for ever in eternity. This may be thought a poor consolation, a sentimental brooding over what might have been; but this is to misunderstand the poem's significance. Though love has been betrayed brutally, even sordidly, the fact that it once existed is sufficient assurance to the poet that "Loue hath Reason," that is to say is an absolute. He will not admit, as he afterwards did in a moment of bitterness, that love's betrayal is a proof that it never existed. Here, he reenunciates the testament he wrote when he suspected that Southampton's affection was cooling:

> Loue is not loue
> Which alters when it alteration findes,
> Or bends with the remouer to remoue.
> O no, it is an euer fixed marke
> That lookes on tempests and is neuer shaken;
> It is the star to euery wandring barke,
> Whose worths vnknowne, although his higth be taken.
> Lou's not Times foole, though rosie lips and cheeks
> Within his bending sickles compasse come,
> Loue alters not with his breefe houres and weekes,
> But beares it out euen to the edge of doome.

Though "Loue and Constancie is dead," the miracle of perfect love exists in eternity,

> *Phoenix* and the *Turtle* fled,
> In a mutuall flame from hence,

so great was their love on earth.

We come now to the more metaphysical parts of the poem, where the problems are of a different order. Let us take the stanzas that express the unity in disunity of the two birds:

> So they loued as loue in twaine,
> Had essence but in one,
> Two distincts, Diuision none,
> Number there in loue was slaine.
> Hearts remote, yet not asunder;
> Distance and no space was seen,
> Twixt this *Turtle* and his Queene;
> But in them it were a wonder.

Shakespeare had already expressed this view of his love in *Sonnet* 36, addressed to Southampton:

> Let me confesse that we two must be twaine,
> Although our vndeuided loues are one.

It was this feeling of the unity of the spirit that enabled Shakespeare to preserve an ultimate faith in love and beauty, even in the inferno through which he was to pass. Cordelia would be impossible without the emotional conviction expressed in *The Phoenix and the Turtle*. As Mr. Murry so eloquently puts it:

> By reason of the mutual disaster which is to engulf them, Lear and Cordelia are lifted up into the condition of *The Phoenix and the Turtle*. Lear's very words: "We two will sing alone like birds i' the cage," contain a trembling mortal echo of their song, and Reason might chant over Cordelia the dirge it chanted over them.

Julius Caesar is the first of the tragedies to be "illuminated by the splendor of the vision," and this brief poem, written during the same period, is the first expression of that vision. In it, the seed of all Shakespeare's later development is contained. Professor Wilson Knight, in his essay *The Shakesperian Aviary*, has attempted to show that the symbolism of the first six stanzas* can be referred to a particular play. But this is to consider too curiously for our purpose. All we would claim is that the mourners at the obsequies are "heraulds sad" of the "tragique scene" on to which the poet was about to enter, and that the essence of Shakespearean tragedy is the conflict between the vision and life as we know it. It is clear that when the poem was written, Shakespeare had a prophetic understanding of the experience he must undergo. Shakespearean tragedy is, in a very real sense, the tragedy of Shakespeare himself.

As we can gather from the *Sonnets*, for example, the idea of sex was tarnished for the poet, and he still clung to the ideal of the marriage of true minds, chaste, and therefore

> Leauing no posteritie,
> Twas not their infirmitie,
> It was married Chastitie.

The poem is a recognition that this love, divorced from its original object, is the motive force behind all his poetry ("So oft

---

*Professor Knight connects the various stanzas as follows:—i, *Romeo and Juliet*; ii, *Macbeth*; iii, *Cymbeline*; iv, *The Merchant of Venice*; v, *Hamlet*; vi, *Antony and Cleopatra*; but *Othello* would surely be a better parallel to stanza iv. *Romeo and Juliet* is the only play written before 1600. We might interpret this by saying that it was a forerunner of the tragic period to which the death of love and constancy gave rise, or, alternatively, that the true parallel to stanza i is *Antony and Cleopatra*.

haue I inuok'd thee for my Muse"—*Sonnet* 78); and it marks the transformation of the lovely boy into the spirit of Ariel. The validity of this love is next established:

> Truth may seeme, but cannot be,
> Beautie bragge, but tis not she.

It was not Truth, for Truth had been betrayed. It was not Beauty, for the Beauty he had worshiped played him false. The answer comes in a brief couplet:

> Loue hath Reason, Reason none,
> If what parts, can so remaine.

Love, it was, to which the others were subsumed, that inspired Shakespeare's plays, a love that would be eventually extended to embrace the whole world. He had not reached that state, but already his prophetic soul looked forward to the ultimate synthesis, the emotional serenity of *The Tempest*. He looked forward to the time when even Reason would recognize that Love was above Reason. As Arviragus in *Cymbeline* says:

> I know not why
> I loue this youth, and I haue heard you say,
> Loue's reason's, without reason.

Though "in itself confounded," it was Reason that made the threne in honor of the co-supremes and stars of love.

About eight years were to pass before Shakespeare was able to embody these co-supremes in a play, but it was no longer a chaste union. The fidelity was founded on sexual love. The proclamation that "Loue hath Reason, Reason none" foreshadows *Antony and Cleopatra*. To Reason, and, alas, to Sir Arthur Quiller-Couch, *Antony and Cleopatra* is *All for Lust,* and Antony sacrifices his honor for the sake of a harlot. To Shakespeare, that actuality was a ludicrous distortion of the reality behind it. He, like the priests, blessed Cleopatra when she was riggish, and Antony is hailed as the Arabian bird. It is noteworthy, too, that bird imagery is more frequent in this play than in any other.

But we must revert to the poem. Truth and Beauty had been set side by side by the poet in *Sonnet* 14. Addressing the lovely boy, he had said, "Thy end is Truthes and Beauties doome and date," and so now

> Truth may seeme, but cannot be,
> Beautie bragge, but tis not she,
> Truth and Beautie buried be.

This must not be taken to imply physical death so much as the admission of the power of Death which faithlessness brings in its train, just as fidelity, by its very existence, conquers Death.

This consideration brings us to the problem of why Shakespeare chose the symbolism of the Phoenix to express this determining experience of his life. The Phoenix has been, from time immemorial, a symbol of immortality and resurrection, and Shakespeare's aching desire to overcome the iniquity of oblivion, so manifest in the *Sonnets,* here finds relief:

> Deuouring time blunt thou the Lyons pawes,
> And make the earth deuoure her owne sweet brood,
> Plucke the keene teeth from the fierce Tygers yawes,
> And burne the long liu'd Phœnix in her blood.

The immortal Phoenix must make this concession to Time. She must burn in a flame of love, and hence, the bird is a love symbol. In Lyly's *Euphues* and Ovid's *Metamorphoses,* the legend is briefly related, and Golding renders Ovid thus:

> One bird there is that dooth renew itself and as it were
> Beget it self continually. The Syrians name it there
> A *Phœnix.* Neyther corne nor herbes this *Phœnix* liueth
>   by,
> But by the iewce of frankincence and gum of *Amomye.*

Shakespeare doubtless took the idea of the turtle as the devoted mate of the Phoenix from Chester's own poem, *Love's Martyr,* the turtle being, of course, the Paphian dove of Venus.

The Phoenix, finally, is a symbol not only of immortality, but also of death, and the emphasis on death and mourning is a parallel to the thoughts of death in *Julius Caesar* and *Hamlet.* Shakespeare, at the turn of the century, stood on the threshold of the tragic period. The experience which finds expression in the poem enabled him to endure to the end. Love was the star that enabled his "wandring barke" to survive the "tempest." In the plays that follow upon this new attitude, notably *Antony and Cleopatra* and *King Lear,* his concept of order in the Universe is expressed as a belief in constancy and faithfulness, a constancy and faithfulness that, in the tragedies, receives death as its reward, and is the antithesis of the betrayal that compassed the death of Caesar. Years later, Imogen, "alone the Arabian bird," escaped the normal penalty for constancy, though she had a funeral, and, in *The Tempest,* Prospero's enemies are compelled to admit that

> In *Arabia*
> There is one Tree, the Phœnix throne, one Phœnix
> At this houre reigning there.

When the validity of the vision of *The Phoenix and the Turtle* had been acknowledged, the poet's task was done.

That, then, is the significance of *The Phoenix and the Turtle.* When Shakespeare finished *Henry V* and *The Merry Wives of Windsor,* he had reached a crucial moment in his career as a dramatist. Both plays were inferior to *Henry IV.* It was, as Mr. Masefield puts it, "slack water" with him. "The personality was worn to a husk."

> Now artists of all kinds exist and progress by destroying those selves of them which, having flowered, have served. They are continually sitting in judgment upon themselves, and annihilating their pasts by creating opposites.

For this self-annihilation to take place, some change in the artist's life must occur. It may be quite unconnected with his art, except in so far as his art must constitute a selection of his experience. The nature of this change, based on a betrayal of some magnitude, will be best examined in the next chapter. All we need say here is that it occurred before the completion of *Henry IV,* and that, at first, its very magnitude prevented Shakespeare from assimilating it into his art. That is the primary cause of the thinness in texture of the plays that immediately followed. It is an inadequate explanation to assume that they were written to order. In a sense, all his plays were written under the same conditions. They were limited by the requirements of his patrons, even when they most obviously expressed the poet's own personality, but in the plays that followed *Henry IV,* Shakespeare dared not, and, indeed, could not, utter what was nearest his heart. In *Much Ado About Nothing,* which came soon after, apart from the plot against Hero, there is little of the new outlook, but in *As You Like It* the imagery is impregnated with the betrayal theme. It was not, however, until *Julius Caesar,* that Shakespeare faced his experience, and, in doing so, produced a play greater than any he had so far written. The confidence gained by the consciousness of achievement, and the detachment that followed on the writing of the play, enabled him to overcome the bitterness of betrayal. It was a noble achievement, one that required not only the courage of acceptance, but also the power of refusing to generalize from his own misfortunes, but the effects of the victory were short-lived. Either before or just after *The Phoenix and the Turtle,* Shakespeare wrote one supreme comedy, *Twelfth Night,* his loveliest and most perfect, so wise, so tender, in its treatment of human frailty, using such gentle irony against self-deceivers, that the less perceptive critics have failed to observe how delicate was the balance of this fine equilibrium. Cast adrift from Southampton, the poet had to make a further journey, and the tragedies chart the voyage. He had seen Illyria in the setting sun, but night came on, and the tempest of his soul.

BRUCE R. SMITH

Just Looking

If *Venus and Adonis* and *The Rape of Lucrece* don't look, by today's standards, like pornography, it is because they are so wordy. Pornography, we assume, is visual: it circulates over the Internet as jpg or mpg files. Yet both of Shakespeare's texts (they pulse through the ether as pdf or doc files) present scenes of sexual predation—an experienced woman's attempt to seduce an adolescent boy in *Venus and Adonis,* a soldier's rape of his friend's wife in *Lucrece*—and both of them grant the reader an ethically safe distance from scandalous events that are represented in alluring, fleshly detail.

Take, for example, this stanza from *Venus and Adonis*:

> O, what a sight it was, wistly to view
> How she came stealing to the wayward boy!
> To note the fighting conflict of her hue,
> How white and red each other did destroy!
>   But now her cheek was pale, and by and by
>   It flashed forth fire, as lightning from the sky.   (343–48)

Subsequent stanzas complete the cinematic sweep of body parts: one of her hands heaving up Adonis's hat, the other hand leaving its print on his cheek, the war of looks as her eyes press upon him and his eyes refuse to see, the combat as his white hand is held back by hers like "A lily prisoned in a jail of snow,/ Or ivory in an alabaster band" (362–63). The white-on-white effect points up how either or both of the figures here—he and/or she—can become objects of the reader's lascivious gaze, regardless of the reader's own gender. And it all happens on the sly. "Wistly to view": the word "wistly" usually means

This essay has been written especially for the Signet Classics edition of Shakespeare's poems.

"intently," but it also suggests silently as well as "wishly" or longingly. This is a scene of voyeurism: I as reader am both *there* and *here*.

That is just the position that the reader takes in *Lucrece*. Having followed Tarquin, and the narrator who trails him, into Lucrece's bed chamber, the reader is invited to stand with Tarquin and the narrator outside the bed curtains that shroud the sleeping woman. Drawing aside the curtains, the narrator observes, is like drawing aside a cloud that hides the silver moon. At first dazzled by the light, Tarquin goes on to paint a multi-hued blazon of the sleeping figure's beauty: her lily hand, her rosy cheeks, her eyes like marigolds that have sheathed their light, her golden hair playing in her breath. Then come the visual details that inspire Tarquin not just to look but to touch:

> Her breasts like ivory globes circled with blue,
> A pair of maiden worlds unconquerèd,
> Save of their lord no bearing yoke they knew,
> And him by oath they truly honorèd.
> These worlds in Tarquin new ambition bred,
>   Who like a foul usurper went about
>   From this fair throne to heave the owner out.   (407–13)

The "owner" of the globelike breasts is, of course, not Lucrece but her husband, Collatine—a fact that fires Tarquin's lust all the more. In touching Lucrece's breasts, he touches not just her but Collatine. The ensuing stanzas let the reader feel Tarquin's drumming heart, his burning eye, his hand "Smoking with pride" as it "marched on to make his stand/ On her bare breast" (438–39). But the hand is Tarquin's, not the reader's. Tarquin quickly discards the role of voyeur for the role of rapist, but the reader holds back, remaining, in the *Oxford English Dictionary*'s definition, "A person whose sexual desires are stimulated or satisfied by covert observation of the sex organs or sexual activities of others."*

In setting up these situations—tantalizingly immediate, yet reassuringly distant—Shakespeare was merely exploiting his stock-in-trade as a playwright. By the time he published *Venus and Adonis* in 1593, Shakespeare had already given theater-

---

Oxford English Dictionary Online, "voyeur" 1 (Oxford: Oxford University Press, 2005), accessed 21 June 2007.

goers the titillations of Proteus's attempted rape of Silvia in
The Two Gentlemen of Verona (5.4), Petruchio's exclamation
"Come, Kate, we'll to bed" at the end of *The Taming of the
Shrew* (5.2.189), Queen Margaret's daringly public kiss when
she is parted from her lover, Suffolk, in *Henry VI, Part Two*
(3.2), King Edward's sexual come-on to Lady Gray in *Henry
VI, Part Three* (3.2), Chiron and Demetrius's display of the
ravished Lavinia in *Titus Andronicus* (2.4), the Bastard of Or-
leans's eroticized sword fight with Joan la Pucelle in *Henry VI,
Part One* (1.3), and Richard Gloucester's verbal and bodily
domination of Lady Anne in *Richard III* (1.2). A perfect record:
seven plays, seven great sex scenes. In each case spectators got
to enjoy what they were seeing at a distance—a distance vary-
ing from ten feet or so (for the groundlings crowding up to the
platform) to fifty feet (for the bench sitters in the third gallery).
Interestingly, it was the bench sitters who had paid the most.
Proximity, in this aesthetic, was clearly not everything. Per-
haps, indeed, it was not even the main thing.

In the medium of print (*Venus and Adonis* marked Shake-
speare's debut in the book stalls) distance was likewise built
into the experience of sexual arousal. The unique surviving
copy of the original 1593 edition in the Bodleian Library, Ox-
ford, presents to the reader's eye a planar surface of 7⅜" x 5¼"
(a little over thirty-eight square inches). The book is thin and
light: only ⅛" thick, it weighs about two ounces. The same was
true of the first edition of *Lucrece*. The Huntington Library
copy has almost the same planar surface, thickness, and
weight. Compared with a folio of Virgil or Ovid, or with the
1623 folio of Shakespeare's collected plays, *Venus and Adonis*
and *Lucrece* are light reading.

The 1593 *Venus and Adonis* and the 1594 *Lucrece* are
"handy" books, and they got even handier in the course of their
publishing history from 1593 to 1655. The first four editions of
Venus and Adonis were quartos, the next six shrank to octavos,
the next edition, dated 1636, was smaller still, a duodecimo.
Surviving copies of octavos average about 5" x 3" (for a sur-
face area of about fifteen square inches, more than 50 percent
smaller than a quarto). The Folger Library copy of the duodec-
imo of 1636 measures only 4⅜" x 3¹/₁₂," giving a surface area
of 12¾ square inches, about 85 percent of the surface area of
the octavo editions, but only a third of the surface area of
the quarto editions. Because more pages are needed for the

smaller-format editions (despite a decrease in the font of the type), the weight remains about the same: two ounces. After the appearance of the original quarto of *Lucrece* in 1594, all subsequent editions (1598, 1600, 1600, 1607, 1616, 1624, 1632, 1655) were issued as octavos—small enough to be slipped into a pocket and carried next to the reader's body. The reader's experience of these two books, now as in 1593 and 1594, is both "out there," in the world, and "in here," inside the body. The printed codex itself is an object positioned in space, something one holds in one's hands, using fingers and thumb as an easel, something one keeps at a certain distance from one's eyes (for most people between twelve and eighteen inches). The reader's relationship to the codex can thus be plotted in geometric space. The text is "justified" in space, in the same way an electronic text is justified in a word-processing program with precisely calibrated left and right, top and bottom margins. A book remains an object even as the reader, literally, *in-corporates* the words printed on the page by taking them in through the eyes.

Psychology in Shakespeare's time—the story that people told themselves about what was happening when they looked and read—posited quite a complicated narrative of what came next. Sense experiences like the feel of the book in one's hands, the sight of the letters and the printed ornaments, and the sounds cued by the letters were thought to be fused in a faculty called "common sense." From there "fancy" took over as the reader drew on his or her personal memories and the workings of his or her own imagination to fill out the story on the page. Fancy's work, in the form of *phantasmata*, was then sent to the heart, which might contract in horror or dilate in pleasure, changing the reader's body chemistry. (Surely it was dilation in the case of *Venus and Adonis,* perhaps a combination of dilation and contraction in the case of *Lucrece.*) The whole process ended in an act of judgment. That happened in the head, but it involved the whole body: eyes, hands, brain, heart, and the nerves or "sinews" that carried *phantasmata* between head and heart and passions from the heart to the head.

Venus and Adonis and *The Rape of Lucrece* belong to a flourishing genre of poetry in late-sixteenth- and early-seventeenth-century England: short erotic narratives that Shakespeare and his readers all identified with their favorite classical poet, Ovid. Ovid's *Metamorphoses* ("Changes" might be the closest English equivalent) provided most of these plots, including the story of Venus's unsuccessful attempt to seduce Adonis; his *Fasti* ("Festivals") provided the plot of *Lucrece*. In the case of *Venus and Adonis,* the promised change comes in Venus's transformation of the dead Adonis into an anemone, a flower that commemorates Adonis's red blood. As for Venus herself, "weary of the world, away she hies" (1189) to her home on the island of Paphos, far from the scene of her intrigue with Adonis. And there the reader joins her, in splendid isolation. Having enjoyed (or imagined enjoying) Adonis's succulent male flesh along with Venus, the reader changes perspective—a change that some male readers may have felt to be especially necessary. Translators of Ovid like Arthur Golding (1567) and George Sandys (1626, 1628, 1632, 1638, 1640) facilitated that change in viewpoint, Golding by padding Ovid's Latin text with Anglo-Saxon moralizations, Sandys by providing a running moral commentary. There is a characteristic edge of judgment in Golding's description of Venus's passion in Book 10 of *Metamorphoses*: "Yea, even from Heaven she did abstain. She loved Adonis more/ Than Heaven. To him she clingèd aye, and bare him company."* As for Sandys, the story of Adonis illustrates the truism "Men of excellent beauties have likely been subject to miserable destinies"—and cites a verse from Seneca's *Hippolytus* to prove it.† The distancing shift in *Lucrece* comes not only in the public display of Lucrece's body in the poem's last stanza but in the blunt politicization that ends "The Argument" before the story even begins: "the people were so moved that with one consent and a general acclamation the Tarquins were all exiled, and the state government changed from kings to consuls." It is changes like these—justifications of the story—that explain why Shakespeare and his contemporaries liked Ovid: he fit perfectly with Renaissance psychology, in which all knowledge begins as sensation, changes into passion, but ends in an act of judgment.

Just *looking*—what we tell ourselves we are doing when we casually view something without getting too involved—is *just*

The.xv.Bookes of P. Ouidius Naso, entytuled Metamorphosis (London: William Seres, 1567), trans. Arthur Golding (1567), p. 131 verso.
†*Ouid's Metamorphosis Englished, mythologiz'd, and represented in figures,* trans. George Sandys (Oxford: John Lichfield, 1632), p. 366.

looking in the case of sexual displays in Ovid's *Metamorphoses* and Shakespeare's *Venus and Adonis* and *The Rape of Lucrece*. We get to have it both ways: the pleasure of giving ourselves up to the erotic spectacle and the satisfaction of backing away in an act of judgment. That equipoise justifies our reading of these, even now, salacious poems.

Textual Notes

The Sonnets

The present text of the sonnets is based on the quarto of 1609, the only edition of any authority; all subsequent editions of the sonnets derive from that of 1609. Two of the sonnets (138 and 144) had been published, in slightly different versions, in a volume of poems entitled *The Passionate Pilgrim* (1599); quite possibly all or almost all of the sonnets were written in the middle '90s, though it is equally possible that some were written only shortly before Thorpe issued his quarto with 154 sonnets. There is no evidence that Shakespeare oversaw the publication; probably the order in which the sonnets are presented is the publisher's rather than the author's. In 1640 John Benson issued a second edition. He dropped Thorpe's dedication and eight sonnets, rearranged the order of the remaining ones, made numerous verbal changes to suggest that the sonnets were written to a woman and not to a man, and implied in a preface that the sonnets had never before been published.

The present edition keeps the arrangement of the 1609 quarto, but corrects obvious typographical errors and modernizes spelling and punctuation. Other departures from the quarto are listed below, the present reading first, in italics, and then the reading of the quarto, in roman.

The Textual Editor wishes to acknowledge his indebtedness, especially in the glosses, to his late teacher, Hyder Edward Rollins, whose indispensable *New Variorum Edition* is as likely as any scholarly book to bear it out to the edge of doom.

12.4 *are* or   13.7 *Yourself* You selfe   19.3 *jaws* yawes   19.5 *fleets* fleet'st   25.9 *might* worth   26.12 *thy* their   27.10 *thy* their   34.12 *cross* losse   35.8 *thy . . . thy* their . . . their   41.8 *she* he   43.11 *thy* their   44.13 *naught* naughts   45.12 *thy* their   46.3 *thy* their   46.8 *thy* their   46.9 *'cide* side   46.14 *thy* their   47.11 *not* nor   50.6 *dully* duly   51.10 *perfect'st* perfects   55.1 *monuments* monument   56.13 *Or* As   65.12 *of* or   69.3 *due* end   69.5 *Thy* Their   70.1 *art* are   70.6 *Thy* Their   74.12 *rememberèd* remembred   76.7 *tell* fel   77.10 *blanks* blacks   90.11 *shall* stall   91.8 *better* bitter   99.9 *One* Our   102.8 *her* his   111.1 *with* wish   112.14 *are* y'are   113.6 *latch* lack   113.14 *mine eye* mine   126.8 *minutes* mynuit   128.11 *thy* their   128.14 *thy* their   129.11 *proved, a* proud and   132.6 *of the* of th'   132.9 *mourning* morning   138.12 *to have* t' have   144.6 *side* sight   144.9 *fiend* finde   153.14 *eyes* eye

Other Poems

Three nondramatic poems (other than the sonnets) are regularly attributed to Shakespeare: *Venus and Adonis, The Rape of Lucrece,* and "The Phoenix and the Turtle." *Venus and Adonis* was first published in a quarto dated 1593, *Lucrece* (thus the title page, but the heading at the beginning of the poem, and on all the following pages, is *The Rape of Lucrece*) in a quarto dated 1594. Both quartos are dedicated to Shakespeare's patron, the Earl of Southampton. These two books were Shakespeare's first publications, and they were destined for a nobleman's eye; Shakespeare apparently read the proofs, and the texts are remarkably clean. There is no reason to believe that he had anything to do with the later quartos, which introduce numerous changes.

The third canonical poem, "The Phoenix and the Turtle," appears (without a title) attributed to Shakespeare in a quarto (1601) whose title page reads in part: "*Love's Martyr* . . . allegorically shadowing the truth of Love, in the constant fate of the phoenix and turtle. . . . A poem . . . by Robert Chester . . . To these [Chester's poem and other materials] are added some new compositions, of several modern writers, whose names are subscribed to their several works, upon the first subject, viz. the phoenix and turtle."

THE APOCRYPHAL POEMS. "A Lover's Complaint" appears at the end of the 1609 volume of Shakespeare's sonnets, published by Thomas Thorpe. No one doubts that the sonnets are Shakespeare's, but many doubt that "A Lover's Complaint" is his. The usual view is that the poem does not sound like Shakespeare, and that the publisher's ascription is of no value. The poem does not do Shakespeare great credit, and a fair number of its words do not appear elsewhere in Shakespeare. On p. xxvi of the present volume, the editor indicates his belief that Brian Vickers has recently proved that the poem is not by Shakespeare.

In 1599 a publisher named William Jaggard issued *The Pas-*

sionate Pilgrim. By W. Shakespeare. The book contains twenty
poems, of which five are certainly by Shakespeare and four are
certainly not by Shakespeare. The remaining eleven are of un-
certain authorship, but there is no reason (other than Jaggard's
dubious word) to believe that Shakespeare wrote any of these,
though of course he may have written one or more of them. The
five poems by Shakespeare are numbered I, II, III, V, and XVI
(I and II are versions of sonnets 138 and 144; III and V are ver-
sions of sonnets in *Love's Labor's Lost,* 4.3.59–72 and
4.2.107–20; XVI is a version of a short poem in *Love's Labor's
Lost,* 4.3.100–20). These five poems are not given in the pres-
ent volume because they are available, in better versions, in
the *Sonnets* section and in the Signet Classics editions of
Sonnets and *Love's Labor's Lost.* The four poems that are not
by Shakespeare are VIII (by Richard Barnfield), XI (by
Bartholomew Griffin), XIX (really two poems, probably one
by Marlowe and one by Raleigh), and XX (by Richard Barn-
field). The remaining eleven poems are given in this volume,
though few people would care to claim them all for Shake-
speare. They are for the most part competent, but only number
XII has aroused much enthusiasm.

Departures from the copy-texts are listed below. The
adopted reading is given first, in italic type, followed by the
original reading, in roman type. The copy-text for *Venus and
Adonis* and *The Rape of Lucrece* is of course the first quarto of
each poem. The copy-text of "The Phoenix and the Turtle" is
Love's Martyr (1601), that of "A Lover's Complaint" is the
quarto of 1609. The earliest known complete text of *The Pas-
sionate Pilgrim* is the second edition (1599), but some pages
of the first edition (perhaps also 1599) survive at the Folger
Library. This earlier edition provides texts of three (IV, XVII,
and XVIII) of the eleven doubtful poems. The copy-text for
the other eight doubtful poems is necessarily the second
edition.

Venus and Adonis   19 *satiety* sacietie   231, 239 *deer* deare   432 *Ear's*
Eares   616 *javelin's* iauelings   644 *Saw'st* Sawest   680 *overshoot* ouer-
shut   748 *th'* the th'   754 *sons* suns   873 *twine* twin'd   940 *dost*
doest   1031 *as* are   1054 *was* had

The Rape of Lucrece   550 *blows* blow   883 *mak'st* makest
884 *blow'st* blowest   1227 *flower* flowre   1312 *schedule* Cedule
1662 *wreathèd* wretched   1680 *one woe* on woe   1713 *in it* it in

A Lover's Complaint   14 *lattice* lettice   80 *Of* O   95 *wear* were
112 *manage* mannad'g   118 *Came* Can   182 *woo* vow   241 *Paling* Play-
ing   252 *procured* procure   260 *nun* Sunne   293 *O* Or   311 *as* is*

The Passionate Pilgrim IV   5 *ear* eares   10 *her* his
VII   11 *midst* mids
X   8, 9 *left'st* lefts
XIV   24 *sighed* sight   27 *a moon* an houre
XV   3 *fair'st* fairest
XVII   28 *back* blacke   33 *lass* loue   34 *moan* woe
XVIII   4 *fancy's partial might* fancy (partyall might)   12 *thy* her
12 *sell* sale   22 *Press* Prease   26, 29 *ere* yer   45 *be* by   51 *ear* are

---

*William Empson suggests emending "A Lover's Complaint," line 311,
which reads: "Showing fair nature is both kind and tame." Mr. Empson
writes: It seems better, though not necessary, to emend *is* to *as,* an easy
change in itself. Otherwise *kind and tame* has to mean "the fact that he could
seduce *any* virgin makes them all look like sheep." Maybe this was Shake-
speare's opinion, but he does not express it so bleakly. Besides, *them* in the
next line has to refer back to *strange forms* (line 303), the pretenses of ten-
derness which the seducer was skilled at adopting; if your mind is cluttered
with tame ladies you miss the grammar. *Nature* here is chiefly the sexual
experience, and he shows it to the virgins *as* not alarming; it really is *fair,* we
are told by the author and the wronged lady, and this should content us.
They can hardly want to assert that it is always *tame.*

Index of First Lines of Sonnets

Suggested References

The number of possible references is vast and grows alarmingly. (The *Shakespeare Quarterly* devotes one issue each year to a list of the previous year's work, and *Shakespeare Survey*—an annual publication—includes a substantial review of biographical, critical, and textual studies, as well as a survey of performances.) The vast bibliography is best approached through James Harner, *The World Shakespeare Bibliography on CD-Rom: 1900–Present.* The first release, in 1996, included more than 12,000 annotated items from 1990–93, plus references to several thousand book reviews, productions, films, and audio recordings. The plan is to update the publication annually, moving forward one year and backward three years. Thus, the second issue (1997), with 24,700 entries, and another 35,000 or so references to reviews, newspaper pieces, and so on, covered 1987–94.

For guidance to the immense amount that has been written, consult Larry S. Champion, *The Essential Shakespeare: An Annotated Bibliography of Major Modern Studies,* 2nd ed. (1993), which comments briefly on 1,800 publications.

Though no works are indispensable, those listed below have been found especially helpful. The arrangement is as follows:

1. Shakespeare's Times
2. Shakespeare's Life
3. Miscellaneous Reference Works
4. The Poems in General
5. *The Sonnets*
6. *Venus and Adonis* and *The Rape of Lucrece*
7. *The Phoenix and the Turtle*
8. *A Lover's Complaint*
9. *The Passionate Pilgrim*

1. Shakespeare's Times

Andrews, John F., ed. *William Shakespeare: His World, His Work, His Influence,* 3 vols. (1985). Sixty articles, dealing not only with such subjects as "The State," "The Church," "Law," "Science, Magic, and Folklore," but also with the plays and poems themselves and Shakespeare's influence (e.g., translations, films, reputation).

Byrne, Muriel St. Clare. *Elizabethan Life in Town and Country* (8th ed., 1970). Chapters on manners, beliefs, education, etc., with illustrations.

Dollimore, John, and Alan Sinfield, eds. *Political Shakespeare: New Essays in Cultural Materialism* (1985). Essays on such topics as the subordination of women and colonialism, presented in connection with some of Shakespeare's plays.

Greenblatt, Stephen. *Representing the English Renaissance* (1988). New Historicist essays, especially on connections between political and aesthetic matters, statecraft and stagecraft.

Joseph, B. L. *Shakespeare's Eden: the Commonwealth of England 1558–1629* (1971). An account of the social, political, economic, and cultural life of England.

Kernan, Alvin. *Shakespeare, the King's Playwright: Theater in the Stuart Court 1603–1613* (1995). The social setting and the politics of the court of James I, in relation to *Hamlet*, *Measure for Measure*, *Macbeth*, *King Lear*, *Antony and Cleopatra*, *Coriolanus*, and *The Tempest*.

Montrose, Louis. *The Purpose of Playing: Shakespeare and the Cultural Politics of the Elizabethan Theatre* (1996). A poststructuralist view, discussing the professional theater "within the ideological and material frameworks of Elizabethan culture and society," with an extended analysis of *A Midsummer Night's Dream*.

Mullaney, Steven. *The Place of the Stage: License, Play, and Power in Renaissance England* (1988). New Historicist analysis, arguing that popular drama became a cultural institution "only by . . . taking up a place on the margins of society."

Schoenbaum, S. *Shakespeare: The Globe and the World* (1979). A readable, abundantly illustrated introductory book on the world of the Elizabethans.

Shakespeare's England, 2 vols. (1916). A large collection of scholarly essays on a wide variety of topics, e.g., astrology, costume, gardening, horsemanship, with special attention to Shakespeare's references to these topics.

2. Shakespeare's Life

Andrews, John F., ed. *William Shakespeare: His World, His Work, His Influence,* 3 vols. (1985). See the description above.

Bentley, Gerald E. *Shakespeare: A Biographical Handbook* (1961). The facts about Shakespeare, with virtually no conjecture intermingled.

Chambers, E. K. *William Shakespeare: A Study of Facts and Problems,* 2 vols. (1930). The fullest collection of data.

Fraser, Russell. *Young Shakespeare* (1988). A highly readable account that simultaneously considers Shakespeare's life and Shakespeare's art.

———. *Shakespeare: The Later Years* (1992).

Schoenbaum, S. *Shakespeare's Lives* (1970). A review of the evidence and an examination of many biographies, including those of Baconians and other heretics.

———. *William Shakespeare: A Compact Documentary Life* (1977). An abbreviated version, in a smaller format, of the next title. The compact version reproduces some fifty documents in reduced form. A readable presentation of all that the documents tell us about Shakespeare.

———. *William Shakespeare: A Documentary Life* (1975). A large-format book setting forth the biography with facsimiles of more than two hundred documents, and with transcriptions and commentaries.

3. Miscellaneous Reference Works

Abbott, E. A. *A Shakespearean Grammar* (new edition, 1877). An examination of differences between Elizabethan and modern grammar.

Allen, Michael J. B., and Kenneth Muir, eds. *Shakespeare's Plays in Quarto* (1981). One volume containing facsimiles of the plays issued in small format before they were collected in the First Folio of 1623.

Blake, Norman. *Shakespeare's Language: An Introduction* (1983). On vocabulary, parts of speech, and word order.

Bullough, Geoffrey. *Narrative and Dramatic Sources of Shakespeare,* 8 vols. (1957–75). A collection of many of the books Shakespeare drew on, with judicious comments.

Campbell, Oscar James, and Edward G. Quinn, eds. *The Reader's Encyclopedia of Shakespeare* (1966). Old, and in some ways superseded by Michael Dobson's *Oxford Companion* (see below), but still highly valuable.

Cercignani, Fausto. *Shakespeare's Works and Elizabethan Pronunciation* (1981). Considered the best work on the topic, but remains controversial.

Champion, Larry S. *The Essential Shakespeare: An Annotated Bibliography of Major Modern Studies* (2nd ed., 1993). An invaluable guide to 1,800 writings about Shakespeare.

Dent, R. W. *Shakespeare's Proverbial Language: An Index* (1981). An index of proverbs, with an introduction concerning a form Shakespeare frequently drew on.

Dobson, Michael, ed. *The Oxford Companion to Shakespeare* (2001). Probably the single most useful reference work for information (arranged alphabetically) about Shakespeare and his works.

Greg, W. W. *The Shakespeare First Folio* (1955). A detailed yet readable history of the first collection (1623) of Shakespeare's plays.

Harner, James. *The World Shakespeare Bibliography.* See headnote to Suggested References.

Hosley, Richard. *Shakespeare's Holinshed* (1968). Valuable presentation of one of Shakespeare's major sources.

Kökeritz, Helge. *Shakespeare's Names* (1959). A guide to pronouncing some 1,800 names appearing in Shakespeare.

———. *Shakespeare's Pronunciation* (1953). Contains much information about puns and rhymes, but see Cercignani (above).

Muir, Kenneth. *The Sources of Shakespeare's Plays* (1978). An account of Shakespeare's use of his reading. It covers all the plays, in chronological order.

Miriam Joseph, Sister. *Shakespeare's Use of the Arts of Language* (1947). A study of Shakespeare's use of rhetorical devices, reprinted in part as *Rhetoric in Shakespeare's Time* (1962).

The Norton Facsimile: The First Folio of Shakespeare's Plays (1968). A handsome and accurate facsimile of the first collection (1623) of Shakespeare's plays, with a valuable introduction by Charlton Hinman.

Onions, C. T. *A Shakespeare Glossary*, rev. and enlarged by R. D. Eagleson (1986). Definitions of words (or senses of words) now obsolete.

Partridge, Eric. *Shakespeare's Bawdy*, rev. ed. (1955). Relatively brief dictionary of bawdy words; useful, but see Williams, below.

Shakespeare Quarterly. See headnote to Suggested References.

Shakespeare Survey. See headnote to Suggested References.

Spevack, Marvin. *The Harvard Concordance to Shakespeare* (1973). An index to Shakespeare's words.

Vickers, Brian. *Appropriating Shakespeare: Contemporary Critical Quarrels* (1993). A survey—chiefly hostile—of recent schools of criticism.

Wells, Stanley, ed. *Shakespeare: A Bibliographical Guide* (new edition, 1990). Nineteen chapters (some devoted to single plays, others devoted to groups of related plays) on recent scholarship on the life and all of the works.

Williams, Gordon. *A Dictionary of Sexual Language and Imagery in Shakespearean and Stuart Literature*, 3 vols. (1994). Extended discussions of words and passages; much fuller than Partridge, cited above.

4. The Poems in General

Later sections of this list of Suggested References will be devoted to specific works; here we list discussions that cover most or all of the poems.

The Complete Sonnets and Poems, ed. Colin Burrow (2002), includes stimulating discussions. For a valuable edition of the nondramatic works other than *Sonnets,* see John Roe, ed., *The Poems,* updated edition 2006. Yale University Press has published, for the Elizabethan Club, *Shakespeare's Poems . . . A Facsimile of the Earliest Editions* (1964).

Cheney, Patrick. *Shakespeare, National Poet-Playwright* (2004).

——, ed. *The Cambridge Companion to Shakespeare's Poetry* (2007).

Dubrow, Heather. *Captive Victors: Shakespeare's Narrative Poems and Sonnets* (1987).

Hyland, Peter. *An Introduction to Shakespeare's Poems* (2003).

Kermode, Frank. *Shakespeare's Language* (2000).

Roberts, Sasha. *Reading Shakespeare's Poems in Early Modern England* (2003).
Wright, George T. *Shakespeare's Metrical Art* (1988).

5. *The Sonnets*

For studies of the *Sonnets* with the other poems, see also above, Section 4.

Especially useful modern scholarly editions of the *Sonnets* are by John Kerrigan (1986), Katherine Duncan-Jones (1997), Colin Burrow (2002), and G. Blakemore Evans (2006). Older editions that are still valuable are the classic two-volume variorum edition by Hyder Edward Rollins (1944) and the very readable volume by W. G. Ingram and Theodore Redpath (1978).

For reprints of essays from books and journals, see *Shakespearean Criticism* 10, 13, 28, 32, 40, 51, 62, 65, and 75.

Booth, Stephen. *An Essay on Shakespeare's Sonnets* (1969).
De Grazia, Margreta. "The Scandal of Shakespeare's Sonnets." *Shakespeare Survey* 47 (1994): 35–49.
Edmondson, Paul, and Stanley Wells. *Shakespeare's Sonnets* (2004).
Fineman, Joel. *Shakespeare's Perjured Eye: The Invention of Poetic Subjectivity in the Sonnets* (1986).
Innes, Paul. *Shakespeare and the English Renaissance Sonnet: Verses of Feigning Love* (1997).
Leishman, J. B. *Themes and Variations in Shakespeare's Sonnets* (1962).
Melchiori, Giorgio. *Shakespeare's Dramatic Meditations* (1976).
Muir, Kenneth. *Shakespeare's Sonnets* (1979).
Pequigney, Joseph. *Such Is My Love: A Study of Shakespeare's Sonnets* (1985).
Schiffer, James, ed. *Shakespeare's Sonnets: Critical Essays* (1999).
Schoenfeldt, Michael, ed. *A Companion to Shakespeare's Sonnets* (2007).
Smith, Bruce. *Homosexual Desire in Shakespeare's England* (1991).
Vendler, Helen. *The Art of Shakespeare's Sonnets* (1997).

6. *Venus and Adonis* and *The Rape of Lucrece*

For studies of these poems with the other poems, see also above, Section 4.

For a variorum edition, see Hyder Edward Rollins, *The Poems* (1938).

For reprints of material on *Venus and Adonis* from books and journals, see *Shakespearean Criticism,* volumes 10, 33, 51, 67, and 79; for material on *Lucrece,* see volumes 10, 33, 43, 59, 71, and 82. For some thirty essays on *Venus and Adonis* (chiefly previously published, but seven are new), see the collection, below, edited by Philip C. Kolin.

For an annotated bibliography of writings about *Lucrece,* see below, under Huffman.

Bate, Jonathan. *Shakespeare and Ovid* (1993).

Belsey, Catherine. "Tarquin Dispossessed: Expropriation and Consent in *The Rape of Lucrece.*" *Shakespeare Quarterly* 52 (2001): 315–35.

Bradbrook, M. C. *Shakespeare and Elizabethan Poetry* (1951).

Bush, Douglas. *Mythology and the Renaissance Tradition.* New revised edition (1963).

Donaldson, Ian. *The Rape of Lucretia: A Myth and Its Transformations* (1982).

Huffman, Clifford Chalmers, and John W. Velz. *The Rape of Lucrece, Titus Andronicus, Julius Caesar, Antony and Cleopatra, and Coriolanus: An Annotated Bibliography of Shakespeare Studies 1910–2000* (2002).

Hulse, Clark. *Metamorphic Verse: The Elizabethan Minor Epic* (1981).

Kahn, Coppélia. *Man's Estate: Masculine Identity in Shakespeare* (1981).

Keach, William. *Elizabethan Erotic Narratives* (1977).

Kolin, Philip C., ed. *"Venus and Adonis": Critical Essays* (1997).

Lanham, Richard A. *The Motives of Eloquence: Literary Rhetoric in the Renaissance* (1976).

Lewis, C. S. *English Literature in the Sixteenth Century* (1954).

Maxwell, J. C., ed. *The Poems* (1966).

Mortimer, Anthony. *Variable Passions: A Reading of Shakespeare's "Venus and Adonis"* (2000).

Nicoll, Allardyce, ed. *Shakespeare Survey* 15 (1962).

7. *The Phoenix and the Turtle*

For a study of this poem with the other poems, see also above, Section 4.

For a thoughtful modern scholarly edition, see John Roe's edition of Shakespeare's *Poems* (2006).

For reprints of essays from books and articles, see *Shakespearean Criticism,* volumes 10, 38, 51, 64, and 76.

Alvarez, A. "William Shakespeare: The Phoenix and the Turtle," in *Interpretations,* ed. John Wain (1955).

Cunningham, J. V. *Tradition and Poetic Structure* (1960).

Empson, William. "The Phoenix and the Turtle." *Essays in Criticism* 16 (1966): 147–53.

Everett, Barbara. "Set Upon a Golden Bough to Sing: Shakespeare's Debt to Sidney in 'The Phoenix and Turtle.' " *Times Literary Supplement,* Feb. 16, 2001: 13–15.

Knight, G. Wilson. *The Mutual Flame: On Shakespeare's "Sonnets" and "The Phoenix and the Turtle"* (1955).

Matchett, William H. *"The Phoenix and the Turtle"; Shakespeare's Poem and Chester's "Loues Martyr"* (1965).

Underwood, Richard Allan. *Shakespeare's "The Phoenix and the Turtle": A Survey of Scholarship* (1974).

8. *A Lover's Complaint*

For a study of this poem with the other poems, see also above, Section 4. John Kerrigan (editor of a volume listed below) has also edited the poem along with the *Sonnets*.

Jackson, McDonald P. " 'A Lover's Complaint' Revisited." *Shakespeare Studies* 32 (2004): 267–94.

Kerrigan, John, ed. *Motives of Woe: Shakespeare and "Female Complaint": A Critical Anthology* (1991).

Muir, Kenneth. " 'A Lover's Complaint': A Reconsideration," in *Shakespeare 1564–1964* (1964), 154–66; reprinted in Muir's *Shakespeare the Professional and Related Studies* (1973), 204–19.

Sharon-Zisser, Shirley, ed. *Critical Essays on Shakespeare's "A Lover's Complaint": Suffering Ecstasy* (2006).

Vickers, Brian. *Shakespeare, "A Lover's Complaint," and John Davies of Hereford* (2007).

9. *The Passionate Pilgrim*

For discussions of the poems in *The Passionate Pilgrim* in a context of other poems of the period see the titles listed above, Section 4. Hyder Edward Rollins has edited a facsimile (1940).